THE MESSAGES AND SECRETS OF THE UNIVERSE

Spiritual Psychoanalysis

Ionel Rotaru

 FriesenPress

One Printers Way
Altona, MB R0G 0B0
Canada

www.friesenpress.com

Copyright © 2024 by Ionel Rotaru
First Edition — 2024

Our civilization has reached the peak of its Materialistic evolution that was based on selfishness, envy, aggression... Now the time has come when we all must decide - to continue the same form of destructive Materialistic Evolution or to accept the Evolution suggested by the Supreme Consciousness of the Universe... My books are a scientific demonstration of the manifestation of the Supreme Consciousness of the Universe in the material world in which we live, which clearly urges us to continue the path of Spiritual Evolution with a Spiritual Thought and harmony between the Human being and the Universe.

ISBN
978-1-03-919916-3 (Hardcover)
978-1-03-919915-6 (Paperback)
978-1-03-919917-0 (eBook)
978-1-03-919918-7 (Audiobook)

1. BODY, MIND & SPIRIT, INSPIRATION & PERSONAL GROWTH

Distributed to the trade by The Ingram Book Company

Dedication

I dedicate this book to the loving memory of my dear departed mother, Anica Rotaru (Anicuta Focsa), who has laid the foundation of the Spiritual Psychoanalysis I describe in my books.

TABLE OF CONTENTS

Introduction

WRITING A BOOK IS AN ART AND AN IMPORTANT TASK. THE WRITER HAS A great responsibility to the reader, who seeks the truth of life through the prism of entertainment. Novelists need to send out messages that can be understood and deeply absorbed by the reader. Whether their epic story is about love or war, those messages should be of optimism, achievement, and hope for another day.

The messages I am sending to my readers are more significant and meaningful, as they span a bridge between science and spirituality; therefore, they should be well understood by the common reader and *adopted* by psychiatrists, psychologists, psychotherapists, and psychoanalysts.

I was not prepared to become a writer. I'm a psychiatrist, a profession I embraced and love with all my heart and soul. But my destiny followed Neale Donald Walsch's, a radio host and writer known for his book *Conversations with God*. Fate forced me to give up my job and dedicate myself to writing books—books that would spread the message of God viewed through my own experience.

At one time I felt bound to give up my psychiatrist job in order to write only one book, *The Destiny and Signs of God* (second edition), which I published in 2020. I never thought that I'd be compelled to write a second book. Unfortunately—or better to say, fortunately—my life took such a turn that I had to go on with my writing assignment and dole out the messages of God our Lord/Universe.

I had barely finished my first book—and I couldn't change anything in it—when a series of situations arranged by God *exceptionally* for me began to develop. They were strange situations, bizarre and incomprehensible.

I didn't have the slightest idea what God was trying to tell me. I didn't understand anything, and I asked myself why they were happening to me, yet I was sure that God was providing me with the information I needed for my second book.

As negative and bizarre as they were, these situations were well organized and structured, precisely in the manner and within the requirements of an irreproachable Spiritual Psychoanalysis.

Strange things occurred from June 2019 to March 2020, when, at one point, I had a kind of revelation in which all the situations came together to help me understand the messages God was sending me. Thus, in March 2020, at the beginning of the pandemic, I had a clear vision of what I was going to write in my new book.

In my first book, *The Destiny and Signs of God* (second edition), I write in general terms about:

- the importance of accepting the spirituality as a science and an integral part of our lives;

- the importance of moving towards a thinking and spiritual evolution of our entire civilization;

- the importance of our collaboration with the Universe; and

- the importance of the signs of God, which are essential to our destiny as well as the destiny of our entire civilization.

The pandemic ravaging the world today is an irrefutable confirmation of what I wrote in my first book and sends a *direct* and *very* important message from God to our civilization to open our eyes, recognize and accept spiritual evolution as an incontestable process for our civilization, and follow *the destiny recommended by God* without hesitation. Otherwise, the destiny *we* might choose, based on our material principles, will give birth to calamities for us and our descendants.

To better understand the message sent by our Lord through the COVID-19 pandemic, in this book I will broaden my attention to include some important details, and I will describe the secrets of the Universe that might enlighten everyone's mind to the truth of who we are and our responsibilities on this earth.

The secrets of the Universe I describe in this book create a bond between all religions, philosophies, and theories regarding the spiritual world in which we live. What is different and extremely important regarding the secrets of the Universe are the secrets of the dark world, which I describe in Chapter Two, "The Secrets of God."

If up until now everyone has been focused only on the Kingdom of Heaven and has become familiar with all its subtleties, the time has come that the world must know about the construction of the Universe in its full splendor. It must know both the Kingdom of Heaven and its opposite side—the World of Darkness. Only by knowing *all* the secrets of the Universe, positive and negative, can we get an idea of *how* harmony works in the Universe. Only *then* will *we alone* be able to create such harmony between good and evil in our society and our family, between our soul and our body.

In this book, the reader will find a revelation of all the secrets of the Universe not written so far, and about the Kingdom of Heaven and its opposite, the World of Darkness. This will give the reader courage and self-confidence to take the first steps towards spiritual evolution, which is based on harmony and love between the good and evil sides of our soul, in our society, and in the entire Universe.

***

I have been asking myself: Why did God specifically choose me to write spiritual books if Neale Donald Walsch has already done it? Just *now* have I found the answer to this question.

Neale Donald Walsch wrote only about the Kingdom of Heaven, about the fate of our soul after the death of our physical body, but neither he nor anyone in the field of spirituality spoke about the dark world of the Universe or about the negative energies of the Universe and everything lurking therein. My mission in this life is to make all people knowledgeable about the dark world of the Universe, which is not so aggressive and despicable as we may think.

Equally important questions are: Why did God choose Neale Donald Walsch to become a messenger of God? Why did He choose me too? Why didn't He choose someone who comes from the field, or some monks or priests? Why didn't He choose people who are interested in the construction of the Universe?

And I answered: God specifically chose both of us to be His messengers because neither of us is involved in religion or politics. If we were believers or politicians, our brains would be populated by all kinds of ideologies that would blur God's messages and turn them into theories based on our political or religious beliefs. But instead, we perceived the messages of the Universe exactly as they are. Of course, we adjust them to a small extent, depending on our jobs, but the essential basis of the messages of the Universe have been faithfully and indisputably shaped.

Thus, as a journalist by profession, Neale Donald Walsch could analyze God's messages from a democratic point of view without altering them. In my case, God chose me to convey His messages to our civilization, because my job allowed me to see God's messages as a Spiritual Psychoanalysis that makes the connection between science and spirituality, and my job entailed dealing with the negative energies of our psyche. This gave me the ability to understand the negative energies of the World of Darkness, of the human being, and of everything that exists in the entire Universe.

Great is my destiny, as it helped me uncover the true purpose of my life, the mighty deed of using Spiritual Psychoanalysis not only to persuade my readers of the significance of spiritual evolution, but also to make the scientists mindful of the magnitude of spiritual analysis and how important it is to accept spirituality as a new form of science.

My duty is to make the scientists and leaders of the world aware that the Universe is a form of consciousness, and that the human being is a form of consciousness. Through the prism of Spiritual Psychoanalysis, we learn to listen to the advice of the Universe, and spiritual evolution remains the only path for the salvation of our civilization. Otherwise, the current materialistic evolution of our civilization will lead us to self-destruction.

The Universe tries to communicate with each of us through the situations in our lives; we just have to open our hearts and souls to listen and live in harmony with Him.

EXPLANATION OF SPIRITUAL PSYCHOANALYSIS AND SPIRITUAL EVOLUTION

In ordinary psychoanalysis, the modes of questioning are directed towards our own person, for example: Why did I do this? Why am I nervous/anxious in this particular situation? These questions are designed to discover the problem embedded in our subconscious. (Note: Even if psychoanalysts ignore spirituality, the problems nested in each person's subconscious are negative energies in our brains.)

The Spiritual Psychoanalysis I describe is oriented outside of our own person, and the questions are asked accordingly: Why did this situation happen to me and not to someone else? Why did this situation happen at this moment and not earlier or later?

In our Universe there are two forms of energy: The Divine Energy of the Universe (of the Supreme Consciousness of the Universe) and the materialistic energies on earth that we ourselves create. Depending on our intentions/activities/thoughts, these are our personal positive and negative energies and the positive and negative energies of our family, our community/locality/country, and of our civilization as a whole.

Imagine that the Divine Energy of the Universe directs all the materialistic energies created by us. Based on the Laws of the Universe, all energies must be returned to the owner. In these conditions, the Divine Energy of the Universe returns to each of us all the energies that we have created so far through the situations in our lives. As a result, depending on the energies we produced, exactly such situations happen in our life. If we created positive energies, then positive situations happen to us. If we created negative energies, then negative situations will happen to us. Also, many situations come to us not only from the energies we produce but from the karma of family energies or energies of our locality/region/country/civilization.

The essence of Spiritual Psychoanalysis described by me is to discover not only the origin of this energy but also the messages the Universe wants to convey to each of us. We should ask ourselves: What did the Universe want to convey to me through this situation? What does He suggest that I correct in my behavior? Which path in life does He suggest for me to take?"

The messages of the Universe are directed not only to teach us to correct our problems and show us the paths of life that we must follow for an ever-ascending spiritual evolution, but also to live in harmony with the entire Universe. Imagine that the Universe is a form of Consciousness, that every human being is a form of consciousness, and that every form of life is a form of consciousness. We are all one with the Universe. We all together are the Universe.

Now imagine that Spiritual Psychoanalysis makes each of us connect with the whole Universe and live in harmony with Him. Living in harmony with the Universe, we will live in harmony with any form of existence in this Universe. Only by living in harmony with the entire Universe will we be able to have an indescribable spiritual ascent.

> As you can see, as a result, Spiritual Psychiatry is able to discover not only the negative energies nested in our brain (in our subconscious) what ordinary psychoanalysis does, but it is capable of discovering all the energies of the Universe with which we are in contact, is capable of making us find our place and our importance in this Universe, is able to find the true path of our spiritual evolution and to live in eternal harmony with our entire family - with the entire Universe. (See also my first book *The Destiny and Signs of God—Spiritual Psychoanalysis*, second edition (Bibliography 36, Ionel Rotaru, 2024)).

For us to evolve spiritually, we must learn not to do what we want to do, and we must learn to do the right thing—to do what the Universe tells us to do. The Universe is with us at every step of our lives and gives us advice through situations, the people around us, and the phenomena of nature. Only by listening to the advice of the surrounding world will we manage to live in harmony with the entire Universe. Living in harmony with the Universe, we will find our place and our destiny in the Universe, and only then will we finally be able to do what we want to do.

To help you to form an idea about spiritual evolution, I will briefly describe the process of spiritual evolution from the point of view of feeding our human body. I wrote much more in detail in *The Destiny and*

Signs of God. Even if we manage to live in harmony with the Universe, we are still in the first phase of evolution in terms of nutrition for the human body. For our body to have life energy, it needs material nutrition, such as proteins, carbohydrates, lipids, and vitamins.

The second phase of spiritual evolution will occur when our body no longer needs material sustenance, because it will feed itself with PRANA—the divine energy of the Universe (such people already exist on earth). Even if in the second phase we no longer consume material energy, we will continue to exist as parasites of the Universe, because our body will need external energy to exist.

The third phase of our spiritual evolution will be the peak phase, because we will no longer be like some parasites of the Universe but will become energy producers ourselves, producers of PRANA. In the third phase, our level of evolution will be so high, and we will emanate so much love and empathy to the surrounding world, that we alone will become the source of energy for the surrounding world.

***

In my first book, I wrote about Spiritual Psychoanalysis and our individual spiritual ascent. In this book I'll write about Spiritual Psychoanalysis and the spiritual ascent of our entire civilization. I'll talk about the origin of the negative energies of COVID-19 and the Russian war against Ukraine, and the messages of the Universe through the prism of these situations (negative energies).

Chapter One

ASTONISHING YET STUPEFYING SITUATIONS

IN THE SPRING OF 2019, I ASKED A ROMANIAN PHILOLOGIST TO TRANS-late my first book into English. My book was finished and ready to go, and suddenly, for reasons unaccounted for, I could hear various objects talk to me. A tide of negative and positive energies was rising and falling before my eyes while God was calling me and challenging me, leaving me in bewilderment.

The Lord was giving me a sense of contrast just to show me how different my life could be from the time I had finished my first book. And He was pressing me to write a second one. I always knew how precious His urges were, and as the turn of events appeared meaningful and persuasive, I started to gather information for my new book.

It was only when the COVID-19 pandemic broke out in March 2020 that I clearly understood what God was telling me through the bizarre things that had happened in the past nine months. In this chapter, I will explain how much our days have changed since the summer of 2019. I will describe one of those situations that, though it may not appear essential, you might find helpful in your communication with your soul.

OBJECTS STARTED TO TALK TO ME

Like many others, I'm faithful to several kinds of food that my mother used to cook when I was a child. Here are some of her best dishes:

- dumplings stuffed with fresh cheese or potatoes, known as ravioli

- fresh cheese or potato pies, like the English pies or French tartes cut in various shapes

- chisleag, which is actually a fermented yogurt from cow milk. (In Canada there is a similar product called the Greek yogurt, but it doesn't taste like the one I used to eat back home.)

In Canada, I can't make the treats from my childhood because both the dumplings and pies require fresh cow cheese, which is made of yogurt derived from the cow milk. Milk in this country comes pasteurized to eliminate pathogens and extend shelf life, and it can't be subject to Moldovan technology. I tried several ferments from the market to make my mother's yogurt but to no avail.

A few years ago, one of my fellow nationals brought me yogurt that tasted exactly like that from Moldova. According to his recipe, I was supposed to use a cup of yogurt for four to five liters of milk and keep it in the basement for twenty-four hours to allow the ferments to spread through the whole quantity of milk. However, I had to retain one cup of yogurt as an ingredient for the next process. Had I used the entire quantity of yogurt, my only genuine ferment would have been gone.

Finally, after several years in Canada, I could make my home yogurt and fresh cheese for my ravioli dumplings and my special pies. I could make my goodies without my wife's help. To make my dough, I used a mixer, and the rest came easy. However, the dumplings posed some difficulty, as making them required meticulous and time-consuming labor for only one meal. I needed my wife to help me cook those things, since she was more skilled in churning the dough. But because Nastia didn't like to cook, we didn't make dumplings very often, maybe once or twice a year, which was not to my satisfaction. I felt frustrated that she didn't volunteer to make my treats. "This is the story of my life," I used to say to myself, and the only consolation was my home-made yogurt that I could enjoy every day and, occasionally, my lovely pies.

I had yogurt every morning, and Nastia had it in the evening. To have fresh yogurt permanently, I used a 4.5-liter glass bowl. I always retaineed a cupful for my breakfast, and I kept a second one to make yogurt for the next fermentation.

One day I went down to the kitchen for my regular cup of yogurt and a slice of home-made bread. Usually I have my breakfast in the dining room, where I can enjoy the sunrise above the Atlantic Ocean. We live in a three-story house and can enjoy the vista of the Atlantic Ocean from our back yard. The windows of the upper bedrooms, the kitchen, and the dining room reach high to the ceiling, giving the eye the liberty to embrace the blue immensity of the Atlantic Ocean.

On that day, I couldn't make it to the dining room because some strange things happened, things I had never encountered before: *the various objects began talking to me.* This is what happened:

I went down to the kitchen to prepare my breakfast and accidentally scooped up three cupfuls of yogurt instead of one. Explanation: a) every morning I take out only one yogurt cup for my breakfast; b) once every three to four days, when the yogurt is almost finished, I take out two cups of yogurt—one for myself for breakfast and the second cup to make another yogurt for the following days; and c) when I want to make fresh cheese for Moldavian dumplings and pies, I take out three cups: one for breakfast for myself, one to make another yogurt for the following days, and the third cup to make yogurt for cheese.

In this case, I took out three cups of yogurt, and I didn't understand why I took out three cups instead of one. I couldn't believe I'd made such a mistake! I'm a perfectionist and do everything by the book. How could I make such a big mistake? This might seem trivial, but if something like this happens only once in a lifetime, things move into the spiritual sphere of the Universe, and an in-depth Spiritual Analysis is required.

The readers of my first book know how the signs of our Lord work and could easily understand what happened, because nothing is aleatoric in this universe. And those who have developed their sixth sense understand even more that as of that moment on, I started to feel the meaning of that message through my sixth sense. What is that message and who sent it? We'll see later in my book.

SPIRITUAL PSYCHOANALYSIS

It was strange to hear the objects talk to me through situations and try to send me all kinds of messages. I was both thrilled and intrigued. "What do they actually want to tell me?" I asked myself.

It wasn't difficult to decode the secret message of the yogurt. I put things together and here is what I found. I use three cupfuls *only* when I make yogurt for my fresh cheese, so I must make fresh cheese. Now, for what kind of food do I make this cheese? The answer is for my dumplings or my pies. But I had made pies several days earlier when my daughters had come to visit, so I was supposed to make dumplings, not pies. But how could I make dumplings during the week when Nastia was at work and no one could mix the dowel? I had to take the brunt. That was the message the yogurt had sent me so adamantly: *I must make dumplings without my wife's help, even though our girls aren't home.*

Our daughters at that time were in their last year of studies at the university a few hundred kilometers from us, and they rarely came home. Sara, the eldest, was in her last year of residency as a family doctor, and Lya, the youngest, was in her final year of a master's degree in physiotherapy.

When I was writing my first book, God was teaching me how His signs work and how He sends us messages. God/the Divine Energy of the Universe sends us messages through life situations, through people, and through natural phenomena. Every time He comes to us from outside and we're involved in a discussion or situation that we didn't initiate, then He is trying to send us a message. To help me learn the ways of communicating with the Universe, the Universe put me through many extreme situations, but never before had messages from the spiritual world come through objects. What I knew from my previous experience was that every time God/Divine Energy wanted to send me a message, the situation came from outside of me to me. But in the yogurt case, the situation came out of me, and I wasn't aware of it.

I asked myself: What was that message about? If God talks to us *only* through situations and people that come from outside, who can send back a message from inside ourselves?"

And I answered: We are made of one body (the representative of the wife of our soul) and one soul (who is the representative of the husband of our body). In my first book, I introduce different Laws of the Universe. As any democratic country needs laws to function, the spiritual world of the Universe needs laws that we should know and respect.

One of the main Laws of the Universe is the "Family Law of the Universe." This law is the basis of the construction of the entire Universe. The Universe is built from the Supreme Consciousness of the Universe (God) and the matter of the Universe. The human being is built in the same way as the universe, from the soul/supreme consciousness of the human being and the consciousness of the human body. This collaboration between two forms of existence is created according to the principles of a family: God is represented as the husband, and the matter of the Universe represents the wife of God. In the case of the relationship between soul and body, the soul represents the husband, and the human body represents the wife. To help us better understand the relationship of the husband-wife couple, the Universe created man and woman so that they could learn to live as a couple and in harmony according to the same principle that the Universe lives by (God with the matter of the Universe)

My body is in love with the dumplings from my childhood, but it doesn't enjoy them very often because Nastia doesn't like to cook, and my body excuses itself for being so awkward when mixing the dowel, so it puts the blame on my wife. As time passed by and my body was getting older without eating the delicious dumplings, my soul decided to make my body cook those dumplings itself, instead of waiting for Nastia to do it.

Conclusion: It's important to train ourselves to live in love and harmony in the family relationship of our body and soul. We should train ourselves to listen to our soul, as it's unique in the relationship with our body, and it knows and sees outside the material world. It knows absolutely everything about all spiritual subtleties.

THE MECHANISM OF THE APPEARANCE OF THE DESTRUCTIVE NEGATIVE ENERGIES

Much later after I wrote this chapter, I understood the mechanism of the emergence of the negative destructive energies because I'd dealt with it before, though on a much smaller scale.

My wife and I had an aunt who was childless. She was friendly and so attached to us that I considered her my second mother. I genuinely felt happy in her presence. I was happy that even if my mother passed away, there would still be someone around whom I loved as my own parent.

At one point, I noticed that negative situations were telling me of danger. For instance:

- I was driving my car, and out of the blue, another car moved in front of me extremely slowly.

- If I entered a store to buy something, someone would stand exactly in front of the product I wanted to buy, and I had no choice but to wait or just give up on the thing.

- When I stood in line at the checkout to pay for my groceries, even if I'd picked the shortest lineup, someone in front of me would be moving slowly and awkwardly, or couldn't find his right card, which held me back and made me envious of the patrons moving faster in the other lines.

Such situations were not sporadic but showed up on every corner of the street and in anything I was doing. Bad luck continued from early morning until late at night, but a major negative energy/situation didn't come.

Through numerous circumstances, God/the Universe taught me how to look at the mechanism of the occurrence of major negative energies/situations, which I described in my first book. But in all the cases I was aware of, the major negative energies/situations usually appeared shortly after the energies/situations announced the appearance of them. For example, if the foreboding energies/situations happened in the morning, within the next twenty-four hours at the latest, the major negative energy/situation would occur.

When bad luck was following me at every step, I didn't understand what was happening. Days passed, and the bad luck kept following me, though nothing bad happened. A whole week had already passed, and nothing bad happened to me.

The Apparition of the Negative Energy

One weekend, Nastia and I called our aunt, and to my surprise, she began chastising me, leaving me speechless. Not wanting to pour fuel on fire, I didn't retort. I only apologized to her, even though I knew I hadn't done anything wrong. I could mitigate the conflict, and I understood the hidden thoughts of our aunt, and this made me feel some disappointment about our relationship. My aunt and I didn't break our relationship. We continued to call one another and talk as before, even if there was a void in my heart.

Explanation: I had invested a lot in our relationship, and I had good feelings for her. We called one another regularly; my wife and I considered her a second mother, and we offered her absolutely everything a real mother could get from her children. We supported her morally and financially, and we treated her like our real mother. We told her about our successes. We contacted her when we were on vacation, and we showed her how we lived too. To make sure that she didn't suffer, I helped her when she was in need. In other words, we invested in our relationship like anyone would invest in a harmonious family.

But I was so disappointed to realize our aunt's hidden feelings, which were so different from what I had thought. It felt like a divorce, when a family member loves his spouse desperately, does everything for him or her, but at some point discovers that his partner never had any feelings for him.

Such a disappointment leaves a deep gap in your soul that you can't close. The opening is so wide that you can never refill it with the same love. In other words, the volume of negative energy building up between us and our aunt was so destructive, God needed a week to warn me about the upcoming peril.

The birth of the negative energy in the case of our aunt was similar to the same mechanism in which the COVID-19 pandemic stormed the world. In both cases, first came the negative energies of smaller magnitude, followed by the negative destructive energy itself. The difference between these two cases is only the caliber of the energies, otherwise the mechanism is identical.

THE FIRST VISIBLE ENERGIES

Let me tell you about the first two energies I saw when I was daydreaming.

A) MY FIRST VISIBLE NEGATIVE ENERGY

In June 2019, we went away for several weeks. We visited two countries in South America and traveled to six places. We visited the most important archeological sites in the region. In La Paz, Bolivia, we visited Tiwanaku and Puma Punku. In Peru, we went to Titicaca Lake, the Scared Valley, Machu Picchu, and the Amazons. We had traveled before, but most of the time we had stayed in all-inclusive resorts without venturing to explore the surrounding world.

That trip was special. We had come a long way from a poor country, and now we were wealthy and traveling care-free. After La Paz, Puno, Cusco, Aguas Calientes, and Puerto Maldonado, our last destination was Lima, the capital city of Peru. We spent two nights there and explored the shore of the Pacific Ocean. We stayed in a small hotel located just a few hundred yards from the International Airport. The room was done in decor from the 1980s by someone who was not a design specialist, but it was clean and well maintained. We didn't need luxury, and we were satisfied with the services provided: safety, cleanliness, proximity to the airport.

On our last day, we visited the downtown and the shore of the Pacific Ocean. We had walked the whole day and absorbed the architecture and the gorgeous vistas. In the evening, we went back to our hotel and started to pack up for the next day, when we were taking off for Canada. I did my part and then went to take a shower. The walls were plated with white tiles, and the shower was separated from the rest of the room by a transparent drape. The color of the tiles made the small enclosure look so bright. I closed my eyes and saw a negative energy floating as an ashen cloud and coming down above my head.

Imagine that you keep your eyes closed in the direction of a strong light, and an object is floating down right there in front of you, blocking the shining rays. Through our eyelids, we still can see a shadow slowly moving down: it was the cloud of negative energy I had just mentioned.

When the dark cloud appeared in my mind, I immediately knew what was going to happen. I knew it was a negative energy because I felt it through a kind of sixth sense. But this was not the sixth sense. I already knew what this feeling meant, because I had experienced this sensation several times, and I knew how it should manifest itself. This new sensation and perception of negative energy was something far superior to my sixth sense.

For the first time in my life, I was looking at a negative energy and it didn't scare me, as it wasn't charging at me with its negative strength to frighten me. On the contrary, it was coming down slowly and silently to give me an explanation about its intentions. Its message came through telepathy, just like an account made by people who've had a near-death experience (NDE) and say that they communicated with the Kingdom of Heaven through some kind of telepathic means.

The same had happened to me now. As if the message already existed in my brain, the process of transmission unfolded. The message brought by the cloud of negative energy was that a major conflict was about to break out between Nastia and I. I perceived that message as if someone from outside had told me we would get into a big argument. But if someone from outside had said it, I wouldn't have believed it, because my wife and I had reached the pinnacle of our achievements and were just finishing the vacation of our dreams.

But because the message was coming directly from the source, from the negative energy that was bringing the conflict along, I became confused and said to myself: *Why would we argue when we feel so well? In the past we have lived in love and spiritual harmony and have never argued. We haven't created any negative energy in our family relationship that could be a source of negative energies like the one descending upon us now.*

9

In my opinion, the message of the negative energy had no logic, yet I believed it, since it was persuasive and worrisome at the same time. I stepped out of the bathroom and didn't say a word to anyone. I was just careful not to do anything that might upset my wife. The next day, on our way to Canada, we had to wait for five hours to switch planes in Mexico. I told Nastia something of which I was very sure, but as always, she disagreed and rejected my proposal. (I can't recall what I told her.)

Before we began living a spiritual relationship, her demeanor touched strings of sensitivity in our relationship, precipitating her fits of anger. I had started to accept her idiosyncrasies and was crazy about her, and now I love her purely and spiritually. It was bizarre to get irritated over such a trivial thing. I knew her negative sides so well and had already accepted and ignored them. But now, for some reason, her reaction made me lose control and aggravated me deeply. And in turn, she got angry, though I hadn't said anything bad. Soon our relationship went sour, and we were talking elliptically about major subjects, but nothing else. This coldhearted period lasted a few days.

Spiritual Analysis

I was aware that the reason for our distancing from one another was not our argument, and neither of us was guilty for what happened. The reason for our conflict was the negative energy that had seized me in the bathroom of that hotel in Lima. I knew that this negative energy settled between us, caused the conflict, and was going to stay between us until it was exhausted.

At the same time, I knew that if during this period of "cold-hearted relations" between us I showed her that I was angry and thought about her negative particularities, I would create more negative energies and fuel what had already permeated our relationship. I knew that the presence of negative energy installed between us incited us to think negatively about each other and caused conflicts between us. All these thoughts or conflicts would have created other additional negative energies, which would have made the negative energy grow bigger and bigger, giving it the opportunity to stay between us much longer than its initial capacity.

ATTENTION! Be aware of the techniques I use in the case of invasive negative energies, as you could use them too. I tried to chase the negative energy away from my brain and my heart through meditations and prayers, and when I felt that negative thoughts about Nastia were getting into my mind, I tried to think of something else. In this way, I stopped the creation of more negative energies that would fuel our conflict; as a consequence, the existing negative energy lost stamina and fizzled out. After a while, my relationship with my wife returned to love and harmony, as if nothing wrong had happened between us.

Before describing the origin of the negative energy sources that invaded me and Nastia, I want to explain one of the Laws of the Universe—the Law of the Wheel of Life. (Further details are described in my first book, *The Destiny and Signs of God*, second edition). According to this law, the life of human beings on earth unfolds in the form of a wheel. One half of the wheel is full of success, positive events, and harmony, and the other half is full of failures, negative events, and conflicts. It was clear that Nastia and I were in the Wheel of Life period of negative events, and for this reason we were invaded by a negative energy. I was very curious where the negative energy came from.

There could be two sources of negative energy that turned us into foes. The first source could be the negative energies we created in time through our negative thoughts and demeanor, which accumulated and degenerated into a conflict.

The second source could be the negative energies created by the persons around us whether the karmas of our family or of our city, country, or civilization.

Why did the negative energies appear in our relationship? There are several hypotheses about why the negative energies generated a conflict between Nastia and I:

The first hypothesis: The negative energies we created over the years through our negative thoughts and attitudes reached a point of brinkmanship and impacted our marital life. Unfortunately, this hypothesis can't be valid because, in the past years, my relation with my wife had been spiritual and full of love and harmony. We hadn't created negative energies at all, so this hypothesis can be taken off the list of possibilities.

The second hypothesis: The negative energies created by the people around us. This is a realistic hypothesis, since the conflicts between Nastia and I fall under the Wheel of Life of the Laws of the Universe. In South America, we had the time of our life, and we had reached the peak of our achievements. Yes, we lived a time of extreme positive energies, but under the Law of the Universe—the Wheel of Life—it was time to deal with the opposite site of this Wheel, the negative energies.

To meet the requests of the Laws of the Universe, God made the conflict energies the most suitable for my relationship with my wife. And because we didn't have negative energies available in our family life to complete the Wheel of Life, He borrowed from the karmas of the people surrounding us, such as our family, locality, country, or civilization. In other words, God gave us negative energies that didn't belong to us.

The third hypothesis: This refers to the abundance of negative energies invading our planet as a COVID-19 pandemic. (I write more on this later.)

B) THE SECOND VISIBLE NEGATIVE ENERGY

We came back from South America, and in September 2019, I went to see my parents in Moldova. They are very old, and I travel to see them every year, hoping they'd be around as long as possible. September in Moldova is nice, with temperatures above 25–30 Celsius in the daytime and a little chilly at night.

My parents live in the countryside and survive from farming the land and raising livestock and poultry. They don't receive assistance from the state, and I am their only support. Every year I go to see them for one month and help them as much as I can.

To make their life and mine easier, I provided their homestead with essential services. Communists never cared about the living conditions of the working people and the peasants, and they never bothered to install running water and sewage systems for them. After communism collapsed, many young people went to try their fortune abroad and later came back to build a house on their native land.

My parents are the lucky ones, as I helped them to connect to the tap water system and sewage installations of the village with money from our own pockets. Thanks to us, they have a bathroom, a laundry machine, a flush toilet, and a shower. We also set up a furnace powered by a gas tank to warm up the water for their shower.

In the fall of 2019, at my parents' house in Moldova, after a day of hard work in their household, I went to take a shower. Suddenly above my head was a small gray cloud like the one I had seen in Lima. This time, the small cloud was quick and not as intense as the first time. It didn't send me any specific message about why it had come to me. But somehow, it must have announced that nothing serious was about to happen.

I knew this energy was harmless, so I continued showering. But in that moment, the water was running cold. I thought there was a problem with the furnace, which broke down occasionally due to water pressure variations. I checked it again and noticed that the propane was dismally low and couldn't heat up the water. I was ambivalent about this situation. On one hand, we didn't have a car to go to a station to fill up the tank. On the other, I had just finished my shower, and no one was waiting to get in.

Spiritual Psychoanalysis

Why did those negative energies come to me? Why did we run out of propane exactly when I was taking a shower? Did I deserve to be punished right there in the bathroom?

The answer may be the following: I didn't deserve to be punished in my parents' bathroom, because I had built that bathroom myself, which was a positive deed, the construction of a positive energy for my parents. The bathroom itself was a positive energy I had made for me and them. And the bathroom had no reason to exact retribution on me, as it was not carrying negative energies against me. Then where did those negative energies come from? You will find the answer in Chapter Three: "The Third Energy and Its influence on the Active Energies." Here I describe the mechanism of overaccumulation of the negative energies for our civilization.

My Conversation with My Mother about My Visions

I was sitting with my mother under a tree in her back yard, telling her about the dark energies I had seen in her bathroom and in Peru. It was one of those sunny days when even the dog was seeking shelter under the fence. I felt well and was explaining what had happened, but I realized that by explaining to my mother, I was making myself understand what was happening to me. My new ability to see spiritual energies in full consciousness means that God has given me a priceless gift. It's a miracle to be able to see all this—a miracle that everyone dreams about.

I said to her, "Mother, do you see how God is training me for another stage of my evolution in the spiritual world? How He makes me see negative energies that don't scare or disturb me?"

"Deservedly so," she answered. "I am so happy that you truly believe in God, and God takes care of you."

I went on. "I believe God is trying to tell me that I've reached a level of evolution where my third eye is coming to life. Only people with a third eye can see the spiritual world. Word goes around that people with the third eye are appalled seeing the spirits of the dead. But in my case, God began showing me the spiritual world in more serene and easier ways."

I finished speaking with my mother and was happy that with the eye of my mind, I could see those things. Even though I was happy with my new abilities, my connection with negative energies scared me. I couldn't understand why God was showing me only the negative energies, so I asked Him:

"God, why do you want me to see only the negative energies? You are the one I'm looking for, and I want to see the spiritual world in which You live. At least let me see my Guardian Angel or someone else from your Kingdom! What You're showing me now are the energies from between the two worlds, the spiritual and the material ones. They are the material energies created by the people living on this earth, the energies of the dead lost between two worlds that all the practitioners of shamanism and psychic reading can see. I don't wish to see these energies. I worked hard and sacrificed so much to come to You, my Lord, and I would like to see the true spiritual world, which Jesus Christ could see.

The Apparition of the Guardian Angel

After I spoke to God, something happened at my parents' place: a new light, totally different from the ones I knew, came shining above my head.

This is what happened. In the dead of the night, when I was half-asleep, I opened the bathroom door but didn't turn on the light. I only switched off the light in the hallway, which could still illuminate the bathroom. In that moment, a white cloud descended on my head. My eyes were mid-closed, and the white cloud was crystalline and so truthful. It sent me a message, like the cloud of negative energy in Peru did. This time that energy was the Guardian Angel.

After I switched on the light in the hallway, a bulb instantly burnt out. Mistakenly, I had turned on the light inside the bathroom, and though everything happened in a few seconds, I understood what was going on, as if someone was explaining everything to me down to the last detail. I knew that the light of energy above me was the Guardian Angel who had answered my plea by showing up. And when I turned on the light in the hallway, I knew that the *energies* of the Guardian Angel were too power-ful for our material world, and they had burnt out that electric bulb. And when I switched on the light inside the bathroom, I knew that the bulb was saved by the Guardian Angel, who had dimmed his energies to protect it. But I also knew that if I had tried to turn on the light in the bathroom for the second time, the Guardian Angel would not be able to keep his ener-gies at bay, and the light bulb would burn out like the one on the hallway.

To my knowledge, the Guardian Angel doesn't have the right to appear in our material world. But on that night, God made an exception, showing me His gratitude for everything I had done for Him.

The apparition of the Guardian Angel in a material way made me the happiest man on earth, and I was hoping that from that moment on, I would forge tighter bonds with the positive energies and God and the spiritual world. Unfortunately, a little later, God created a series of circum-stances that left me in total disarray.

IONEL ROTARU

DISTURBING CIRCUMSTANCES

1) My Friend's Wife Had a Terrible Accident

A few days later, I decided to pay a visit to some friends in Gasca village at the outskirts of Bender Moldova, where Nastia and I had built a house and lived for several years. We befriended many people there, and George and his wife, Maria, remained our dearest ones.

I was going back to Canada soon and was budgeting my time, planning to see my friends in the middle of the week and spending the last Saturday and Sunday with my parents. Ideally, I should have seen my friends on Tuesday evening, and next morning I would have gone to Bender, where I had practiced medicine for a while. I had planned it because my parents had a dental appointment and we could have spent some time in the city together. I wanted to invite them to a restaurant and take a taxi back home. It sounded like a perfect plan, but it was not meant to be.

I called George on his cell phone to inform him about my intentions and find out if he was available to host me. I called him on Monday morning at ten, but he didn't answer. I couldn't leave him a message, since he didn't have a voice-mail set up. I tried a second time, and since he didn't answer, I suspected that he wasn't happy to welcome me on that day. I waited a few more hours, but no one answered that number, making me think that I should pick another day for my visit. So I decided to leave on Thursday afternoon and head back to my parents' place at noon on the following day.

Well, leaving on Thursday would have been good too, though not as good as on Tuesday to Wednesday. The problem was that my parents had to be in the city that Wednesday, and I wanted to invite them to a restaurant and then come back home by taxi together. They had never had dinner at a restaurant or ridden a cab, two luxuries they could never afford. Now that I was there with them, they would have certainly enjoyed the evening in the city with me.

After I called George the third time, I understood what God was telling me, and I was hoping that my friend's silence was just a pure coincidence. I was still hoping he would call me back before midnight, but no one did and I went to bed. I was convinced that the Lord didn't want me to pay my visit on Tuesday. Bitter-sweet and confused, I fell asleep.

16

George called me next morning, asking me if I'd tried to reach him. It was almost noon, and I could have gone to see him by taking the bus at 12:05 or even at 15:00. But as I knew what God wanted me to do, I said to George: "I called you to let you know I was coming to you today, but because you didn't answer, I scheduled my visit for Thursday, if you're available."

"No problem," George said.

On Thursday morning, I was ready to step out when George called me to tell me that he was going to see his wife at the hospital, and he'd be at home after 18:00. I found it convenient, because I couldn't be at his place before 18:00 anyway, but I was surprised that Maria had been admitted to a hospital.

"What happened?" I asked George.

"She fell down the basement steps," he said.

I arrived at his residence shortly after 18:00, and he told me the whole story. On Wednesday morning, she decided to clean up the basement, and she slipped and rolled down the steps. As a result, she fractured her right femur. Now pay attention to the following details.

We went to bed at 21:30. George was leaving at 6:00–6:05 to catch his bus at 06:30. There was one bus leaving for the city every hour, and I would take the 07:30 bus to go to the city. The next day, George walked out at 06:05, and I left his place one hour later.

In the city, I bought some flowers and went to the hospital to see Maria. She looked scared but was happy to see me. She was lying on that bed—pale, immobile, scared, and helpless. She had been scheduled for surgery and now she had to wait a few days.

I asked her what happened, and she told me that she had fallen down the basement steps at 07:00 in the morning. She'd been in terrible pain from a broken bone and was about to lose consciousness. There was no one at home at that time to help her up, so she remained on the floor for a couple of hours. Eventually, with her leg bone creaking, she crawled up the steps on her hands to the outside and cried out for help. At 09:00, a passerby heard her and came in to help her.

Her explanation left me speechless. Technically, her accident had to do with me 100 percent, since I was supposed to stop this tragedy. I had planned to see George and Maria on Tuesday evening and ride a city bus next day at 07:30. I was supposed to wake up between 06:20–06:25, take a shower, and wait for Maria to make my breakfast. I was supposed to walk out the gate at 07:05. Maria wouldn't have had enough time to clean up the basement, because at 07:00–07:05, she was seeing me to the gate. So the negative energies couldn't have put their diabolic plan into action.

**

Those who read my first book know that when a negative energy is coming upon us and something bad is going to happen, these energies know the *time*, the *place*, and the *person* to be visited by the bad things. And they also know how the accidents are going to come about. If we can change at least one of these elements, the negative energy too will change its destination. In my first book, I mentioned several cases when God was trying to help me alter the time or place where accidents were expected to occur. If I had changed at least one of these elements, I could have fended off the accidents.

The first situation God organized for me when I was just starting to write my first book was the accident with Ramona, a Romanian friend from Montreal who along with her family was in a state of discouragement and pessimism. She'd recently had cancer surgery, her husband was unemployed, and they didn't know what the future held for them.

My wife and I insisted that they and their family come to our house for at least a few weeks to regain their confidence in life. Our house, located on the shore of the Atlantic Ocean with nature and beautiful views, would have made them forget about their troubles. My wife and I told them that we'd take care of all the expenses for their transportation and vacation.

Ramona announced that she wanted to come with her family on a Thursday by bus from Montreal. On the same day, my family and I were to return by ferry from New Brunswick. When Ramona found out about this, she wanted to change the day to a later day. I didn't allow this but promised that everything would be fine. We would arrive by boat at 06:00 p.m. and they'd arrive by bus from Montreal just after midnight, so there was no need for them to change their arrival day.

On Thursday, the day we were returning from our vacation in New Brunswick, I had calculated the distance and the time to arrive at the ferry almost two hours before departure. On the way, all kinds of things happened that prevented me from arriving by car on time to the ferry. The signs of God were so obvious that you couldn't help but see them. It was as if God was shouting at me not to go home that day. At one point, I thought that if I didn't manage to get to the ferry on time, I'd send Ramona and her family to our Ukrainian friends for a night.

In the end, my arrogance and my desire to fulfill my promise prevailed. For the last thirty kilometers, I drove at 140km/hour just to get to the ferry. We arrived just as the ferry was closing the doors. My wife and our girls were the last to board the ship. I stayed with the car for the next day.

Arriving home, my wife met our friends at the bus after midnight. They came home and all went to bed. Ramona, in the dark, not knowing the interior of the house, fell and rolled down the stairs to the basement, fracturing her spine, ribs, the basin, etc.

The situation unfolded in such a way that God/the Universe showed me that I must listen to His advice/signs, otherwise people will suffer because of me. Because of my disobedience, Ramona suffered. Through the same experience, God showed me not only that I must listen to His signs, but also that negative energies turn into disastrous situations at the exact time, in the exact place, and with the exact person. If I had listened to God's advice, the accident wouldn't have happened. God organized several situations of this kind for me, through which He demonstrated to me how negative energies work and how we can avoid them if we pay attention to God's signs.

***

Maria's case affected me deeply. God had taught me that life is the most precious thing on earth, and He'd stood by me numerous times to help me avoid the negative energies.

Ramona's case and Maria's misfortune were identical, but God's intentions were totally different, as He'd insisted that I change Ramona's place to avert her tragedy.

In my first book, I wrote about several situations through which God helped me understand how to avoid negative situations. I had a car accident, for example, through which I learned again that I should change the time when misfortune comes. I had a situation with a careless pedestrian. God did everything possible for me to change my time to avoid running into the careless guy.

But in Maria's case, there were no benefits. It was just a terrible misfortune that involved the health of a human being. Maria remained physically challenged for the rest of her life, and she needed a walker to move along.

I couldn't understand what was going on. Why had God let this happen? Why did God insist that such a calamity should happen? Why did He involve me—the one who knows about the signs of God and who writes books about God's relationship with the people of the earth?

This event must have been essential for everybody, as God wanted me to get involved in it and write about it in my book. Maria's misfortune made me realize that God was asking me to write my second book. Was I ready to go for it? I wasn't ready to write my first book either, let alone proceed with another one. But God made the impossible possible and trained me in how to write them. He insisted that I begin writing, and I listened to His signs and did exactly what He asked me to do.

Now I had some knowledge about His intentions, but I had no idea what subject to approach in my second book. Luckily, I had made notes each time I dealt with a bizarre situation, and I decided to use them. I reviewed my notes from June 2019 in Peru, where I saw a negative energy for the first time in my life, until March 2020, when the COVID-19 pandemic was spreading around the world, and I discovered God's message hiding behind them, so I started to scribble my second book.

Let's analyze all these circumstances, commencing with Maria's accident.

Spiritual Psychoanalysis

Before I start the spiritual psychoanalysis, I'd like to introduce to the reader some details about the configuration of materialistic energies on earth and about the Laws of the Universe that govern them. I described in my first book a scheme according to which the energies are structured. Every form of existence in the Universe is an energy, and each of them creates energies. Inanimate forms of existence create energies through their movements. Animate forms of existence create energies not only through their movements but also through their actions, intentions, adaptation capacities, etc.

Human beings create energies through our thoughts, words, actions, desires, intentions, etc. All the energies created by us accumulate in a kind of "Personal Box." This box has three departments: the department with positive energies, the department with negative energies, and the department with accomplished energies. In the Universe there is a law according to which energies from the box are directed. This law is called the "Boomerang Law." It makes the energies created by us return to us. Every energy returns to its creator. If we do good, then positive situations will happen to us, and if we do bad, then bad situations await us.

The negative energies from our Personal Box return to us until we realize that what we're doing isn't good. When we realize that we have to stop doing harm (stop being aggressive, for example), the negative energy (of aggression) turns into accomplished energies, and this energy passes from the department of negative energies to the department of accomplished energies. The accomplished energies" from the Personal Box make us evolve spiritually in the material world on earth.

The same principle of a Personal Box exists in every family, society/community, and country. Each has its Personal Box, including our civilization. The Boomerang Law of the Universe behaves identically with all the energies in any box.

a) Why did the Lord want Maria to have this accident?

The accident was a result of the negative energies Maria had created during the course of her life. The energies had grown exponentially and reached a point where they had to discharge their power in the most devastating way. Definitively, Maria had done so much wrong in her life that God wasn't able to forestall the accident. On the contrary, He had an obligation before the Laws of the Universe to protect the negative energies by letting them charge at Maria.

In the material world on earth, each of us is influenced not only by the energies from our Personal Box but from all the other Personal Boxes already mentioned. In other words, negative situations can happen to us not only because of us, but also because of our family/community/country/civilization. When this happens, God/Divine Energy of the Universe helps us avoid the negative situation that awaits us (as happened in the case of Ramona, the accident, etc.). But when we accumulate an overflowing amount of negative energy in our Personal Box, like in Maria's case, then God can only let terrible things happen.

The Universe is obliged to obey the Laws of the Universe, because not only does He alone direct the energies of the Universe, but there's also a Third Energy of the universe, which I talk about in Chapter Three: "The Third Energy and Its Influence on the Active Energies."

The Universe is also obliged to respect the Boomerang Law and return to us all the negative energies created by us, because the human being is very hard to convince. He doesn't want to understand that it's not good to do harm until he personally confronts his energies. Only by going through the most difficult temptations does the human being realize that he must change. Even if Maria was forced to face all the negative energies created by her until now, and even if she was left with a physical challenge for life, still the intention of the Universe is to make her aware that she has to change, that she must transform her negative energies into accomplished energies.

As you can see, the evil that the Universe distributes to us isn't really that bad. It's for our good, to help us realize that we must focus on our spiritual evolution by eliminating from our habits the evil that it hurts.

b) Why did God want me involved in this unfortunate accident?

I was the innocent who knew His signs perfectly and wrote books about Him. Let's try to find an answer together.

When Maria got injured, God was trying to send a message through me. At that time, I was writing about His signs and was planning to achieve a true Spiritual Psychoanalysis. He wanted to wake up me and all of us on this planet to warn us about the peril of staying in our material world, away from spirituality.

In my first book, I wrote about the stages of evolution of each individual and our entire civilization. At this time, our civilization is living the age of adolescence, when negative and positive energies take possession of us and give impetus to our physical temptations. They boost the energies we create as we crave for more comfort and material satisfaction. As we pursue these goals, we destroy what's important from a spiritual viewpoint—namely our family and natural environment. For a hundred years, we've damaged our planet, our family relationships, and so many of our spiritual bonds that we have almost nothing left of what God created on this earth. I believe that through Maria's accident, God wanted to send a warning message to us and our entire civilization.

God's Message on a Personal Level

The Lord wants us to change our way of thinking and demeanor. If up until now we've lived in a stage of material evolution against the backdrop of the material thinking, where our ego and selfish interests prevailed, the time has come to switch to spiritual thinking that gives prominence to the surrounding world of animals and plants, the entire planet and the universe, and to all the signs of God, our Heavenly Father. Unless we give up our self-centered thinking and tame our physical temptations, we will continue to generate negative energies and meet the same fate as Maria.

God's Message Worldwide

The Lord wants to warn each individual in this world about the negative energies we will face unless we stop generating negative energies at a world level and overload the Personal Box of our civilization (see detailed explanations in Chapter Four).

Unless our civilization heeds the message conveyed by God through Maria's accident and draws the right conclusions in the wake of the COVID-19 Ppandemic, and unless it changes its material principles and egocentric behavior, God cannot resist the negative energies spawned by our civilization. He will follow the Laws of the Universe and give support to the overloaded quantum of negative energies, like He did in Maria's case.

Remember that during the adolescence of our civilization, the negative energies we produce are in abundance, and they continue to pile up and multiply at an astronomic pace, like they did in Maria's case. And our stubborn refusal to obey our Lord will spell disaster for our chances as a human race.

But we should know that nothing is lost and everything is still in our power; we are still capable of preventing the catastrophes, and we should do something right now!

2) My argument with my friend

When I visited my parents in the fall of 2019, my wife called me and told me that Boris, one of our family friends in Canada, wanted me to bring him a special dog he had purchased for his own breeding business in Canada, where dogs of that kind were tremendously expensive. Boris knew that I was in Moldova, and he was trying to save himself a trip.

I had befriended Boris fourteen years earlier, and I agreed to help him provided that all the papers were in order and the customs officers would let me board the plane with a dog that didn't belong to me.

It wasn't easy to fetch a puppy from Moldova, and Nastia was surprised that I accepted. There are formalities to go through, and a thorough check is required at the border. She would never have agreed to it. Boris contacted me and gave me the information about the man who was bringing the puppy to the airport. He also told me that all the documents would be in my name. This was all he said.

My plane was taking off at 5:30 in the morning. As my parents live 170 kilometers away from the Chisinau International Airport, I went to spend the night with a former alumnus who lives in the capital city. This would make it easier to get to my plane in the morning. We woke up at 03:00, and my friend gave me a ride to the airport.

I was on my way to the airport when Boris called me.

"Ionel, the man is coming to meet with you, and he will give you a bag of food for the puppy. He will provide you with two sets of documents, two passports, and two health cards. One set is in my name, and one is in yours. I placed mine at the bottom of the bag, but don't show them at the customs. Show them yours," he said to me.

I wasn't very excited about his convoluted monologue. His words took me by surprise, but there was nothing I could say. Everything smelled fishy. I was expecting that the documents were in Boris's name, and I didn't expect that he would make me bring the dog to Canada with false documents in my name.

"You mean the puppy is in my name?" I asked him. "This is not my dog; it's yours. Now you want me to lie at the customs? I never do this! Not for a single minute. You'd force me lie for your dog? Please never ask me to bring you anything from Moldova again!"

Boris tried to ingratiate himself with me. "Please, only this time. I promise that I will never ask you anything else."

I was upset and hung up.

Definitively the papers were fake and could have resulted in criminal charges being brought against me. For a second, I thought I could show the officers the papers in Boris's name, and once in Canada, Boris would be there and I would be let right through. But there was another issue. It suddenly struck me that the convoluted situation was a sign of God. When we're ready to take up on a new road in our life, God shows us which way to proceed.

The intricate situation with the puppy had begun exactly when I was on my way to the international airport. I was certain it was a sign from God and I should not take the puppy with me. There was no doubt in my mind about it, and I decided to refuse my friend. I felt relieved that God was asking me to do the right thing. But on the other side, I was afraid that I would lose one of my best friends in Canada. With a broken heart, I chose to listen to God rather than Boris' plea, just to stay on the safe side of life.

I met with that man at the airport and I said to him, "I'm sorry but I had no idea about Boris's two sets of documents. He told me about them just fifteen minutes ago, and I don't want to cross the border with fake papers. Sorry, I've decided not to take the puppy to Canada."

The man tried to convince me that the documents were original. He showed me the two passports and the medical sheets, saying that they had the original stamps. Then he attempted to call Boris in Canada.

I had to stop him. "I'm sorry that you got yourself into this, but my decision is final. I am not going to take the puppy to Canada." I turned back and proceeded to the check-in area.

From Canada, my friend Boris was sending me one text message after another. He was calling me names, and to stop him I had to block his number and take the chance of losing him forever.

Two weeks later, Boris went to Moldova to fetch his puppy. When he tried to board his plane back to Canada, he had to pay a fine of a few hundred dollars for his lies. Also, I found out that the documents he had made in my name weren't for a pedigree puppy. Boris had lied to me just to skip the customs fees in the amount of a thousand Canadian dollars. On top of everything, at the bottom of the bag with dog food someone had cozily stashed medication that would have certainly put me in a very delicate situation at the border. Imagine my situation at customs had I brought Boris' puppy and the bag as he had planned: two sets of documents, of which one was fake, plus expensive medication stuck under the dog food. It would have been a good chance to bring a case against me.

Spiritual Psychoanalysis

God spared me a big inconvenience at the Canadian border. However, He began sending me other messages through His signs—much more complex messages than before.

In a spiritual world, evolution never ends. It's in continuous motion, just like how we learn in school. In the first grade, for instance, we learn the fundamental significance of His signs. In the second grade, we learn the hidden significance conveyed through God's messages as we're trained to analyze the signs of the Lord in an abstract form.

The case of Boris's puppy falls under the hidden significance delivered through the signs of God. Let's see what these significances are.

THE FIRST SIGNIFICANCE:

I'm a resourceful guy, and I could have made it through at the border based on Boris's documents. But since I'd been initiated in the signs of God, I'd learned that I should never disparage those signs or try to get kickbacks from them for my personal interest or pleasure. We should faithfully listen to all His signs and do the right thing, not only what we would be pleased to do.

If God had been interested only in protecting me at the Canadian border, He would have found another solution to warn me, and He would have ordered Boris to call me two days prior to my departure. Then I could have called Boris back in due course. God always has numerous mysterious options, but He was interested only in protecting me, because what mattered to Him was the hidden message delivered through Boris's situation.

Why did He make such an effort to preclude me from bringing that puppy to Canada, knowing that I would lose an invaluable friend? He knew the consequences, but why did He want me to lose a friend? I believe He forced me to change my destiny patterned on His personal principles. Moreover, He had forced me to live my life at the far end of the North American continent, where I know no one, far away from all my friends in Montreal and Quebec. So not only did He take me away from my friends, but now He removed the best one from my life. Why did He do that?

When I came back from Moldova, I stopped at the apartment of my daughter Lya, who lived in Quebec, and I answered this question. I told my family about Boris and the argument that ruined our friendship. My daughters and my wife liked Boris's family a lot, and the news saddened them. I tried to explain what had happened from a spiritual point of view and from the perspective of God's intentions:

According to the Laws of the Universe, to win something, we must lose something first. In other words, in this Universe, there is a Wheel of Life that brings around prosperous periods followed by times of loss and dire need. I believe that God wanted to announce to me that a big surprise was coming, and before that happened, I needed to lose something precious in my life. So now the Wheel of Life was telling me that I had to lose a valuable friend, and the following spin would repay me with the accumulation/acquisition of new friends.

Usually the Wheel of Life is a succession of energies of the same kind; for example, if we live in love and harmony with someone, then at a given moment, this energy turns into a period of conflict and hatred. If we earn a lot of money, then at a given moment, we must expect significant losses of money. In the case of the loss of my friend, this suggests to me that the Universe is preparing another category of friends for me who could bring a lot more value than the lost one.

Equally important is that with spiritual evolution, with our ability to produce increasingly enormous amounts of positive energies, the Law of the Wheel of Life causes negative energies to be created against us of the same magnitude as the positive energies created by us. I tell you this not to discourage you but to inform you that with our spiritual evolution, we will be forced to live in harmony with many kinds of negative energies. Our spiritual evolution is based on our ability to live in harmony with negative energies and on our knowledge to find their positive parts that could shape our thinking, decisions, and behavior for our future. Let's see when this accumulation is going to happen.

As I told you, my book will be published soon. I hope it will be successful and that instead of the friends I lost, I'll gain other kinds of friends, ones with spiritual minds and aspirations. I had always wanted to have them in my presence. So I believe that in exchange for Boris, I will acquire friends who will make me feel like I'm in the Kingdom of God right here on earth.

THE SECOND SIGNIFICANCE:

Now, what did God want to tell Boris?

Not only I lost a good friend, but Boris lost one too. He lost me. Why did God want him to lose me as a friend? Why did God have Boris put on the customs black list? What was the reason for all this? Let me tell you something about Boris's negative side. Boris never hesitated to dodge the law and lie for his material benefits.

First and foremost, when you open a pedigree business, you make sure the pets are pedigree and buy them from a reliable source. Boris didn't buy his dog from Canada, where pedigrees are guaranteed 100 percent. He bought it but from Moldova, where a lot of stuff comes with forged documents.

Secondly, when you acquire a couple of dogs you intend to breed to sell their puppies, you must have all their supporting documentation, including their breeding line and true origin. Boris didn't have any legal proof that the dog he'd brought from abroad was a pedigree, because he didn't have any papers, nor did he register his dog or pay for him at customs. Boris wasn't interested in going legal for his business. He didn't care if his dogs were purebreds. He just wanted to make money off his business, however undeserved that money may be.

Boris managed to circumvent the Canadian laws, since no one at the border bothered to check up on him thoroughly. But nothing can pass unnoticed, because each time we lie, dodge, deceive, or mislead the surrounding world for our personal interest, we inevitably create negative energies that, pursuant to the Laws of the Universe, will rush back towards us, particularly when huge negative clouds build up in the air. In Boris' case, the cloud of negative energies grew so big that the Universe was forced to send it back to him and teach him not to do what he had done again. God punished him at Canadian customs and stripped him of one of his best friends—me.

This was the explanation I gave to my wife and daughters.

THE THIRD SIGNIFICANCE:

I'm trying to understand if I deserved the negative energies that ruined my relationship with one of my best friends in Canada. "Did I really deserve it?" I kept asking myself.

In the past years, I hadn't created any negative energies in my personal relations with my friends, or my enemies either. I had tried hard to change my way of thinking and look at God through the surrounding natural scenery and all the situations of my friends and enemies. I viewed the surrounding world as the harmony of a whole (*like God together with the Universe to which we all belong*), and I perceived the ongoing situations as messages from God, and the persons in my entourage as little mischievous, though innocent, children. So there was no way I could generate negative energies that would destructively impact on my friendship with Boris. But why did God want the undeserved negative energies to descend on me?

The answer to this question can be found by continuing to read this book.

When a negative energy is charging at me and ignites a conflict between me and someone else, I realize that neither of us are at fault for the argument, but only the energy is to be blamed. So I don't pass judgment on the other person, and I discard any negative thoughts from my head and let the negative energy fizzle out helplessly.

I used this kind of technique during my argument with Boris. Unfortunately, he never stopped chastising and judging me in front of our mutual friends, which fueled the negative energies and precipitated the termination of our friendship.

THE FOURTH SIGNIFICANCE:

Eight months after I finished writing my book, I realized that God was trying to send me the message that the loss of my good friends was a foretaste of a very important loss of my life (see details in Chapter Four).

HOW I HANDLE NEGATIVE ENERGIES

I came back from Moldova in early October and stayed in Montreal for a while to accommodate some friends who had just arrived from Romania. I had good memories of them, and now they'd come to spend two weeks with us in Canada. My wife joined us, and we went together to Niagara Falls, the Thousand Islands, Old Montreal, Quebec City, Montmorency Falls, and the gorgeous regions around my place.

After my friends returned to Romania, I became the target of negative energies and couldn't fight them in any way. But before I tell you about their invasion, let me recount what happened while my friends were here, which demonstrates that sometimes I can handle the negative energies in my life.

In *The Destiny and Signs of God* (second edition), I describe how God warns us about the apparition of negative energies and catastrophes in our life. After I finished my first book, I believed that I knew a lot about this subject, but the apparition of the visible energies and then the disturbing situations I've mentioned left me in total darkness. I knew that whatever happened to us, and whatever negative or positive energy came upon us, we must respond with love and kindness to create positive energies. Here's an example of how to handle negative energies.

Tatiana, our friend from Romania, has an elderly brother whose wife had left him when their son was just a teenager and immigrated to Canada in the highest secrecy. Before Tatiana and her husband, Gicu, came to Canada, their nephew, who was thirty years old and had not seen his mother since he was in his teens, asked Tatiana to meet with his mother and tell her that he wanted to see her. The boy missed his mom desperately, and his father was still in love with his wife. They both wanted to meet with the estranged woman.

But Tatiana and her husband didn't really like her. They actually hated her for what she had done to her family, and they loathed seeing her. As Tatiana and her husband were thinking of a way to avoid that woman, I insisted that they send her a text message. I said, "At this moment, your opinion in this matter is irrelevant; you promised the boy that you would meet with his mother, so you don't have a choice now. You're obliged to meet with her. Even if you hate it, it's your duty to make the first step. She'll answer and tell you if she wants to come to see you, and you'll be there to wait for her. But if she doesn't answer your call, or if she declines the invitation, you can give a sigh of relief, and no one will blame you for not having met with her."

Reluctantly, Tatiana sent that woman a text message, hoping that she wouldn't answer. But the boy's mother responded quickly that she was coming to the meeting. This scared my friends, who intended to cancel the plan by pretending that something happened and they were no longer available.

Then I gave them a technical explanation about how to handle the energies of our life:

"In any relationship with another person, we act like it's a tennis game. We are creators of positive and negative energies through our thoughts, words, desires, love, and hatred. So when the ball falls in our court, we should treat it with love and send it back to where it belongs. In your case, when the young boy asked you to help him meet his mother in Canada, he sent a ball of energy into your court. Now it's your duty to treat this ball with love and answer this energy with positive thoughts and serve the ball back where it should successfully land.

"Your duty is to contact the boy's mother and invite her to come to the meeting. If she doesn't answer your message, or if she declines your invitation, it won't be your fault; it will mean that the energy ball failed its mission because of the boy's mother, not because of you.

"But if this woman answers your message and wants to meet with you, it means that the energy ball is back in your court. And pursuant to the Spiritual Laws, you don't have a choice. It is your duty to respond favorably to the woman's request and meet with her. But if you lie to her and cancel the meeting, you will destroy the energy ball and turn it into a negative energy, which will cause evil both to the boy and to you, who failed to deliver on your obligations.

The negative energy you create will weigh hard on your conscience for the rest of your life because you did nothing to help the boy see his dream come true. But if you go to that meeting, you will fulfill your duty, and the boy's energy ball will successfully drop at its destination. That will make the boy's wish come true and give birth to the most beautiful, positive energies on earth.

"However, there is always something. If you meet with the boy's mother and argue with her and tell her what you think about her, instead of giving her warm regards and love from the boy, the boy's energy ball will turn into a negative energy. Your argument will shatter the boy's hopes, and his energy ball of love will never hit its target as it had initially planned.

"In other words, you must see the boy's mother and treat her nicely."

My friends met with that lady in a restaurant in Saint Foy's neighborhood, not far from Lya's place. It was an unexpectedly cordial meeting that left the road open for a new relationship between the boy and his mother.

I have always been skillful and resourceful and could handle the energies easily. Unfortunately, the visible energies that came into my life and the disturbing situations that have occurred from the spring of 2019 struck deep fear in me and made me lose my temper every so often, as seen in the following situations.

THE PARADOX OF LIFE

I finished writing my first book with the conviction that I am wise enough and capable of handling the energies of life. Ironically, in that moment, a series of situations with new energies in my life indicated that actually I didn't know anything.

After our Romanian friends left, a string of negative energies started to rain down on me, and I had no clue about their meaning. I was scared and in total disarray. The first energy coming out of the blue was the issue of Nastia's car.

After we saw our friends to the airport in Montreal, I took my wife's car to the Honda dealer to have the oil changed and the winter tires installed. The car was ten years old, and based on my experience, it wasn't worth driving anymore. Old cars break down often, and lots of money is required for maintenance. I was already planning to trade it in for a new one. At the same time, I was engaged in paying instalments on Lya's apartment, and I was waiting for her to finish her studies and remove some strain from our savings.

The dealer checked the car and found that it needed serious reconditioning. He said the car had a manufacturing defect, and he suggested that I trade it in for a new one. I had no intention of buying a new car, but I accepted a pre-owned, two-year-old one with 38,000 kilometers on the odometer. Though we weren't ready to pay so much, we accepted the deal and became the owners of an almost brand-new vehicle.

I had no idea that our acquisition had marked the beginning of the invasion of a long series of negative energies, which I thought I could easily handle. I even told my wife not to worry too much, because we'd win back more in the near future. But later on I realized that what had come upon us was an unknown and undeserved energy I had never seen before.

Shortly after we bought the new car, I had a strange feeling that something new, like some alien force, was taking possession of me and my entire place. It happened on a November night when the sky was dark and the wind was gusting. At two o'clock in the morning, a terrible noise woke me up, suggesting that a slate from the roof had been ripped off by the wind. At dawn, I went out to check my roof. I was right: a shingle had been torn off exactly where I had thought, and I had to call a tradesman to fix it.

I understood what was going on. I had to deal with very powerful negative energies, which came upon me undeservedly, and I couldn't protect myself against them. Previously, I had hoped that the invasion of these energies would help me grow the third eye, but I was so scared that I immediately gave up that foolish thought.

Our house is built on a hill sloping downward to the Atlantic Ocean. The air currents are strong, and many houses in this area are damaged by the storms during the cold season. Gusting winds and heavy rainfalls rip off the roofs and loosen the plastic boards from the exterior walls. Our house was the only one untouched, and the unexpected scarring caused by the violent wind was giving me the creeps. We had replaced our roof two months earlier, and the installers had used high quality material with a lifetime warranty. Strangely, for a decade our house with an old roof stood firm before the elements, and now with a new replacement it was partially damaged! And no other house on our street was hit!

All this while, I used a series of methods to protect our house from these negative energies. I prayed, proceeded with meditations, and sprinkled holy water around like priests in Eastern Orthodox churches do. I was convinced that our house was safe! But now I was frightened and confused.

I knew that my family didn't deserve the negative energies that stormed our place. After all, my way of life was transcendent and should protect us from all the evils. Certainly those negative energies that didn't belong to us were precipitating the opening of my third eye. So I prayed the Lord: "God, I don't want the third eye, so if this is the protocol, please don't send them to me anymore!"

THE FIRST NEGATIVE VISIBLE ENERGY I PERCEIVED WITH EYES WIDE OPEN

Came the first snow and we began using our fireplace. One night I started the fire in the living room. Nastia was already dressed in pajamas and was sitting in bed in front of the fireplace watching TV, and I went up to change. I turned on the lights in the bathroom, and suddenly a dark gray square, like a small cloud, was silhouetted against the white walls, just like the one I had seen in Lima. The object was moving fast and escaping my gaze, like the spot the ophthalmologist asks you to follow during an eye test. It was quick, like a living organism, and it suddenly vanished through the bathroom ceiling.

I searched for it for a short while, but it was nowhere to be seen. Through my sixth sense, I knew that the negative energy had come to me to bother me, but I wasn't worried at all, since it was nothing but a whim. I was frightened by all the previous negative energies, and I was trying to convince myself that the small cloud in the bathroom was just an illusion or a trick played by my imagination late at night.

I came down to the living room to cuddle my wife. Then I could hear noises from outside. It wasn't the wind; there was something else knocking on the walls and scaring me to death, like on the night our roof was torn. I couldn't believe that in less than two months, our house was damaged again. That thought was frightening me, and impossible questions were flooding my mind, shattering my confidence that my house was safe and secure. I stepped out and saw that a loose board on the front wall was being flipped off by the wind. It wasn't serious damage, and I used a screwdriver to tighten the board back in place.

Analysis:

I was scared and fed up with my spiritual evolution and the development of the third eye, and all I wanted was to be left alone. I didn't know what kind of negative energies had been storming my mind for almost a year, but I was sure that I didn't deserve them.

While I was writing my first book, everything that happened and all the signs I'd received from God were so logical, I could find an explanation for each one. But now they were all absurd and striking deep fear in my bones. Why would they do that? After all, I didn't deserve any of them. On that night, I didn't say anything to my wife.

God was so good to teach me how to defend myself against the negative energies, and He showed me how to live in harmony with them.

a) At least once a year, I sprinkle the house with holy water, like Eastern Orthodox Church priests do in Moldova and Romania. Also, I pray to the Lord to cleanse our house and family of all the negative energies and turn them into positive ones. I pray to all the negative energies to leave us alone and, unless they turn into love and spiritual light, go where their service is needed. Sometimes I spread burnt incense and holy water through the entire house to chase the negative energies away.

b) Also, I successfully meditate, like in *The Archangel Guide to Ascension,* which was registered by Diana Cooper on October 15, 2018. I am using now using this on a monthly basis.

c) One of the most important things I've learned from God is that we should train ourselves to live in harmony with the evil and the good, because we all are making one single Whole in this Universe. Therefore, the good and the evil belong to us, and everything that lives and goes around us is a part of us, and we are a part of it too!

Practically, all the good and evil people do and all the situations in which we find ourselves, positive or negative, are a result of our deeds and a sign that indicates which direction we should take on the road of our spiritual evolution. My God-given knowledge helped me see the Lord and myself from the perspective of all the persons around me and all the events that happened in my life.

Therefore, when I interact with someone and develop a relationship with him, and he tries to do something evil to me, I don't judge him. I simply welcome God's message through that person and examine myself to see if my own mistakes could have started the conflict. I look at evil persons with love, like I'm looking at an innocent child, and I show compassion to them, because they will have to take many risks and face unfortunate incidents before they realize what they did wrong.

When I'm involved in a negative situation, I don't pass judgment on anyone. I only try to find the origin of the negative energy and understand the message of our Lord to see what I did wrong. I treat the negative energy with love and respect for its message, which is essential for my spiritual evolution.

Attention: After the effect of the negative energies is consumed and God's message successfully sent across (meaning I understood the message, applied it in practice, and shook off all my bad habits), the negative energies turn into Godly, positive energies. Each time it happens, I am happy for what I achieve from these challenges, and I thank those energies and God from the bottom of my heart for their strenuous efforts.

d) To cleanse my house, I also use the Tibetan bowls, whose singing makes the lingering energies dissipate quickly. I bought two sets of such instruments, with fourteen singing bowls in all, and took a training course in the sound massage therapy the Tibetans use in their monasteries to cleanse charkas and cure illnesses.

I use these bowls every day, and each session lasts at least one hour. These bowls have enough power to chase the undeserved negative energies out of my house and not let them ever come back in.

Summary statement:

God has taught me that we are *one whole* all together, and we must live in harmony with everyone around us. Sadly, we tend to embrace the good and ignore the evil. We pray to our Lord and are grateful to those who do good to us, and we try to do good to them and want to be well off, but we ignore the negative energies completely.

To live in harmony with the whole world, we must take into consideration the negative energies, not only the positive ones. After all, God told me to pray to the negative energies too, and thank them for their contribution to my spiritual education. Also, He taught me that the sacrifice is a special way of telling the negative energies how grateful I am to all of them. Through sacrifices, we show our debt of gratitude for the good they do to us, and this will keep their vicious spirit at bay and eventually tame it. Just like we feed a hungry dog who then befriends and paws us, the negative energies turn into energies of love and harmony.

The sacrifice of the Easter lamb is an old tradition. By this gesture, we're not giving gifts to our Lord. We're only giving a small present to the negative energies to make them feel that they belong to the one whole of the Universe and to feel elated on the day of our Lord's celebration.

For seven years, since God began teaching me the phenomenon of the sacrifice, I have offered a daily sacrifice to the negative energies for my family: I give them a slice of bread and I give out clothes and stuff I no longer need. Each time I do it, I ask the Lord to accept my sacrifice for the negative energies, and I ask the negative energies to turn into positive ones for my family or leave me and withdraw to the levels of evolution where they can be of use.

MY ACTIONS TOWARDS THE NEGATIVE ENERGIES ARE CONFIRMED AS TRUE

Recently, I watched a few episodes of the documentary *The Story of God* with Morgan Freeman. In the episode "Search for the Devil," Morgan Freeman speaks with various religious groups about their view of the evil man and negative energies. Most of these prelates resented these energies and said they were trying to discard them. But the Tibetans gave a different approach.

Morgan Freeman discovered that monks at the Tibetan monasteries in Katmandu don't pray to chase away the negative energies. On the contrary, they lure them to their monastery and turn them into positive energies. Once they have turned, these energies become highly protective, since they know the bad habits of the negative energies very well. The Tibetans, therefore, ask them to kick the reluctant negative energies out of their place.

An analysis of the monks' attitude towards the negative energies:

I was happy that what God was teaching me was similar to the methods of the Tibetan monks. In my first book, I deemed the negative energies as our protectors. Up until now, we've all lived in a time of material evolution of our soul, in which everything is driven by the Law of the Jungle, which dictates that only the stronger, wiser, belligerent, avenger, pusher, selfish, and mean can survive. All these negative energies have been useful, but from now on, we don't need them and we don't need to be belligerent, frightened, or cocky because in the age of spiritual evolution, the negative energies are pointless. From now on, we should turn our aggressiveness into love and compassion, and our revenge instincts into kindness and help.

We should eliminate the fear from our bones, because in a spiritual world, there is no evil. The worst of all evils will be for our wellbeing; therefore, we should turn our selfishness into generosity, because the Laws of the Universe say that the more you give, the more you get back. Our tricky habits won't help in a spiritual world, where fair-mindedness and dependability prevail.

The most important thing I gleaned from the episode "Search for the Devil" was a clear image of the classification of negative energies.

The first category includes the negative energies willing to turn into positive ones. These are the protection energies I described above. Throughout our material evolution, these energies meant well to us. They took all the necessary steps to safeguard us, and now that we've reached the threshold of the spiritual evolution, they won't change their principles and will continue to be our guardian and do everything for us—even turn into positive energies to please us and make us happy.

But in order to do that, they need our specific explanations, and we will have to respond from A to Z. So when we're fearful, envious, aggressive, or judgmental, we must explain to them that we want to change our life for a spiritual evolution in which life unfolds at a more meaningful level than in our material existence. We must explain our wish in full detail and let them know what the Laws of the Universe are. We must also tell them that during our spiritual evolution, they have a negative impact on us personally. In the end, we must ask them to metamorphose into positive energies of love, compassion, understanding, etc.

Included in the second category are the negative energies that don't wish to change and continue to cause harm and destruction in our life. This category has two parts.

The first part is made up of the deserved negative energies, which we create ourselves and want to live with all the time. Drugs, alcohol, and sex addiction are such energies. We should challenge them and ask them to go to the material evolution levels, where they might be needed. If they refuse, we should ask the Lord and all our positive energies to free us of these negative invaders.

The second part is made up of the undeserved negative energies, which are the product of the surrounding world: our family; our cities, villages, and towns; and our entire civilization. Usually they manifest themselves as diseases, conflicts, arguments, accidents, financial crises, wars, catastrophes, pandemics, terrorism, etc.

MY LAST VISIBLE NEGATIVE ENERGY

In the past ten years, we spent the holiday season in the Caribbean. We had bought a two-bedroom condominium with underground parking in Quebec City, and we spent a night there before we took off. The building is located in front of the university where our daughter Lya is studying, and each time we go abroad, we park our car in her underground garage, particularly in winter time. Once when we came back from vacation, we spent a night in Lya's condo. The next day, our daughter Sarah was going to her place in Malbaie, and we were leaving for our home in Chandler.

In the morning, I was refreshing myself in the bathroom, and suddenly I saw a negative energy of the same color as the one I had seen at my place. I was angry and stepped out of the bathroom without saying a word.

After we kissed our daughters goodbye, we went down to the basement, got in our car, and drove away. Half an hour later, the tire pressure indicator lit up, warning me that something was wrong. A few minutes later, the spray nozzles froze, making it impossible to clean the windshield. And then there was another problem: the wrench indicator, together with its five figures, lit up on the dashboard. Disheartened, I asked Nastia to check the significance of those figures in the car manual.

We found that there was nothing seriously wrong. The figures under the wrench indicate that we must change the engine oil, the air filter, the transmission fluid, and the oil filters, which was nothing bad but had to be done as soon as we got home. The tire pressure was normal, and the warning was caused by a layer of rust deposited on the wheel discs, making imperfect contact with the light indicators on the dashboard.

The only urgent issues were the spray nozzles covered in ice. As the highway was wet, the windshield got muddy easily and needed to be wiped clean, which couldn't be done without spraying some washer fluid on it. So repeatedly I had to pull over and clean the windshield with a piece of cloth.

The thought of spending almost a thousand dollars on repairing the car bothered me. We had bought a pre-owned car that had come with a five-thousand-kilometer or two-month guarantee. The two months had lapsed, but I didn't know if we had put five thousand kilometers on this car, and I was hoping that the dealer would fix it free of charge.

We arrived at our Honda dealer in Chandler a few minutes before closing. We reported to a service advisor and explained to him what had happened.

"You got the winning ticket," the service advisor said to us. "You've won free service for many issues in one shot.

We all burst into laughter. Our car had seven issues, of which five were registered with the wrench key on the dashboard; also, the spray nozzles for the windshield weren't working, and the tire pressure was inaccurate.

The advisor took us to the agent who had sold us the car. The general manager was there too. We told them that the former owner of the car must have used water instead of fluid, as the nozzles had frozen, now that the temperature was below zero.

"As for the wrench indicator," I said, "We've driven less than five thousand kilometers, and we haven't changed the oil yet. With regard to the tire-pressure warning, I used the winter tire discs from another car, and now the issue isn't the sensors on the wheels but the discs themselves, as they developed rust and fail to make accurate contact with the warning system. This isn't something you should fix.

The agent and the general manager listened to us carefully and then went to a back room for a private consultation. They returned shortly and assured us that they would service our car for free. "You can make an appointment now," they said to us.

We gave a sigh of relief. We made an appointment for the next day and then shook hands and left. The next afternoon, we got our car back. Unbelievably, it was like a brand-new car.

Spiritual Psychoanalysis

I made a thorough review of everything that happened.

God knew that I was angry at the negative energies that were invading me so aggressively. He knew that I was angry with Him too, and He kept sending me only negative energies that could be of essence only to shamans and medium readers—not to me, who was interested only in pursuing His positive energies along my spiritual evolution.

Therefore, God organized a special situation to soften my heart and make me look at the negative energies with kinder eyes. He wanted to show me that the evil and the negative energies coming down on me (us) aren't as bad as we think, and that difficult situations in our life presage better times.

Before they sold me the car, the dealer tried to save money and skipped check-ups that fell under his obligation. He provided water instead of windshield washer fluid, hoping that I would have used it completely before the end of the warm season. He didn't change the engine oil either. But all this was for our benefit. The wrench indicator and all the figures under it came on sooner than he had predicted, and I didn't have to pay for the repairs from my own pocket.

When you commit something bad, you commit it against yourself. The dealer did something bad to me, but he actually did it to himself. I caught him red-handed, so he lost more than he expected: he had to pay for the full repair of my car.

THE MESSAGES AND SECRETS OF THE UNIVERSE

Literally, the dealer did a good thing to me by sparing me a huge expense from my own account. And now I had a brand-new car with a five-year warranty.

This negative energy God was sending to me was the only one He used to give me a *direct* message. And the message was that the negative energies are actually for our wellbeing.

Even if His message had opened my heart to the negative energies, I was still confused, as they continued to come down on me.

MEANINGLESS NEGATIVE ENERGIES

One night, shortly after midnight, a most bizarre thing happened. Strong cracking noises were coming from the wood structure of our house and startled us out of sleep. Everything was blaring and blasting, and I thought the whole house would come apart.

"Ionel, what's going on?" my wife asked me with fear in her voice.

I knew that the undeserved negative energies continued to pummel our place, and I tried to calm down my wife. "It's nothing, my dear. Go back to sleep. It's only the uneven shrinkage of the old cranky structure of the house."

I was looking up to the half-lit ceiling and could see the shadows of the negative energies coming down. I had never seen them before that night. They had been present each time I woke up because of the creepy sounds from the cracking structure in the walls, and it had been like this throughout January and February of 2020. If you doubt what I'm telling you, I can assure you that what I saw was real. I'm a psychiatrist by profession, and I know that people's minds can create illusions and hallucinations. But what I saw there was in no way a psychiatric symptom.

When things from the spiritual world manifest themselves in our material world, I remain rational and logical, and I analyze the unfolding situations and all the internal and external factors involved. What I saw there were definitively the shadows of the negative energies rampaging out of control. Each time I heard those terrible noises, I understood that God was trying to send a message straight into my heart. Deep inside, I was hoping the flow of energies pouring down upon me since June 2019 would finally come to a halt.

I could hear those scary noises only at night, two or three times a week, from January through February 2020, and I saw the shadows exactly at the same hour. As of March, they all vanished.

FINAL SPIRITUAL PSYCHOANALYSIS OF ALL THE UNDESERVED NEGATIVE ENERGIES

In early March 2020, Canada was bracing herself for the fight against the COVID-19 pandemic. I had debunked the undeserved negative energies and suddenly started to understand what message God had been sending me since June 2019 to late February 2020.

What are the undeserved negative energies? The negative energies challenging us are our own product on earth. They're the result of our negative actions, thoughts, wishes, and words. The energies we create join the cloud that floats above us our family, our home, our country, or our entire civilization. They are known as karma, and they turn into diseases, accidents, conflicts, catastrophes, pandemics, wars, etc.

When undeserved negative energy is visiting us (for instance the karma energies of our family or locality), God is trying to prevent bad things from happening, just like I mentioned in my first book when He warned me of Ramona's upcoming accident and my own crash, which I could have avoided.

If the negative energies are a result of our actions and come down intensely, God cannot protect us or build a sanctuary for lives (see details about the forces of the Universe in Chapter Three "The Third Energy and Its Influence on the Active Energies"). *Maria's appalling accident is a perfect example.*

Important: There was a reason why the Lord had me involved in this accident and, in a way, made me accountable for Maria's permanent physical challenges. He did it so that I could tell you what will happen to us if we continue to act materially and generate negative energies, or continue to think materially instead of accepting spirituality as the essential center-piece of our existence.

Through Maria's misfortune, God warned us about what can happen to us on a personal plane if we continue to produce negative energies. The COVID-19 pandemic is an admonition from God warning us of the fate of our civilization if we go after the same material principles of evolution that have been our guide since the dawn of the ages.

To understand that our society hasn't changed its principles of thinking and behavior for five thousand years, I invite you to watch the documentary movie *Ötzi, le mystère révélé* (2020).

The mummy in the film shows the whole world that nothing has changed in our psychology and behavior. People's belligerence nowadays is the same as in Ötzi's age. We believe that we have made tremendous progress, but in reality, we're the same, with the same mindset, mentality, principles, and demeanor. The only things we've changed are our instruments of operation, but the outcome is the same as five thousand years ago. Also, our greed has grown intense and so has our drive for power and revenge. All these things increase the volume and density of the negative energies.

The undeserved negative energies that flowed down on me from June 2019 until late February 2020 were those accumulated by our civilization during the course of its life, especially in the past century when Modernism damaged the nature God and the Mother Matter have modeled since the beginning of our memorable age. What they created in 4.28 billion years (Wikipedia "Abiogenesis") was destroyed by the Modernism of our civilization in the span of a century.

Through the undeserved negative energies that pummeled my life, God wanted to demonstrate that if our civilization continues to accumulate negative energies following its primitive principles of evolution, these energies will turn around and impact the entire population of the planet, whether we deserve it or not! In my case, over the years, I had created only positive energies, yet the negative energies of our civilization continue to come to me with unabated vigor.

I believe we should genuinely devote ourselves to changing the principles and direction of our civilization. If we don't, nothing will save us, because not being wrong doesn't necessarily mean saving ourselves. To save ourselves, we must commit ourselves to changing and show devotion to our entire civilization.

We must begin with ourselves and change our own pattern of thinking, moving from a selfish, material thinking to a spiritual model of thought: one of love, wisdom, generosity, and kindness for whoever lives around us. And then we should promote the spiritual principles to everyone from all the walks and stations of life, beginning with our family, our friends, our workmates, and our leaders.

To recap:

1) Classification of personal negative energies for the human being:

    a)   The negative energies deserved by the human are the energies we have produced in this life or in previous lives. We meet with the exact situations as we have previously created for other people. Such situations appear in our lives when another person does something bad to us. When this happens, we don't have to judge this person, but let's force ourselves to forgive and then determine what problem related to the situation needs to be solved. Aware of our problem, we will create energies accomplished, which will make us evolve spiritually.

    b)   Negative energies undeserved by the human are those that come from our family/locality/country/civilization. Even if they harm us undeservedly, we must realize that this is our sacrifice for our family/locality/civilization. Any sacrifice is highly regarded in the spiritual world and is a step forward in our personal spiritual evolution.

2) Negative energies of families/localities/countries/civilization:

Usually, here on earth, most people don't deserve to be punished or to suffer. The people who sacrifice themselves here on earth have a great advantage in their spiritual evolution, and the people (leaders of the world) who create global negative energies, even if they don't suffer in this life here on earth, they still have no way to escape or hide in the spiritual world. All of them will pay in full for all the global negative energies they have created.

No matter the origin of the negative energies, whether deserved or undeserved, regardless of whether we came into this life to face the negative energies created by us or to sacrifice ourselves for the negative energies of others, our duty is to learn to live in harmony with them. First of all we have to look for our position in all the events that are taking place around us, to look for our problems that we have to solve and for our positive position in all this negative.

We must look as a spectator and not as an actor at any negative situation in our life. As an actor, we will be able to more easily see the solution to the problems. We don't have to judge anyone but try to understand them and forgive them, even if they don't deserve it. If we do judge, this is a negative energy created by our thoughts—energy that will attract us into the vortex of negative energies from the dark. By forgiving and looking for positive solutions to solve the problem, we create positive energies that will keep us at our current level of spiritual evolution.

If we came into this life to sacrifice ourselves for the negative energies of the family in which we live, this doesn't mean that we must suffer all our lives under the pressure of aggression. We must look for positive solutions to solve the problem. First of all, we must build an energy wall that separates us from the aggressive person in the family. We must look for positive solutions to the problem, and if we fail to defend ourselves from the aggressive person with the imaginary energy wall, then we must not be afraid to separate ourselves from this person in reality.

Important: One of the most important keys to our spiritual evolution is our ability to live in harmony with the negative energies of our life and to have a positive approach to any negative event/energy.

Final Psychoanalysis

Shortly after the COVID-19 pandemic became a national problem in Canada, forcing the government to take harsh measures and impose safety protocols in mid-March 2020, I clearly understood the message that God was sending me through the undeserved negative energies.

THE FIRST CONCLUSION:

All the negative energies that came against me from June 2019 to early March 2020 belonged to our civilization.

THE SECOND CONCLUSION:

The dynamics of their effect depended on how big or small they were. Initially, they had big dimensions, but in time, they shrank to simple fractions. For instance, the first negative energy I saw in that hotel in Lima was as large as a sombrero (Mexican hat). The second one, which I saw in my parents' bathroom, was a cloud the size of an ordinary hat. The third one, which I saw in my bathroom at home when a board on the exterior wall of our house loosened its hold, was as little as a matchbox. And the one in Quebec City was just the size of a mail stamp. The last multiple energies, which I saw on the ceiling when the cracking noise woke me up in the dead of the night, were tiny little spots, like fingernails.

When the pandemic hit Canada and all the undeserved Negative Energies had vanished from my life, it became clear what God was trying to tell me. Exactly when I finished with the visions of my undeserved negative energies was exactly when the COVID-19 pandemic started in Canada. To convince yourself, look at the Bibliography (7): health-InfoBase. Canada COVID-19 epidemiology update: Summary (updated: 2023-09-06).

What a striking coincidence between the negative energies that hit me and the backlash of the ones that came upon the whole world! It's clearly a message from God, especially since I'm the one He has chosen to write books about Him. God tried to send us global information about the apparition of the negative energies on the globe.

Just imagine that a giant meteorite is falling towards the earth. It's surrounded by rocks of various sizes and is so powerful that it could destroy the whole planet in a minute. The big rocks are the avant-garde and are dashed upon the earth ahead of the giant meteorite. Behind them come the middle-sized ones, followed closely by the small ones. The big rocks will be the first to hit the earth. The middle and the small ones will follow. This is a perfect example of what happened to me. At first, I was challenged by the huge energies, and later on by the middle and small ones. And in the end, the COVID-19 pandemic made its grand appearance.

THE THIRD CONCLUSION:

On the same day—March 17, 2020, I clearly understood God's message regarding Maria's unexpected accident. It was not by chance that He associated her injury with my undeserved negative energies and the COVID-19 pandemic. Maria's misfortune demonstrates that when a world negative energy hits our civilization, none of those who gathered negative energies in their personal karmas will be spared. We will all be swamped in our own negative energies before the negative energy of the world collides with the earth.

If our society remains enslaved to its material-primitive principles and resents spirituality as a fundamental basis of our evolution, the negative energies of the world will shatter our earth to pieces.

THE FOURTH CONCLUSION:

In the summer of 2020, the pandemic was in full swing. One day, Nastia and I were walking our dog in the woods. It was a beautiful sunny day, with the temperature above the freezing mark, so ideal for a long stroll. The trails were familiar, providing a welcome escape from home. As we were trekking along, I started to share with my wife my opinions about the messages God had graciously delivered to me. I was trying to make it intelligible, and suddenly I was surprised to see that I was actually talking to myself and explaining to myself, not to her, the attributes of the negative energies coming down on me.

"Nastia, the meaning of this message delivered by God may differ from what I said, and the pattern of the events involving me and the pandemic may be a mini model for what the future holds for us if we don't change our sense of purpose and demeanor. The pandemic today could be the equivalent of the negative energy as large as the sombrero hat that challenged me at that hotel in Lima. If the COVID-19 pandemic is just like a sombrero compared to the super-giant negative energy coming down on us, I don't know what could happen to our civilization if it gets hit by the blast," I said to her.

Nastia didn't say anything. She only gave me a quizzical look, and for the next couple of minutes, she remained wrapped in thought. She looked frightened, and I tried to quiet her down.

"I don't know if my theory is right. I hope it isn't and that our civilization will draw lucid conclusions about God's signs and pursue a new way of development—the spiritual way of evolution that can keep us from any pandemic such as COVID-19," I said to her.

Dear reader,

I could be wrong, but if we continue to generate negative energies as much as we have the last one hundred years, my premonition might become true. I may have some doubts about my last conclusions, but I assure you that I was right when I drew the first three about the message of God.

I am asking you to look into your heart and accept the signs of God and the spirituality into your life as a unique process of evolution in this Universe. Start to steer the course of your life as God advises you, and share your expertise with everyone wherever you may be, as the future of our civilization hinges entirely on each of us, on every action we take, every thought we think, and every word we utter.

What I'm telling you is serious. There was a time when I viewed the signs of God as a joke, but as I continued to collaborate with Him, the Lord artfully persuaded me on *how important his signs were.* If God sends us a global message, such as the COVID-19 pandemic, we definitively have to take Him seriously and look inward and examine our thoughts and feelings.

Looking at the COVID-19 pandemic spiritually, I can say that it doesn't do us any harm. On the contrary, God dispatched it to do us well and spare us the overloading negative energies our civilization has created. He offers us measures to protect our future and the future of our descendants. To be successful, we must proceed with a Spiritual Psychoanalysis of the signs He is sending through the COVID-19 pandemic (see details in Chapter Six).

Chapter Two

THE SECRETS OF GOD

THERE WAS A SECRET ABOUT OUR LORD THAT I FEARED TO UNRAVEL IN my previous book, so please let me do it now in this part of the book. Whoever read my book knows the history of my life, including the epiphany I had in agonizing times.

That revelation concerned the construction of the Universe, and it occurred in the fall of 2005, shortly after landing in Canada. My daughters were in a state of depression after the loss of their best friends from Romania and Moldova. I had found a job in construction that fetched me a pittance. It was miserable work, renovating old apartments that had been occupied for a very long time and now were full of the remnants of other people's lives. It didn't bother me to work in deplorable conditions, but it's not what I had trained for. In Romania, I had been a doctor. On top of this, my workmate was pig-headed, arrogant, and belligerent, bullying me all day long. I couldn't fight back, as I feared that things would escalate and I'd lose my job.

I was totally hopeless. I had abandoned my medical profession to come here and do dirty work together with a lout. I had left behind a quiet and prosperous life and come to Canada, where the future was bleak and prospective-less. And worse, I was desperate because my daughters were depressed after their separation from their best friends.

One day I was coming back from work to get ready for my French language classes. It was a gloomy, cold, and cloudy autumn day. I was walking along the road and was a prisoner of my own mind, and I couldn't tell my family and friends. I was in a state of despair with no hope and no vision of a real life for my family and me in this country. I didn't see any light at the end of the tunnel of my life. I felt like a worm underground that can't see the light of day. And suddenly I had an epiphany, a revelation, as if someone had opened my skull to pour knowledge into my brain. That knowledge was about the construction of the Universe, the identity of God, and who we are and what our purpose on earth is.

My revelation was frightful, and I thought I would die. People have such profound disclosures about the spiritual life before they pass away. But I was in good health and not expecting to die soon. Later on, I understood that my revelation was actually an invitation to write my first book about God, which I did.

While I was writing it, I was afraid to unveil the secrets our Lord had exposed to me during my epiphany. I was afraid that once they found out the truth about God, people would abandon their admiration for Him and get wrong ideas about spiritual evolution, and they'd skid backwards, befogged and stupefied.

I went to seek advice from my daughter Sarah, to whom I had explained Spiritual Analysis from my book *The Destiny and Signs of God*, second edition.She looked pleadingly into my eyes and said: "You shouldn't tell them anything."

But now that the COVID-19 pandemic is ravaging the globe, I believe that people should know the whole truth. Whether they like it or believe it or not, my duty is to tell them everything God wanted me to know. Only by knowing the truth can people open their hearts to accept the spiritual world as a unique process of evolution in this universe.

THE CONCEPT OF SECRETS

What compelled me to unveil the secrets of God was the very concept of secrets and their manifestation in our civilization. To better understand this, let's consider what children think about it and how they feel when we keep a secret from them.

Children don't understand why secrets must be kept, and they can't do it anyway. As the popular adage has it, "The truth comes out from the children's mouths." They can't lie, because they were born innocent into a spiritual world where no one lies or keeps secrets. Only later do they learn from the grown-ups and from our lie-based society how things should be hidden.

What do the children understand by the concept of hiding something or keeping secrets?

Children don't know how to hide things, and they lie and keep secrets when something isn't good or goes wrong. What if behind the secrets is something that doesn't go well? Let's draw an analogy with the strategies developed by our politicians and religious leaders, who built their master plans on prevarication and confidentiality. Why do politicians work secretly on taxpayer's money? How much do they invest in defense projects to destroy our planet? What do the Christian religions conceal in their archives? What is in the mind of some Muslim leaders who enslave and degrade women? Why don't they stop emphasizing that their religion is superior to all other religions?

Now let me answer these questions. The secrets of politicians and religious leaders are a means of maintaining the evil on earth, in our society and civilization. Only when our politicians and clerics learn to tell the whole truth will our civilization begin the Era of the Spiritual Evolution.

I have recently discovered that the spiritual world doesn't have any secrets. Let me make a comparison between humanity's material world and the spiritual one. During our material evolution, we can't see anything around us because we're absorbed by our own interests that blur our vision and perception. During our spiritual evolution, we get to know the world, beginning with our communication with the Lord through His signs. And then we go on with the opening of the third eye, which makes way to a new dimension of the spiritual world.

The more we advance in our spiritual evolution, the better we see the world. If we abandon the material principles of our thinking, we will grow a third eye and will see the spiritual world like Jesus Christ could see it.

Important: There are no secrets in a spiritual world, which stays open permanently to provide us with any information we need. The partition between us and the spiritual world is due to the rigidity of our thinking and our material, selfish cravings. We are the ones who reject the truth about the spiritual world.

Look what politicians, clerics, and scientists think about spirituality. We're all made of a body and a soul, but no one wants to accept the soul as a component that should be examined like we examine the human body. No one wants to accept spirituality as a Science.

GENERAL INFORMATION ABOUT OUR WORLD

We're all energies and we create energies and consume energies and live in a world of energies.

1) We all are energies: Our soul is a spiritual energy. Our material body with its seven chakras is a material energy.

2) We create energies: Every thought, word, action, or wish is a process of generating positive or negative energies.

3) We consume energies: Other than the food we eat, which is energy, we also consume the energies created by ourselves or the persons we interact with, such as our family or home, our country and civilization, and finally, that which comes from the Mother Matter of Universe. All these energies turn into situations that mark our life.

4) We are living in a world made of two forms of energy:

   a) Passive energies—with a soul, matter, and a *third energy*. The Universe is composed of two major energies: one from God/the Supreme Consciousness of the Universe, and the other from the matter of the Universe with its consciousness. The Third Energy is as important in the Universe as the two described. This energy is an independent energy that makes the connection between God and Matter; she is the one who sets in motion all the Laws of the Universe and makes sure that they are respected. This energy is the prosecutor and judge of the Universe. I will talk about the Third Energy in full detail in the next chapters.

b) Active energies—These are created by the active processes of matter, including thoughts, cravings, words, and actions of people on earth.

Passive energies include our spiritual forefathers and our human body. Our spiritual forefathers refer to our Mother Matter, who constitutes all the matter of the Universes fitted with the chakras and the magnetic fields of the Universe, and God our Father, who constitutes the whole free space of the Universe, both material and spiritual (see page 61, Fig. 1 "God and the Universe")

Secondly, our human body is made of the physical body, with the seven chakras, and our soul, which constitutes the whole material space of the human body and the one in the free spaces of the matter, the spaces between atoms (see Fig. 2 "The Human Body and the Soul").

Along with our human being and spiritual forefathers, there are numerous forms of life that belong to the passive energies of the Universe. These forms of life are structured after the same principles as the human body and the Universe: they have a soul and a matter, and the matter, in turn, is provided with chakras.

Any form of material life in the Universe is provided with chakras only if it's alive—in other words, if it has a soul. When the soul leaves the living matter, the chakras spread away and vanish, and the matter is considered deceased.

Here are the forms of life in the Universe known by me as being included in the passive energy category:

a) The first form of life made of a soul and matter are the galaxies of the Universe. Any galaxy is provided with chakras. Any galaxy has a soul, which is the entire material space and the free space inside the matter.

b) Another form of life made of a soul and matter are the solar systems inside the galaxies. They are composed of the following elements:

– the matter of the sun and the planets revolving around it, fitted with charkas

- the soul of the solar system, comprising the entire material and nonmaterial space of the solar system.

c) The third form of life made of a soul and matter are the planets inside the solar systems containing the following elements:

- the matter of the planet provided with chakras
- the soul of the planet comprising the entire material and nonmaterial space of the planets;

d) The fourth category of forms of life made of a soul and matter are the beings populating the planets and able to create other forms of life. On earth, they are the following:

- plants
- animals
- insects
- birds
- human beings

I will give you more details about the above later in this chapter.

CONSTRUCTION OF THE UNIVERSE/ MANIFESTATION OF THE SUPREME CONSCIOUSNESS IN THE MATERIAL WORLD

The Universe is built from the matter of the Universe and the Supreme Consciousness of the Universe (God). Until now, various scientific evidences prove that the construction of the Universe is not a random event, and it has also been proven that the Universe has a form of Supreme Consciousness. In this section, I will try to convince the reader that the Universe really has a form of consciousness. I will give some examples that demonstrate the ways of manifesting the Supreme Consciousness of the Universe in the material world.

The first example:

Let me tell you a story about one of our vacations in Mexico. My wife doesn't like to sit in the sun for too long or swim in the ocean and she hides in the shed reading books. Recently, she has developed a passion for spiritual books. I had read numerous such books when I was training myself to become a psychiatrist, and I was intrigued by what Nastia was reading now. It was *La Formule de Dieu* by Rodrigues dos Santos (July 2019), a well-known novelist and journalist from Portugal who wrote this book based on facts. According to the author, some scientists, including Einstein, attempted to prove that God and the Supreme Consciousness exist. They wanted to prove this thing scientifically, with the criteria of their material thought.

All the information presented in that book is accurate. According to the author, the whole Universe is well-organized chaos, and the chemical formulae on which our life is constructed are so precise that any deviation, however little, would have delayed the birth of this Universe. The Big Bang scientific theory about how the Universe began is made with absolute precision. All the scientific information about the construction of the Universe is irrefutable evidence of the existence of God and the Supreme Consciousness of the Universe, but what impressed me the most was the idea that due to exterior influences, any point in this Universe is different.

On pages 335 and 636 of *La Formule de Dieu*, the author shares an example from meteorology, which is an exact science. However, meteorology remains inexact, because if we measure the exterior temperature in two different points, close to each other, the findings will always be different. The deviation can be fractionally small and is always determined by external factors; leaves blown by the wind or butterflies flapping their wings can change the outside temperature. Jose Rodrigues says that a butterfly flapping its wings can cause a hurricane on the other side of the planet.

The second example:

We were walking by a river that empties into the Caribbean Sea through a vast lagoon. We picked a nice spot and sat down to watch the fish. My wife started to wade in the ford, slowly and gently, fearing that her moves could scare the little colorful creatures. It was a beautiful image to see her feeding the fish with crumbs of bread from the buffet. When she entered the water, the fish swam back, but they returned to her shortly, waiting for their food.

In that moment, I understood the theory of chaos in the Universe mentioned by Jose Rodrigues dos Santos. Looking at Nastia feeding the fish without considering any external factors was making everything seem chaotic. However, everything was coordinated with precise calculations, and in spite of all the chaos, every little fish got a crumb of bread, and none of them remained hungry. Here are factors that determined the trajectory of the crumb of bread from Nastia's palm to the wave:

- The crumbs of bread my wife was tossing in the water were never the same in shape and weight.

- The crumbs were blown by the breeze, which was never the same due to the influence of the sea waves and the trees swinging continuously and impacting the trajectory of each crumb flipped off from my wife's palm.

The little fish were moving chaotically and were permanently changing their location. The river was running down, altering its course around the objects coming its way. Also, the waves of the Caribbean Sea were pushing its tidal waves inland after a pattern that was never the same. The fish themselves were laboring against the currents, and their sense of direction was always different.

I explained my observations to my daughters:

"Look how God is careful about feeding every fish in the water; look how He makes His presence in every tiny spot of this Universe. God was present each time your mother was breaking a crumb, and He made sure that each crumb had the *right* weight and shape to go with the wind, *right* to the hungry fish. He was there along the entire trajectory of the crumbs, and He calculated the accurate speed of the air currents that took and kept the crumbs suspended until they landed before the hungry fish. He professionally calculated and directed all the water currents crossing the lagoon inland from the sea. Therefore, all this chaos is actually not chaos. It is a correct calculation by the Lord of all the factors that made each fish receive a small little ration. This demonstrates the presence of God and the Supreme Consciousness in every spot of this Universe."

The third example:

As I was looking for the one who said that any spot in the universe is different, I came across some interesting theory written by Ernst Mach in 1893, called the "Mach's Principle" and endorsed by Albert Einstein in 1918. According to this theory of the crossing cosmic energies, everything interacts in this Universe. Though this theory can't scientifically demonstrate the presence of God and the Supreme Consciousness anywhere in this Universe, for me it marked a first step to discovery. We should keep in mind that astrology was created based on the interaction of the energies of planets, stars, and sky configurations.

In my opinion, scientists should not ignore Chinese astrology or the astrology of the Maya civilization only for the sake of their material thinking. I believe they should implement spirituality in their research and accept God as a Supreme Conscious of the Universe, and the soul as a component of all existing beings.

The fourth example:

A few weeks ago, in the spring of 2020, after the COVID-19 pandemic hit the world, I watched several episodes of the series *L'histoire de Dieu* starring the American actor Morgan Freeman. The episode I watched was called "Vision de Dieu" (2019). This show was about Ian Ball, a character who had an epileptic seizure for forty-eight hours. His disease was caused by a bone tumor that spread to his brain. Ian Ball underwent surgery, and his tumor was successfully eradicated. However, every morning Ian started to behave weirdly, claiming mental encounters with the Universe. He was living under the impression that the wall was alive and had some form of consciousness. But what impressed Ian Ball the most was that this consciousness encompassed everything around him. Everything was like *one whole* coordinated by *unconditional love* coming from the Universe.

He had this vision every morning for almost four months, and he presented his case to scientists at Cambridge University, but no one there could give him a scientific explanation. As you can see, not even Ian Ball's case could *convince* scientists that they should change their attitude towards the material principles of scientific research.

Let me tell you about the vision I had in the fall of 2005. From what I said before, you can clearly see that the Supreme Consciousness of the Universe, namely the Lord, exists in every one of us. The Lord exists in us and the surrounding world, in the planets and stars, and in the free spaces between the planets and the galaxies. He is everywhere, which means we all and the Universe are *one whole.* So we are God, and God is us. This is clearly proven by the miraculous states of Ian Ball.

We hear such accounts of miraculous aspects of the surrounding world from people who experienced a near-end death (NED). And if we could call the visions experienced by people in clinical death "spiritual visions," namely from another world, a world where God lives, Ian Ball's vision is definitely not from our world. His visions demonstrate that the whole Universe is structured after the principles he envisioned. I have seen the construction of the Universe and the surrounding world myself, after the same principles as Ball, only the forms and the dimensions were different.

In my first book, I write about the general principles of the construction of the Universe and the human body. The human body is provided with seven chakras: muladhara, svadhisthana, manipula, anahata, vishuddha, ajna, and sahasrara. Our earth too is provided with the seven chakras mentioned above; our solar system has its own chakras, and all the animals and plants are fitted with chakras as well.

If all of the above are fitted with chakras, our galaxy must have its own chakras, and our whole Universe too. Actually, no form of live matter could exist without chakras. And when someone dies, or a plant or an animal dies, the chakras fade away. The same thing will happen when the earth or the solar system exhaust their resources: they will die and their chakras will fade away. And the same death will visit the whole Universe when it exhausts its resources completely.

Here is our present Universe:

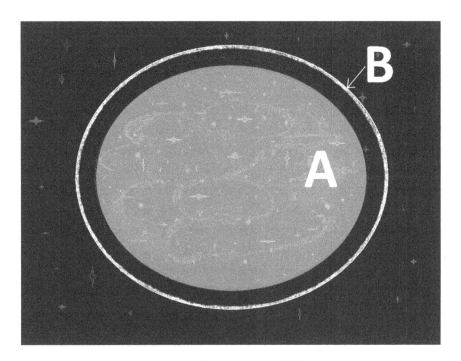

FIG. 1 "GOD AND THE UNIVERSE"

Considering that the matter of the Universe and the Universe itself are living forms supported by their chakras, and the Universe wouldn't exist if it didn't have a soul/God, and that God or the Supreme Consciousness of the Universe is omnipresent both inside any form of matter and outside it, we can conclude that *God is everything*. He is the matter of the Universe, the spaces between matter, the galaxy we live in, our solar system, the planet we live on, and each of us, so He is within us.

In the image above, at letter (A), we have the Universe described by scientists, and at letter (B), in the white circle drawn around the Universe, is God. God appears as a balloon and represents the whole interior and the matter of the Universe, together with the free spaces inside the matter. Looking at this image, everyone should realize that everything is God, everything is one whole—all the galaxies, all the black holes, all the dark energies, all the solar systems, all the planets, including all the living creatures on earth, are God, and everything is one whole.

As we can see in the image above, God is everything, and the matter of the Universe is like one of His internal organs. Consequently, the matter of the Universe is one of God's achievements. Everything in this Universe was built based of the Laws of the Supreme Consciousness of God our Father. And He would not have achieved anything without the matter of the Universe.

Attention! In my first book, I revealed the Theory of the Essential Law of the Universe—the Family Law. In the image above, we can clearly see the correlation between God and His wife, the matter of the Universe. Even if God is everything in this Universe and His wife is only a minimal part of this whole space, neither God nor the matter of the Universe can exist without each other. If God/Supreme Consciousness of the Universe is light, love, and the essential laws of conduct in the Universe, then the matter of the Universe is the complete opposite of God.

The matter of the Universe is darkness, the holder of both positive and negative energies. If there were no negative energies of the Universe, then there would be no conflicts, no counter-traditions. In other words, if there were no "whims" of the matter of the Universe, there would be no spiritual evolution of God either. Only through contradictions and trials can God and the matter of the Universe find other paths of evolution; only through the contradictions of the matter of the Universe is there true life in the Universe. Practically, God's wife is the one that decides the destiny of His life.

JUXTAPOSING OF SOULS OF THE SUPREME CONSCIENCE

In Fig. 1 "God and The Universe," we have a simple formula of representation of the matter of the Universe and the Supreme Consciousness of the Universe. God is shown as a white balloon.

As we discussed at the beginning of this chapter, all the forms of passive energies, namely all the forms of life in the Universe, all the galaxies, solar systems, planets, living creatures on all the planets, etc., are made after the same principle as God, together with the matter of the Universe, and have a soul and matter inside them. Knowing this, we can imagine the juxtaposition of the souls and the matter at every level of evolution in the Universe.

For a better understanding of the meaning of living creatures, including humans, see Fig. 2 below, which represents the man and his soul, which comprises the entire matter of the human body, including the spaces between the atoms of molecules within the matter.

FIG. 2 "THE HUMAN BODY AND THE SOUL"

Inside the gastrointestinal tract are various bacteria helping with the digestion of food. From a spiritual point of view, each bacterium is a form of life inside our body, and each of them is made of matter and soul. As the soul and matter juxtapose, the ones belonging to bacteria are included in the whole human body. Consequently, the analysis of the juxtaposing of all the human creatures in the Universe indicates that *we all are one single whole*. In other words, we all are a part of God, and God is a part of each of us.

Considering our material way of thinking and our ego above all and all the people around us serving as molding clay to our judgmental minds, what conclusion should we draw from the explanations given above? I believe we should discard the materialistic way of thinking, because each time we're judgmental, steal from somewhere, or destroy something, we actually judge *ourselves* and destroy ourselves simply by stealing from us.

EVERYTHING IS US AND WE ARE EVERYTHING

Everything in this Universe belongs to everyone—everything is ours and we belong to everyone.

Everything is a part of Us and We are a part of everyone.

Now we know where the Boomerang Law begins, about which I wrote in full detail in my first book. This law deals with all the energies that have been created here on earth by each of us. She is the one who takes care that each energy returns to its producer or to the community where the it comes from.

When we see that we are everything, everything is ours, and everything is us, it's clear that:

- when you hate someone, you hate yourself

- when you ignore or offend someone, you ignore or offend yourself

- when you judge someone, you judge yourself

- when you steal, you are stealing from yourself

- when you deceive, you deceive yourself

Now I'll say a few words about the composition of the Supreme Consciousness of the human body—the soul. I hope scientists will give up the rigidity and conservatism of their material thinking and accept the soul as a component of the human body in their scientific approaches. If they can't find the exact place of the memory in the human brain, this memory must be located elsewhere; if they can't pinpoint the function of emotions in the rain, they should seek it elsewhere.

I applaud everything scientists do, but I would invite them to give up the material principles and criteria of their contemporary politics in scientific research. It's time to open our heart to spirituality and the soul as essential components of scientific research. If we all know that the soul exists, then why shouldn't we welcome other forms of scientific vision? Why shouldn't we approach scientific research from a different position than the old conservatism and selfish materialism?

To better understand the old fashioned nature of our scientific research, we should ask ourselves a very simple question: Why are we so impressed by the scientific results of the Egyptians and the Maya civilizations, which were based on astronomy, spirituality, and the human soul, while we still consider these domains as taboo for our civilization? Who doesn't want us to open our horizon towards spirituality?

The soul of the human body is a form of consciousness that exists in every cell of the organism. When we deal with the pathology of the body, like a disease or a cut, our body reacts both generally and locally, and all its functions get into motion to eliminate the disease and recover the impacted tissues. This general reaction testifies that the Supreme Consciousness of our body is everywhere in it. When the whole body responds, the Supreme Consciousness is committed fully. When we accuse just a small pathology and our body responds *only locally*, the Supreme Consciousness exists everywhere in our body down to its tiniest part.

Of course, contemporary scientists attribute all these merits only to the evolution of our body as a result of the material evolution. Unfortunately, like any other beings in this Universe, the human body cannot exist without a soul, namely without the Supreme Consciousness.

Consider Fig. 2, which shows "The Human Body and the Soul." Like in the construction of the Universe, where God is everything and the matter of the Universe is like an internal organ of the Lord, we have exactly the same model for the construction of the Human Body. Our soul is everything, and the Human Body is like an internal organ of our soul.

Pursuant to the Essential Law of the Universe, which assigns the soul as the representative of the husband, and the human body as the representative of the wife of the soul, the wife always decides his destiny.

THE WAY OF LIFE OF OUR SOUL

In my first book, I wrote that our soul lives in two worlds:

- the material world when he is inside our human body

- the spiritual world when the soul returns to the Kingdom of Heaven during our sleep

What happens to our soul when it abandons its material body and moves into the spiritual world where time does not exist? To answer this question, we should know what our Universe looks like from the perspective of the spiritual world, namely from a place where time doesn't exist. See the image below.

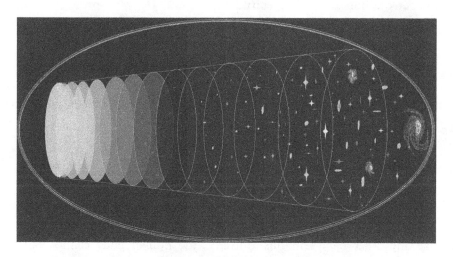

FIG. 3 "THE UNIVERSE OUTSIDE THE TIME FACTOR"

If we stamp out the time factor from the Universe, any moment in the evolution of the Universe exists eternally. And anytime we take a look at the Universe from a spiritual point of view, we will see it entirely from the Big Bang to the end. In other words, the Universe has existed and exists entirely from its birth to its death in every second of our life.

What happens to our soul when it breaks free from our body during our sleep? It returns to the spiritual world, where it has ample vision of its body and its course of life on this earth. If any moment of our life exists in the spiritual world, our soul can be present in all the stages of our life, from birth to death. Being outside the time when we sleep, our soul has the capacity to connect itself to all the moments of our life in its entirety, and it becomes one single whole. See the picture below.

I can only give you examples from my personal life. In recent years, I have started dreaming of events that will take place the next day or in the near future. If before I dreamed abstract dreams with different interpretations, then now I dream the exact people and actions that will take place. For example, the night before my daughter's birthday, I dreamed that the families of her new friend all came to our house and congratulated her all together. The next day, they all called at once through Facebook and congratulated her on her birthday. My dream was so real, and the event of the next day was so identical to my dream that I couldn't believe what I saw.

On another note, I can tell you that "deja vu" is proof that our soul has already visited the moment/event.

FIG. 4 "THE SOUL OUTSIDE THE TIME FACTOR"

Unlike our soul, our body doesn't have the ability to travel in time, nor does it know what the future holds for it or how to proceed to avoid catastrophes during its life. Because of this, each of us, each body of us, needs a message from the spiritual life to give it advice. The messenger of each of us, of each body of us, is our soul itself. Not by chance, our body has the feeling of deja vu. This feeling is a message from our soul to our wife, the body.

Attention! Important! Every soul is a messenger of the Lord here on earth, for both our body and the surrounding world—friends, enemies, colleagues, neighbors, but most importantly, family (children, parents, and life partner).

Becoming one whole, our soul knows not only what will happen to us tomorrow, but also everything about our life in general. Having full access to all the information, our soul tries to warn us that something could go wrong. It warns us about the events in the near future; it tries to send a message to our body through the intermediary of our dreams. It also warns us about the most serious situations that will take place in a distant future and tries to send us a message through the intermediary of the signs of God and through the intermediary of the sixth sense, like the message it sent to my Uncle Ilian that he would die and his body would decompose in his house, and no one would ever know. I was the only one who could have spared him this ominous end.

The readers of my first book know the story of my Uncle Ilian very well. All his life, he had been afraid that he would die alone in his house, and his body would rot without anyone knowing about it. Ilian didn't have children, and I was his only help. He hoped that I would take care of him when he got old in exchange for his wealth.

Before he died, we had an argument, and I declined his inheritance. He died alone in his house as he had expected, without anyone knowing what happened. Two weeks later his neighbors were alerted by the stench of his body throughout the building, and they notified the superintendent. I would have been the only person to know that he was dead, had we not argued on that day. Ilian knew through his sixth sense that he would die alone in his house, and I could have spared him this degrading end.

THE WAY OF LIFE OF THE UNIVERSE TOGETHER WITH GOD

God is everywhere. He is everything, and He knows the entire past and future of everyone. But no one is asking what God looks like. Let's take a look at the relationship of our spiritual forefathers—God and Mother Matter—from a spiritual viewpoint, namely without the time factor.

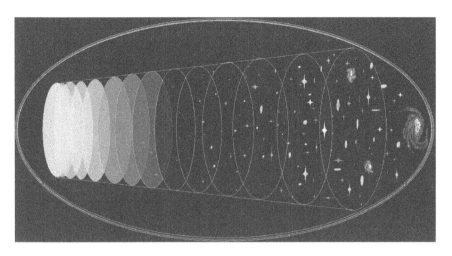

FIG. 5 "GOD AND THE MATTER OF THE UNIVERSE OUTSIDE THE TIME FACTOR"

The above image represents the Universe together with God outside the time factor: the Universe, which begins with the Big Bang and finishes with the end of its existence, and God, who is represented by a white circle and encompasses absolutely all the space in the Universe, from the Big Bang to the end of its existence.

The soul has the capacity to travel in time, while the human body in this life can't travel in time and lives only in the present. It takes many lives until the human being will be able to travel in time together with his physical body.

Unlike the human body, the Universe is more advanced. God has the power to be everywhere at any time and at any stage of the evolution of the Universe. The matter of the Universe can travel from the past to the present time and from the present time to the future. Scientists have already demonstrated some of these capacities of the matter of the Universe, and soon they will use the Material bonds of time to travel to the past through a worm hole, for instance, and to the future through trips around the black holes. (see "How the Universe Works season 8 E, 5 *Secrets of Time Travel* (2020).

LIFE AND EVOLUTION OF OUR SOUL IN THE UNIVERSE

In my first book, I wrote about the stages of evolution of our soul, which are similar to the stages of a man's life on earth:

- the stage before being born as a human being on earth, which is similar to the pregnancy/birth of a human being
- the stage of being born and living the first period of childhood
- the stage of childhood
- the stage of adolescence
- the stage of maturity
- the stage of old age
- the stage of death.

In this section, I will speak about the voyage of the soul through the spiritual world and the stages of evolution of the human being in this Universe.

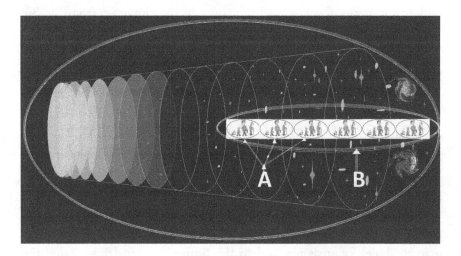

FIG. 6 "THE EVOLUTION OF THE SOUL IN UNIVERSE"

Fig. 5 "God and the Matter of the Universe outside the time factor" represents:

- God, who is absolutely everything and everywhere in and outside the Universe

- the Universe outside the time factor.

New in this image are the various lives of our soul, which was reincarnated in various individuals. For a better explanation of this picture, I will break down this subject in several parts.

The first part: The soul of the human being is a part of the Supreme Consciousness of the Universe/God.

The first thing that draws our attention in Fig. 6 is that both our soul and bodies are part of that one single whole—God. Through this image, we can see that God is us, and we are God.

Our bodies are a small piece of the matter of the Universe, which, in turn, is a component of God's achievements, and our soul is a tiny particle of the Supreme Consciousness, God Himself.

Imagine that the white circle in Fig. 6 is an air bubble, and we are like a cubic meter of air in this entire Universe; also, each person around us is like a cubic meter of air.

In conclusion:

- God is us, and we are God.

- We are a part of God, and God is a part of us.

- We are the surrounding world, and the surrounding world is us.

- We are a part of the surrounding world, and the surrounding world is a part of us.

The second part: The capacity of the Soul to see life as a whole.

In Fig. 6, we see that our soul has two forms. At letter (A) there is a representation of our soul being present only during the course of one life, and at letter (B) there is a representation of our soul accessing all its lives, both past and future. As long as our soul is married/reincarnated in a body on this earth (in this image at letter A), it doesn't have access to the information of previous or next lives.

When our souls leave our bodies during our sleep, or when they experience an NED, they have access only to the information of our current life. Our souls can see only what's in store for us in *this* life and in *this* body. The soul has this restriction of the vision of its evolution only during the material evolution.

As for letter (B) in Fig. 6, our soul has access to all its lives, from its apparition as a form of life in the material world to the death of our Universe. It has this vision after its death, when it abandons a body and has not reincarnated in another body yet.

The third part: Prophets and religions have a wrong image about the relationship between husband and wife and man and woman.

Some religions and prophets who entered in contact with the spiritual world saw our soul like the one represented in Fig.6, letter (B). By seeing that the soul has access to all its previous lives, they created a wrong image about the relationship between men and women:

- They believe that men, the representatives of the souls, are superior to women, and women have no rights before men.

- They believe that men must control, lead, and play with women the way they please without being challenged.

- They believe that they can sell out their spouses and buy them like they buy cattle

- They believe they have the right to buy as many wives as they can afford.

This made the prophets and the creators of religions behave irrationally when it came to the messages transmitted by God to humans on this earth. As you know, I am one of God's messengers on earth, and I wrote my books upon the Lord's specific request. I never thought to write them, but the Lord insisted that I do so and elaborate on all our relations and everything He was telling me.

But …

What God is trying to communicate through me is His *enormous* message—the Message of the Essential Law of the Universe—the Family Law that demonstrates that at the base of spiritual evolution stays the woman. According to this law, the woman is the one that decides the course of life here in the material world:

- in the relationship between God and His wife, the matter of the Universe, she is the one that decides her destiny;

- in the relationship between the soul and our body, the wife of our soul is the one that decides her destiny;

- in the relationship between man and woman, the Woman should make the essential decisions regarding the course of her family, because the spiritual evolution of the whole family depends on the accomplished energies the woman created for herself and her family.

Regardless of the life path the wife chooses, the man must always be by her side to support her. Only loved and supported will the woman be able to create those accomplished energies necessary for the spiritual evolution of the whole family.

Here is an example of the relationship between the human soul and the body. Imagine that when the soul is born in a human body, it comes from the world of God, where time and secrets don't exist. Basically, before being born, the human soul knows absolutely everything about what will happen to it in this life, regardless of the choices the body will make along the line. It knows what paths will be good or bad for its future.

Compared with the soul, the consciousness of the human body knows nothing about the future the soul can see; instead, it's endowed with those seven chakras through which it relates directly with the consciousness of the matter of the Universe. This connection makes our body sense our life as real, and feel through the sixth sense the true pathways of evolution.

Although many times our human body choses the wrong pathways of life, that doesn't mean they will destroy the destiny of our evolution. NO. On the contrary, passing through the negative energies of life, the consciousness of the human body represents the accomplished energies from the Personal Box. The accomplished energies are the energies that evolve not only the consciousness of the human body in the material world, but also the evolution of our soul in the spiritual world.

Men should learn to accept the idea that their wives need to fulfill their wishes, and they should provide them with all the conditions needed to accomplish this both in their family, personal, and professional lives. Investing in the future of their wives, men invest in their personal future, because men's destiny lies in the hands of their wives, just like the destiny of our soul is in the hands of our body.

Our civilization should be led by *women*. I don't mean that parliaments should be composed only of women, but from a spiritual point of view:

- Women are the ones who should decide our destiny here on earth.

- Men should lay out signal flares and landmarks to make women aware of the consequences of their choices and the importance of spiritual evolution in this Universe (see my first book for further details on this matter).

In other words, the relationship in the governing parliaments of our civilization should correspond to the relationship between husband and wife described in the Bible (Ephesians 5:22–33). Women should be very careful about the consequences of their decisions, and men should be respectful of women and show them love and warn them about the consequences of their decisions.

I believe that an optimum parliament must be composed of 50 percent women and 50 percent men, and all these members must be elected based on their spiritual visions and principles, not due to extremist criteria used to manipulate masses.

Specification 1: Everyone, our leaders included, must know the advantages and disadvantages between men and women. For instance:

Women have an advantage over men, as they can predict the future with their sixth sense and are ideal candidates to see the signs of God, but sometimes their carnal temptations, which are intense beyond control, prevent them from seeing the signs of God.

Men have the advantage of keeping temptations at bay, and they can see the signs of God, while women are overwhelmed by their own urges. But men's capacity to see the reality is sometimes diminished by their own invasive thinking. Due to the sharpness of their thoughts, they lose contact with the real world. Fully convinced of the "perfection of their thinking," they call on everyone to do what they believe it is best. This fuels their hatred and aggressiveness against the world and makes them blind before the signs of God.

Specification 2: Let's take a look at any normal family where love and harmony prevail. Who makes decisions regarding their relations, the husband or the wife? I would say that women make the major decisions, in all situations and families.

Men's decisions versus women's decisions: Imagine there are two different parliaments, one made of women and one made of men. They have to make an important decision regarding the use of antibiotics in livestock.

For many decades, it has been scientifically proved that antibiotics used in livestock make the human body resistant to antibiotics. This situation is getting worse, as infections can't be treated with antibiotics. This untoward resistance is passed from one generation to another, leading to a global pandemic. Within thirty-five years, the planet's population will be completely unable to treat any infection whatsoever. For more details, see the television show *Les grands reportages*, episode "Antibiotiques: la fin du miracle?" (2020).

The pandemic generated by the use of antibiotics in livestock will be followed by a global catastrophe that will destroy our civilization, and the COVID-19 pandemic will sound like an innocent nuisance compared to what the future holds unless we stop injecting our livestock with antibiotics.

The pharmaceutical companies nowadays don't want to give up the production of antibiotics for the animal industry, as billions of dollars in revenues are at stake. Let's think of the differences in decisions between the two kinds of parliaments. Which one would vote against the production of the antibiotics used in livestock? I will invite the reader answer this question.

Let's take a look at letter (A) in Fig. 6. It shows that our soul, currently in its material evolution on earth, can't see all its lives as a whole. It can only see its progressing life, from the birth of its body to its death. What I mean is that such limitations of our soul's vision are determined by our body's presence in the Period of Material Evolution. Our body will have a *full* vision of all its lives *only* when it discards all its carnal temptations and enters the age of its spiritual evolution. Even in this case, the human body—the wife of our soul—is the one that decides her husband's destiny.

The politics of many religions are so demanding towards women; some even insist on a style of dress. Some religions insist on completely hiding the woman behind clothing. Looking at the "clothes" of our Mother-Earth and her husband, and our galaxy and her husband, and the Universe with her husband, God, we don't see any forms of matter hiding behind their garments. On the contrary, we see the beauty of the Universe, because of Mother the Matter is resplendent in its natural skin.

Let's ask ourselves why some religions show such a demeaning attitude to women by hiding their wives from the eyes of the society? Isn't it because of their material thinking, which is selfish, possessive, and eager to manipulate everyone? I believe so!

I don't mean that our society should walk naked in the street. No. What I mean is that we should become aware that the spiritual world is not an old-fashion form of manipulating the masses but a democratic form of eternal evolution and discovery of new values of our body and soul. We can't advance and have the third eye opened if we continue to follow the old religious ways written thousands of years ago.

Stepping into the spiritual world can be done only by seeking God's ways in our present personal life and living in direct harmony with the Universe. If we evolve, we'll see how captivating the surrounding world is, and we'll lose interest in the exterior beauty of our material bodies.

Remember Ian Ball, who talked about his early morning capacity to see the world in its full splendor and full of Godly love? At a certain moment, we'll all have the capacity to see the surrounding world using the same criteria as Ian Ball did. When our civilization attains such a level of spiritual evolution, no one will be interested in what our wives are wearing. Until that happens, we should let our wives wear whatever they please, and men should train themselves not to look at women's bodies with lust. Instead, be mature and start seeing women as spiritual creatures of a soul in this Universe.

To reach this point of evolution, we should explain everything to our children from their first years in school. I believe that if we manage to instill a spiritual way of thinking in our civilization from the first years of their childhood, at maturity they'll be able to put into practice the spiritual theories far more easily and turn our civilization into a spiritual one that is subject to perpetual evolution in Universe.

Note: I would like to remind the reader that our civilization is built and manipulated according to the principle of material thinking. The greatest forces of manipulation of our civilization are religions and politics.

Let me say something about the aberrations of some religions who insist that the words in their scriptures are written by God (see the documentary film *L'histoire de Dieu*, episode "Dieu existe" (2019). God does not consider the words as a form of communication in the spiritual world because they don't represent reality and can always be misinterpreted. He is sending all His messages through senses, feelings, and situations in our lives.

To be more specific, listen to those who had an NED experience. No one who met God ever spoke with Him with words. All of them used senses, some sort of telepathy, but they never used words. Based on my personal experience in my relationship with God and the messages He sent me, I can say that He never talked to me with words but through situations and people from my entourage, which made me truly and clearly understand His message.

Whoever created religions had the same revelations and contacts with God as I did. However, unlike me, they didn't have access to the scientific and spiritual information like I have now. So they came up with the religion from their own mind. In other words, they used their aterial thinking and interpreted the visions of the spiritual world for their personal interest. They degraded the woman by turning her into man's slave and bundled her into isolation. In order to maintain the monopoly of his religion, the creators of religions made the world believe that their religion is the most important in the world.

Attention! Important! We all should know that none of the prophets/ apostles are holier than we are. Each of us is a saint and a Guardian Angel and a messenger of the Lord. (For more details see "The Sixth Part: The Messengers and the Angels on Earth" and "The Second Part: The Evolution of God after the Death of our Universe.")

The only difference between us and the prophets/apostles or the saints invented by the religions is our age in the material world here on earth.

They lived several lives as human beings and acquired more experience than we did, which helped them reach a spiritual level of evolution, while we're still groping though the material stage of evolution, hoping that our sixth sense will grow. We're still incapable of communicating with the Universe, and we don't know how to confer with God through His signs. We also don't have direct access to the spiritual world yet.

A time will come when everyone can reach the spiritual level of evolution, like any apostle born on this earth, and communicate with God directly, as shown in my first book.

THE FOURTH PART: REINCARNATION CRITERIA

Let me get back to several subjects from my first book.

The first subject:

This deals with the unveiling of the details of the Personal Boxes. We're all like a machinery system that generates energies through our thoughts, words, wishes, and actions. All the energies we produce belong to us and accumulate in the so-called Personal Box. Each of us has one. These boxes are classified in three compartments:

- a compartment for all the negative energies we produce

- a compartment for all the positive energies we produce

- a compartment for all our accomplished energies

When we promise ourselves not to repeat the wrongs we did, such as going on drinking binges for a long time, the negative energy accumulated for decades in our Personal Box turns into an *extremely* positive energy, an eternal and accomplished one that stays in the compartment of the accomplished energies of our Personal Box.

On a general plane, this energy becomes a law for our future as human beings and for our soul as well. On a specific-circumstantial plane, all the negative energies from our Personal Box, in connection with our addiction, will dissipate and turn into positive energies of harmony and love. In other words, once our addiction is cured, all the negative energies our alcoholism created will disappear forever.

The Personal Box of every soul finds itself in the third space, between the spiritual world where God exists and the material world where the matter of the Universe is settled. (I will provide you with more details about this form of energy in Chapter Four.)

From the very beginning of the human being, the soul has built its Personal Box, together with all the bodies in which it was reincarnated. Before it dies, our soul has the right to become reincarnated in the body that corresponds to the energies accumulated in its Personal Box, whether negative, positive, or accomplished. For instance, if our soul manages to cure its alcohol addiction from its previous lives, but it still has a lot of negative energies in stock within its matrimonial relations, he can pick up a new body that will still be affected by the negative side of the family relationships. This reincarnation will be repeated until our soul achieves a matrimonial relationship imbued with love and harmony and creates an accomplished energy between husband and wife for its Personal Box.

The second subject:

In my first book, I wrote about the stages of evolution of our souls as human beings. As you know, our souls follow the same stages of evolution here on earth as the humans: pre-birth, childhood, adolescence, youth, maturity, and death. Our first period is the "pre-birth," which begins with the apparition of the first forms of life and ends with the naissance of Homo sapiens. Practically, the apparition of our soul coincided with the birth of the first algae or the primeval forms of life. This form was meant to assist our soul in giving birth to its charkas. It was reincarnated in the plants on this planet so many times until it managed to generate its first three chakras. Then, based on the primeval chakras, it became entitled to be reincarnated in animals, and this went on until all the chakras of the animals were produced. In the end, our soul created the last seven chakras in the ape-human body to which Homo sapiens was born.

To create the seven chakras, our soul:

- lived in harmony with the forms of matter in which it was reincarnated

- persuaded these forms to produce love and harmony between the Matter and the Spirit; and

- created accomplished energies in the third compartment of its Personal Box.

Now that we all know that plants and animals are potential human beings in the process of evolution, what should be our attitude towards them?

Another period of evolution of our soul on earth was the stage of the material evolution, which began with the Homo sapiens and lasted until today, the stage of the soul's adolescence. In this period, the creation of the accomplished energies in the Personal Box is more complex than the prior stage, because in the period of material evolution, our soul had more things to teach to our body:

- learn trades;

- learn how to study;

- learn how to behave in society;

- learn what spiritual principles are and how they can be dissociated from the material ones

In other words, our soul's reincarnation in the material world depends on the chakras created together with all the forms of life on earth and the accomplished energies in the Personal Box accumulated over the course of its life. The more accomplished energies the soul has in its Personal Box, the higher it can be reincarnated in the House of God (see "The House of God" from my book *The Destiny and Signs of God*, second edition).

Our soul cannot be reincarnated at a higher level than it deserves based on its evolution on earth. However, it can be reincarnated lower than it's justified.

Who decides in what body we will be born? In the documentary film *Mon enfant, son fantome* (Canal D august 13, 2015), many children remember what happened to them before they were born. They could select their own body for reincarnation only with help from God.

Practically, our souls decide their own future destiny. If they want to stay in the Kingdom of Heaven, they can stay, and if they want to continue their evolution in the material world here on earth, they can choose the bodies in which they'll be born after the following reincarnation criteria:

Even if our soul chooses its next wife (the body), it can't be reincarnated higher than the merit it has earned during its evolution. Our soul's possibility of choosing falls within a scale dictated by achievements and accomplishment, and it runs from maximum to minimum levels.

THE FIFTH PART: WHO TAKES INITIATIVES IN OUR LIVES?

I will try to explain who is the organizer of the situations through which God sends His messages into our life.

Another major factor for the selection of the body is our soul's access to all the lives from its past and future. In Fig. 6 "The Evolution of the Soul in the Universe," at letter (B), we can clearly see our soul's capacity to embrace all its lives as a whole. Therefore, before being born, our soul will check for future spouses through all the above factors and, *with god's help*, it will try to forge its own destiny. By using the positive and negative energies of its previous lives, and the ones of the family it's supposed to be born to, our souls will pray the Lord to help it create those situations that will fittingly help its future wife/body produce accomplished energies for the third compartment of the Personal Box. Together with God, our soul will select the entourage and the circumstances for an appropriate atmosphere for its wife.

As you see, everything that happens in our life is the choice of our soul. We're the only ones who can select both the body we will live in and our destiny, and those situations serve as beacons for the decisions the wife of our soul is going to make.

Important: Even if our soul selects its wife/body and its destiny by itself, the final decision belongs to the wife of our soul, the body. Therefore, in the spiritual world, manipulation and dictatorship don't exist. God doesn't force the soul to pick its destiny. He only helps it organize situations in its life depending on the volume of positive and negative energies from the Personal Box and the Family Box of the body in which our soul will be born.

The soul doesn't force its wife/body to make any unwanted decisions. It only creates situations that suggest and lay out beacons along the path of life in such a way that our body *alone* can make the right decisions for its own destiny. As a result, the wife of our soul will make the *final* decision for its destiny and the destiny of its future husband. Our soul lies in its hands.

Conclusion No. 1: The soul sets up the beacons" for its wife, the body; in other words, it creates the signs of God along the path of its life to guide her onto the best avenue.

The wife of the soul-body is the only one that makes final decisions about the roads of her life. Practically, the fate and destiny of our soul are completely in the hands of the wife of our soul-body. If the body decides to go on a wrong path, on a different path of life than the one suggested by the soul, then the process of evolution will be much longer. If we choose to create negative energies in life, we won't be able advance in spiritual evolution until we reach the stage when we transform our negative energies into accomplished energies.

Consequently, we reach Conclusion No. 2: For the wife of our body to make the right decisions, our soul must love its wife/body from the bottom of its heart and make her feel loved, important, wise, and accomplished. Only the husband's love for his wife can make a family great!

Conclusion No. 3: If our soul is the creator of the signs of God with the help of God, we should not accuse God of dictating our fate/destiny, but we should be grateful for the effort He makes to fulfill our wishes, the wishes of our soul. We also should not neglect the signs of God, as they are the most comfortable ways recommended for a spiritual evolution in this Universe. They are thoroughly and meticulously analyzed down to the last details by both our souls and God Himself.

THE SIXTH PART: THE MESSENGERS AND THE ANGELS ON EARTH

The soul knows our destiny. Definitively, it's a part of the Supreme Consciousness of the Universe and *is* the Supreme Consciousness itself, which means that it knows everything about the spiritual and material world alike.

Then why did our soul land here on earth? Did it come down to learn from his wife, the body, and from the material world how to live a primitive life? Or did it come here just to teach its wife and the surrounding world about evolution in this Universe?"

Of course, our soul came to earth to send us a message from the Universe, from God Himself. He came to share his knowledge to his wife, the human body, and the world in which it lives. Every soul reincarnated on earth is a *direct messenger of God!*

Let's talk about their mission as angels here on earth. Before its birth, our soul picks its body and family and the society it will live in. It chooses its own destiny and assumes responsibility not only for its wife, the body, but also for the surrounding world it's going to live in for the rest of its life. It assumes accountability for the members of its future family and its classmates, workmates, etc.

To understand our soul's responsibility for these people, we must be aware that when God creates a situation for someone, He uses people from that person's entourage. In my first book, I provide several examples about the manner in which God speaks through the people around us. Our Souls are responsible for the members of our family above all. Therefore, they are the Guardian Angels for our gamily and for the surrounding world as well.

Knowing that our souls are messengers of God and the Guardian Angels for the surrounding world, we should reflect deeply over our thoughts and demeanor. First, we should change our material thinking for a spiritual one. Secondly, to discover ourselves and our soul, we should dedicate more time to the latter by reorganizing our schedule of work to have more free time for ourselves so we can meditate and analyze ourselves. Thirdly, we should train ourselves in how to listen to the signs of God, which are direct messages from Him and from our soul.

The following questions are essential for a Spiritual Analysis:

- Why doesn't our body want to listen to its husband, the soul?
- Why do our bodies insist on training our souls on how to behave and not vice-versa?
- Why does our society refuse to accept spirituality as a science?

THE SEVENTH PART: GREED-LADEN PURSUIT OF WEALTH

From the birth of our civilization, greed, envy, hatred, belligerence, and the pursuit of wealth have been some of the causes of wars and major conflicts on this earth. Our insensitivity and lust for power and wealth, and our craving to be superior to the others, brought about discord and irremediable separation among the people on the planet. This is particularity true of our body. We "erode" ourselves, and our personality destroys us as a nation and civilization entirely. We have the same vision and the same principles of life as five thousand years ago, even though we deem ourselves a modern civilization (see *Ötzi, le mystère révélé*, 2020). This is due only to our material, self-centered, selfish thinking. But if we change our material thinking for a spiritual one, we will realize that we don't need to be greedy, selfish, and crazy about health, because everything is ours.

Back in Fig. 6, I underlined that absolutely everything in this universe is a part of us, everything is us, and we are everything. Now we will embark on a true spiritual evolution. What we have to do now is to accept what we are, to accept our level of materialistic evolution, and to start thinking spiritually. Only by having a spiritual mindset will we be able to listen to the signs of God. And listening to the signs of God, we will start to walk on the true path of life that we must walk. By following this path, we won't only be able to evolve spiritually much faster, but we'll also get what we want from our lives much faster. Even if we want something other than what the Universe offers us, we must trust that none of our desires are ignored by the Universe, that He will give us everything we need when the right moment arrives.

THE EIGHTH PART: THE UNIVERSE DEPENDS ON OUR DECISIONS

As we can see in Fig. 6, "The Evolution of the Soul in Universe," we are one whole, and when something from that isn't going well, the whole is going wrong; for example, when someone hurts his finger, the entire body will be in pain. The same thing happens to the Universe in which we live: each time we stray from the right path and do something wrong, we do it to the entire Universe.

When someone suffers, the Universe and God suffer.

When someone is in pain, God is in pain.

When we destroy our own environment, we destroy ourselves, together with our spiritual forefathers.

When we design wars and begin wasting lives, we are actually wasting our life and our God too.

Of course, justice is served in this Universe (see Chapter Four) when the negative energies we create return to the producer based on the Boomerang Law described in my first book, but this can't be a solution. To solve this problem, we should understand that with our stupidity we make ourselves suffer and bring suffering to God Himself and to those who live in this Universe.

THE NINTH PART: THE RISE OF THE SUPREME CONSCIOUSNESS

In Fig. 6, we can clearly see our evolution in the Universe and the evolution of the Universe together with us.

Let me tell you what I have noticed over the course of my life. I was young when my wife gave birth to our daughters, and I had material thinking in my mind. I believed that I was smarter than all three of them, and I had become belligerent and manipulative. But my daughters were growing up, and I realized that they were playing the educator, not me. Yet I was scolding them and yelling at them, arguing that they should change their attitude. And when they reached the age of maturity, I reached the same maturity myself. Up until then, everything had been endless confusion, as I had lived under the impression that I knew everything, while in reality I was ignorant.

Looking at Fig. 6, let's try to imagine that we're all children of the Supreme Consciousness of the Universe, and let's try to imagine that during hundreds of thousands of years of evolution, the human being will reach such a high level of consciousness that we can't even imagine. Along with the evolution of the human being's consciousness, the Supreme Consciousness of the Universe will also grow. Imagine how big the Supreme Consciousness of the Universe will grow when each of us has an indescribable level of consciousness? As the understanding capacity of the parents increases as a result of the education of their children, so does the consciousness of God increase as a result of the evolution of human beings.

THE SECRETS REVEALED

It is high time that I unveiled the secrets of God of which I feared to speak for many years. Since the fall of 2005, when I had that revelation regarding the construction of the Universe, until this day, I haven't said anything to anyone about it, not even to my wife. I only told my daughter Sara. And now I am going to confess to you.

As I said, I was afraid that once they know the truth about the construction of the Universe, people would start talking disparagingly about our Lord.

The secrets of God begin with:

a) The Secrets of the Evolution of the Human Souls in the Universe, followed by

b) The Secrets of the Evolution of God Himself.

We are children of God:

To find out what the human being is, we just have to ask ourselves the appropriate questions. Let's ask ourselves a few simple questions and then proceed with a short analysis

"Who are the descendants of fish and animals and humans? What can they beget and bring about?"

Well, the fish create fish, and the animals bring about animals, while humans give birth to humans. I haven't seen any fish create a human being, or a human being give birth to a fish or an animal. If the answers to these questions are so simple, it will be the same for the following questions:

"When we pray to God and solemnly request a favor, we know He is our Father, don't we? And if we know that we all are His children, what can He create and who are His descendants?"

You will find the answer to these questions in full details if you continue to read my book.

THE SECRETS OF THE EVOLUTION OF HUMAN SOULS IN UNIVERSE

Sooner or later, we will have to take the spiritual way of evolution, because in this Universe there is only one way—the way towards God. We will get there, whether on this earth or another planet. The question is what do we want to do here on earth or on another planet. What do we want to build here on earth? What do we intend to leave for our descendants, a planet ruined by greed, aggressiveness, and egotism, or a prosperous civilization laden with love and harmony?

To find the spiritual way of evolution, we must train ourselves to behave in our family after the Essential Law of the Universe, the Family Law. We must learn to live in love and harmony in the relationship of a husband and his wife, or a soul and his body.

Attention: Trying to find the spiritual way of evolution doesn't mean that we are pursuing perfection. No, because perfection does not exist. Wherever we may find ourselves, we should feel that something is missing.

This is the charm of spiritual evolution: the farther we progress into the spiritual world, the more numerous will be the things we need. And we should keep looking as we pursue the spiritual way of evolution, as we may discover new things around us with the signs delivered by our good Lord.

If during the stage of adolescence of our soul we opt for the spiritual way of evolution and continue to evolve towards one life or another, within decades or hundreds of years we will attain the same spiritual level as Jesus Christ had when He ascended to Heaven with His body and soul.

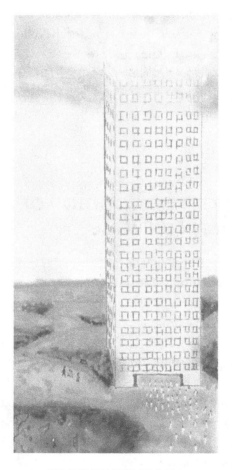

FIG. 7 "THE HOUSE OF GOD"

The image in Fig. 7 represents the House of God that I saw in my dream while I was writing my first book, *The Destiny and Signs of God*. It contains all the stages of evolution of our soul as a human being, from Homo sapiens to the moment we step into the spiritual world with body and soul, like Jesus Christ did when He ascended to Heaven.

Each floor in the House of God stands for a different level of evolution in the spiritual world. During our life, we can go up or down a number of floors. Everything depends on the wishes and decisions of our soul's wife, our body, especially now in the adolescence period when our carnal temptations are so intense and the risk of going down several floors is great. Sooner or later, regardless our failures during the time of evolution, each of us will attain the top floors of evolution in the House of God, and we will all reach the Cloud of Godly Light, represented in this drawing.

Very interesting in the drawing is the aureole of the cloud above the house. This cloud is not a usual one. It is the brilliant spiritual light from the Heaven of God. So if we reach up to the top floor in the House of God, we will walk into the Cloud of Heavenly/Spiritual Light with body and soul like Jesus Christ did two thousand years ago.

Another aspect of the evolution of our soul as a human being in the House of God is the power of our soul, together with the bodies in which he will be reincarnated, to gather more chakras, up to twelve maybe, to the seven we already have.

THE EVOLUTION OF OUR SOULS IN THE KINGDOM OF HEAVEN

Once in the Kingdom of Heaven, in the Cloud of Light represented in Fig. 7, our souls will begin a new form of existence. Before being born as a human being, our soul lived as a plant or animal, and it ought to create the seven chakras in order to become a human being. As a human being, he will need to reincarnate hundreds and thousands of times until he develops other, better chakras, in order to reach into the Kingdom of Heaven (the Cloud of Light). During his stay in the Kingdom of God, he will begin a totally new stage of his life as a human being.

Currently, our soul is crossing through the period of evolution in the House of God and must learn how to abide by the Essential Law of the

Universe—the Family Law. Once in the Kingdom of Heaven, he will continue his evolution after the same principles of the Family Law and under a different form of existence. To understand what I mean, please take a look at Fig. 8 and the explanations that follow.

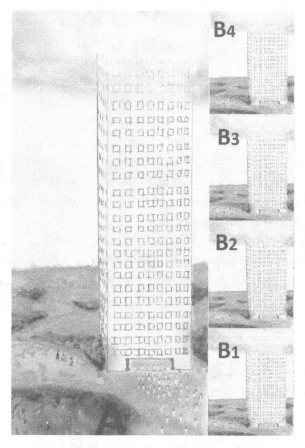

FIG. 8 "STAGES OF EVOLUTION OF OUR SOULS IN THE KINGDOM OF HEAVEN (THE CLOUD OF LIGHT)"

In the drawing above, we can see the representation of several stages of evolution of our souls in the Kingdom of Heaven, about which God spoke to me during my epiphany in the fall of 2005. In Fig. 7, I spoke about the evolution of the human being from Homo sapiens until the moment we step into the Kingdom of God, which I portrayed as a house, the "House of

God." Now try to imagine that the house I mentioned found itself in Fig. 8, at the right bottom part of the drawing as B1.

The first stage of evolution of our souls in the Kingdom of Heavens

After our souls step inside the Kingdom of Heaven, the Cloud of Light represented in Fig. 7, they will start a new way of life. The same House of God will be there waiting for them, like in their period of evolution as human beings. This stage is represented in Fig. 8 at letter B2.

Once in this house, our souls will begin a new form of existence that unfolds after the same principles of the Essential Law of the Universe—the Family Law. This new form could be the planets composed of matter and soul. In other words, we will exist as a relationship between husband and wife. Our souls will be reincarnated om various planets as many times as needed to rise from the B2 level up to the top of the House of God, as long as they create all the chakras required for admission to the next Cloud of Spiritual Light and be ready for a new form of existence. When they reach the top floors of the House of God, they will enter the stage represented at letter B3 in Fig.8.

The second stage of evolution of our souls in the Kingdom of Heaven

Once they get into the second stage of the Kingdom of God (letter B3 in Fig.8) our souls will find themselves in another House of God, where they will begin a new way of life patterned after the same principles of the Family Law of the Universe, in a husband-and-wife relationship. In this stage, our souls could become solar systems, in which the matter represents the wife, and the soul represents the whole space inside and outside the solar system. Our souls will live and reincarnate as solar systems as many times as they need to evolve spiritually and go up through all the stages in the House of God, from the second stage of the Kingdom of Heaven, and create all the chakras required by these stages to be ready for the next ones.

The third stage of evolution of our souls in the Kingdom of Heaven

Once in the third stage, shown by letter B4 in Fig. 8, our soul enters another House of God and begins a new stage of evolution under the form of galaxies. He will be reincarnated in various galaxies as many times as he needs to reach up to the top floors in the House of God and thus embark on a new stage of development.

The fourth stage of evolution of our souls in the Kingdom of Heaven

Once in the fourth stage, represented by letter A in Fig. 8, our soul enters another House of God and begins a new stage of evolution under the form of the Universe. This passage from stage B4 to stage A is like a new birth under the form of our spiritual forefathers, God and the Matter of the Universe.

SPECIFICATIONS

First specification:

Our soul has a spectacular evolution. Whatever stage we're at, we feel like children, young, mature, and old every second of any stage of our evolution in this Universe. When we conclude all the stages of evolution in the House of God, shown as B1, and we switch to letter B2, we will die as human beings and, for the first time, be born as planets. When we conclude stage B2, we will die as planets and, for the first time, be born as solar systems, etc.

Let's take a look at the stages through which our soul has gone.

When they finished all the stages of evolution at the level of plants, our souls reached the stage of death and, for the first time, they were born under the form of animals. When they finished all the stages of evolution as animals, our souls were born as human beings.

Other than the general stages of evolution, our souls have stages of evolution at every floor. For instance, our civilization is currently going through the adolescence stage and finds itself at the end of the material evolution era and the beginning of the spiritual one.

Considering all the stages of evolution we have gone through, and the level we have reached, we can conclude the following: We are so close to our death from the viewpoint of our material evolution, and we're about to be born from a spiritual evolution point of view. At this point, we are adolescent human beings in the House of God, but we find ourselves in the pre-birth period in comparison with the following stages in the Kingdom of Heaven (B2). Also, considering B1, B2, B3, and B4 as four stages of a lifetime, one whole, we can say we are living our early childhood period.

Second specification:

The second specification of the stages of evolution of the human beings in Universe is Depression.

As you know, a new disease is now ravaging our civilization: *depression*. Under normal conditions, depression is settling in the brain of people who've lost all hope of living. It happens to those who attained the climax of their material achievements. The loss of hope for the tomorrow of our lives, the loss of hope for material, family, or professional achievement in this life is the last stage of the evolution of material thinking. It happened to me when I landed in Canada. I had made my utmost material achievement, and now I had missed any chance of becoming a psychiatrist, a profession I missed so much. Usually this happens in developed countries, where everyone can fulfill their dreams. In the less developed parts of the world, people must struggle to survive every day and have no time to get bored. They hope more and expect to get higher than the rich on the scale of material evolution. Reaching the top of their material realizations, many lose hope for living, as they have no further goals or forms of evolution of interest, because everything was achieved from a material point of view.

It happened to me here in Canada. I had lived in poverty-stricken Moldova and then in Romania, and I know what depression means, but there was always something to achieve there, and I was always hoping to get higher on my career scale. But here in Canada, I was overtaken by depression. Why would people in developed countries become depressed sooner than those in the impoverished parts of the world?

Answer: I had everything I needed from a material point of view, and the only thing I missed was my profession as a psychiatrist, which precipitated my period of depression. However, because I knew how to follow the signs of God, I found my destiny. God helped me find it, and I wrote about it in my first book. Now this destiny helped me find another form of happiness and evolution, an infinite evolution that would give me hope to live my life: the spiritual evolution.

As you can see in the first specification above, the spiritual way of evolution is a permanent source of hope for life when we have permanently something to learn and find ourselves before our birth, childhood, maturity, old age, and death. Therefore, anticipating something new and interesting and unknown is our greatest satisfaction.

By accepting spiritual evolution in our minds, we accept the eternal evolution and gratification for the unknown, interesting, and mysterious things, for the world without an end and depressions.

THE SECRETS OF THE EVOLUTION OF GOD

The first part: The rise of the Supreme Consciousness of God

I've already said that parents mature and grow wiser along with their children. The older their children get, the higher their parents' consciousness becomes.

Let's take a look at Fig. 6, which represents the evolution of the soul in Universe. If each of us elevates the consciousness of his own soul, he will also help the Supreme Consciousness of God grow. If during the evolution of the Universe everyone raises their personal consciousness to a maximum level, they will also raise the Supreme Consciousness of the Lord. Imagine how big the Supreme Consciousness of God will grow with His children's help from their birth in the Universe until the disappearance of the latter.

Practically, when the Universe comes to an end and God leaves His wife, the Matter of the Universe, the Supreme Consciousness of the Lord will grow bigger and higher than in the Big-Bang moment. Like the human soul unloads accomplished energies in the third compartment of his Personal Box, God will have His Personal Box stuffed with accomplished energies from the evolution of His children in the Universe.

The second part: The evolution of God after the death of our Universe

After the energies of our Universe are completely depleted, God and all the energies of His children will be reborn under the form of a larger and more complex Universe. God will be reincarnated from one matter into another, and from one Universe into another, and will continue to grow, thanks to His children—thanks to *us*, who are the human beings and individually become a universe in the Universe of God.

Until then, God our Father will grow into a MEGA-UNIVERSE and a MEGA-GOD. In other words, we who are now human beings will become GODs and multitudes of Universes as a part of our Father and our Mother: mega-Universe, Mega-Matter, and MEGA-GODS.

We are the Children of God, which means we are the future Gods.

First, if we are all the future Gods, we have the essential duty to learn how to conduct ourselves like God, our Heavenly Father. Just like He accepts us and loves us and helps us and doesn't interfere in our personal decisions and or judge us, whether we're good or bad, we should treat ourselves and the surrounding world nicely.

Second, if we all are Gods, it means there will never be another one better or worse than us, because there are no idols, stars, prophets/apostles, or saints. There are no lower human races or backward or primitive minds or more stupid or wiser people. Just because *we all are the future gods.*

The difference between the primitive minds and the great prophets/apostles, or those described by religio, lies only in the time and life our human body experienced in the material world. But in the end, we all will become the faithful child of the Lord our Father and of our Mother, the matter. We will all become Gods.

Attention! Important! Even though we know that we are the future Gods, it doesn't mean that we should scorn the surrounding world and treat it with haughtiness, or denigrate the Lord and the people with illuminated minds. On the contrary, we should know that our mission in this Universe is to provide love, harmony, and esteem for anyone, irrespective of their level of evolution.

We should love and treat the lower ones as if they were our own children, still innocent and having no idea of what they are doing.

We should treat our equals as if they were our brothers or sisters, from whose expertise we could get inspired.

We should hold those of a greater spirit in high esteem and respect them as if they were our mentors or parents wishing well to their children. Some religions turned them into idols and made you kneel to them and kiss their feet. But in the spiritual world, no one does it, and no one bows and crawls before the illuminated ones. No one saw this happen, not even those who had an NED experience. I didn't see it in God's attitude towards me either. Each time He appeared in my dreams to send me a piece of information, or speak His feelings about me, He looked like a humble man about my age and height. And each time He talked to me as if I were His peer or one of His best friends. I am telling you these things so that you will be respectful of yourselves and of God and the surrounding world.

Also, to find the truth of the Surrounding World, we *should not* seek it in religions, prophets/apostles, or saints described in many books, but in the surrounding world. If we seek it in ourselves, we will find it in our soul, and if we seek it in the surrounding world, we will find it in the signs of God, and thus we will find God.

Only by discovering our soul within us and by discovering God in our entourage can we find the true way of evolution in this universe.

THE END

THIS WAS THE MESSAGE GOD SENT TO ME DURING MY EPIPHANY IN THE FALL OF 2005

I hope you understand why I was so scared when I found out all these things. Actually, I never wanted to know them. My only goal was to provide my family with a decent living, nothing else. I had never been inclined to abandon my profession as a psychiatrist, which I desperately loved, or to become a writer, something I had never done before.

But, notwithstanding my principles, I faithfully obeyed the signs of God and accepted my destiny under the guidance of our Lord. I accepted this destiny because I knew that if I didn't send God's message across, no one would ever do it, and our civilization would be in torment.

Please listen faithfully to the signs of God and change your destiny according to what God tells you to do, or else the destruction of our civilization *cannot be avoided.*

As you can see, we are all one whole. We are a whole family. The entire Universe is a whole family in union with us eternally and is anxiously waiting for the moment when we all turn our face towards it and begin living together in love and harmony with our own families and the surrounding world. It is waiting for us to start listening to our good Father, who gives us precious advice at any crossroad we may be at. Please spare the Mother Matter of our irresponsible exploitation, as she is always ready to sacrifice down to the last drop of energy in her body. Let's listen to our soul, who takes good care of his wife, the body, every second of our life.

HOW TO LIVE IN HARMONY WITH THE UNIVERSE

In the winter of 2019–2020, we were spending a vacation in Mexico. I already wrote about it, when Nastia was feeding fish in a lagoon in the Caribbean.

One day, we were hanging out and went there to watch the fish. There were people on that shore doing the same thing. Immobile, they were staring at the water in amusement, speaking in low voices to not to scare the fish away.

At a certain moment, a couple came to the shore in a hurry. They were carrying goggles and swimming fins, and they didn't say anything. They put on their equipment and began fidgeting and talking loudly, sending the fish in all directions and making everyone leave that place. We were the only ones who stayed there, staring at the young couple as they were wading in the shallow water looking for the fish. But the tiny creatures were nowhere to be seen. So after a while, the Americans decided to go back to their hotel.

I said to my wife and my daughters: "We should not treat the Universe like this. To live in harmony with the Universe, we should be careful about everything around us, just like these people who watch the fish from the shore. Before they came close to the water, they looked around and checked all the details of the environment. It is only by answering the fish's requests that we will manage to live in harmony with them. Thanks to this wise policy, the people on shore could enjoy the beauty of the exotic fish.

"We should do the same in our relationship with the Universe. We should be careful about absolutely everything that happens around us. We must watch and feel any breeze and listen to the advice of anyone around and try to adapt to any situation, because God is permanently with us at any crossroads, and He guides us on the road of our evolution to prosperity. It is only by integrating ourselves with the surrounding world, like we did with the fish, that we can live in harmony with God, the whole Universe, and our Soul, which is the coordinator of the signs of God.

"But look at what's going on in reality. We are all like that American couple—self-centered and proud of our superiority over the others. Just like those two, who believed they could see the fish better because they had the best equipment, we think that we have the most sophisticated technique and are free to cut down the secular forests of the planet, extract all the natural resources from the soil, and raze every natural thing from the ground to erect luxury residential complexes and wage destructive wars against other countries.

"Look what we have done in a hundred years since our modern civilization has fitted itself with advanced technology! We have destroyed the natural environment and multiplied like rats, invading the planet like hungry parasites. There's nothing left from what our Mother Nature has created from the beginning of the earth. There's no more room for the wildlife except some abridged National Parks and zoo parks where the occupants, unable to migrate to strengthen their DNA, cannot survive."

GOD'S PASSIONS AND FATHERLY LOVE FOR US

Let me give you some examples to demonstrate how God expresses His feelings at sensitive times of our life. My younger daughter, Lya, has never been a fast learner, and she had to study hard to graduate from high school. Because of that, she couldn't dedicate enough time to her parents, though we knew how much she loved us. Each time she came to see us, she was dewy-eyed, and when she had to go, she was literally sobbing.

Towards the end of her studies, she was doing much better and had more time to spend with us. She even brought her boyfriend with her and stayed with us a whole week. When they went back to Quebec, we had breakfast together and saw them to their car. Lya was crying and we were doing the same. We hugged and bid adieu while our dog was bouncing around us. Then Lya got in the car and they drove away.

We followed them with our gaze until they disappeared behind the houses ahead. We got in our car and moved away. We were driving silently towards the woods at the town boundary, so overwhelmed by our separation from our daughter. Before we reached the light stop, I saw Lya's car running on a side street, and now our daughter was ahead of us. We arrived at the stop and the light turned red. At that moment, the radio was playing a song in French called "Il est où le Bonheur." The name of that song in Romanian is "Where Is the Happiness?" It is a sentimental, nostalgic tune with devastating lyrics: "Where is the happiness, where is it? It is here."

Suddenly, our cars were moving side by side. We stopped and rolled down the windows. The sentimental melody filled the air and seized Lya and her boyfriend with a devastating effect that we could feel deep inside our bones. I was struggling hard with my tears, hoping she would understand that God was telling us that happiness was there for us. After the last notes were played, we all burst into tears, such was its beauty and tenderness.

The light turned green, and our roads forked off. God had created that sentimental moment to fill our hearts with immeasurable joy. This breakaway was similar to how I felt when I moved to Canada, leaving my parents behind. At that time, I didn't know if I would ever go back to see them. Yet almost two decades later, I managed to travel back to embrace them.

I came back to my senses and called Lya. "You see, Lya, how God organized our separation? You see how much He loves us and suffers together with us?"

"Yes, Daddy, I see," she said.

And I went on. "All the feelings God created for us are actually a token of how He feels for us. This affection is His affection. He knows how much we love one another, and He always stands by us when we're in pain. He suffers when we suffer, and He feels our pain when we're in torment. It's not the first time He's shown His empathy and love for us. Years ago, when your maternal grandfather passed away, I had to go with your mother to buy things and, according to the tradition, give them out to the needy. The whole day we drove around from one shop to the other, and each time we got in the car and started the engine, the radio was playing classical music, a sign that God was kind and compassionate to us. You see?"

"Yes, I do," Lya answered.

Spiritual psychoanalysis

This is an analysis of my separation from Lya and the pain caused by the death of Nastia's father. Why would God show empathy for us only in situations involving our family? I believe He does it because the Essential Law of the Universe is also the Family Law, which states that the *family* always comes first. The most important aspect of this interrelationship is the alliance between husband and wife, parents and children, and children and parents as well.

It's not a coincidence that God *insisted* that I write my first book, *The Destiny and Signs of God*, in which I described the Family Law in full detail to let our whole civilization know about it and start focusing on this way of thinking and learn how to live in the family and create tighter and healthier inter-family relations based on affection and understanding.

As you can see, God commiserates with us and shares His joyfulness with us and wants to live in harmony with us. But do we really want to live in harmony with Him? Do we really care about His feelings and predicaments?

Chapter Three

THE THIRD ENERGY AND ITS INFLUENCE ON THE ACTIVE ENERGIES

DURING THE WRITING OF MY BOOKS, IT WAS EASY FOR ME TO DETECT God and Mother Matter as forms of existence, because I had my knowledge of the construction of the world that was enhanced with the help of my revelation of the fall of 2005 and enhanced with all the situations organized by God for me. The Third Energy of the Universe is a very sensitive topic, and it took me a long time to understand it. God had to make me go through different radical temptations so that I could become aware of the existence of this energy.

This energy is independent and is located between two worlds, the material world and the spiritual one. It doesn't take sides with either one but only creates harmony, balance, and fairness among them.

As you know, the Universe is made of two forms of passive energies: the energy of the matter of the Universe, and the energy of the Supreme Consciousness, which is God. The Third Energy is the third passive energy, which belongs to the couple of husband and wife, of God and Mother Matter.

- All the laws of the Universe exist in this energy.

- It plays the justice role in the Universe and also serves as police, prosecutor, lawyer, and presiding judge.

- It distributes the active energies we and the entire Universe create.

THE GENERAL PRINCIPLES OF THE THIRD ENERGY

What is this energy? Honestly, I can't answer this question. I know what its role and functions are, but I can't give a clear explanation like I did for the representatives of the husbands and wives in Universe.

Initially, I believed that this energy was the Personal Box I described in my first book. But later on, I realized it was way more than that, as it contained the Laws of the Universe governing the spirit and matter relationship.

Then I believed it was the energy of love and harmony that grows from the relationship between the spirit and the matter, but this wasn't convincing enough because, like in the first case, it contains more than love and harmony; it contains the Laws of the Universe.

And now I believe this energy could be the Holy Ghost chronicled in the religious literature. The Third Energy, or the Holy Ghost, makes the Trinity described in the religious books, and the Trinity is composed of the representative of the Husband, and of the Wife, and of the Holy Ghost. In other words, any form of life in this Universe is composed of the representatives of the wives and those of the husbands. Practically, they are not just a couple made of two energies but *a third* composed of the three passive energies described above.

THE ROLE AND FUNCTIONS OF THE THIRD ENERGY

The first function of the Third Energy is the role of justice in the Universe, and it also serves as police, prosecutor, lawyer, and presiding judge. The second function is that of a supervisor of the reincarnation of our souls in the material World.

The First Function of the Third Energy

Even if the Third Energy is a part of the Trinity of the Matter, the Soul, and the Third Energy, its functions and duties are completely different.

Together with the soul, the matter creates active energies for the Personal Box for all three compartments. However, the Third Energy *cannot* create active energies, as its role is to operate with them in accordance with the Laws of the Universe.

This is consistent with:

- The Family Law of the Universe

- The Boomerang Law, which makes the energies return to their maker

- The Wheel of Life Law, which makes the positive and negative events in life recur in circles

- The Paradox of Life Law, which demonstrates that nothing is what we are convinced it is.

Abiding by the above laws, the Third Energy plays the justice role for any form of life in this Universe, from the most primitive to the couple of God and Mother Matter. She also plays the role of police, lawyer, prosecutor, and judge.

The Third Energy operates with all the positive and negative energies from all the Personal Boxes of any form of life in this Universe. She decides the time, the place, and the person/society where those energies from those should land. She also decides the quantity that should be allotted to a person or society. She decides the source, the Personal Box from where the energy should be taken.

For instance, the Third Energy can send to a person/society negative energies from the Personal Box, the Family Box, the Community Box, or the Personal Box of our civilization on earth. For instance, from June 2019 to March 2020, the Third Energy sent me negative energies from the Personal Box of our civilization, about which I wrote extensively in the first chapter of this book.

Important: Irrespective of the discretion used in the distribution of the negative energies on earth, no energy is meant to harm us. And even if they affect us seriously, they're meant to do us good and help us seek the right ways of evolution. All the negative energies are apportioned by the Third Energy to guide us on the spiritual way of evolution in Universe.

To what extent does God get involved in the decisions made by the Third Energy? God cannot disapprove the decisions made by the Third Energy and must let her perform her functions liberally. He has three options of collaboration with her:

A) THE FIRST OPTION:

This applies when the Third Energy sends to someone negative energies from the Personal Box or the Family Box of the target person. Our souls too are familiar with these energies because before our soul is born and decides in which body he should reincarnate, he takes into consideration the energies from his Personal Box and his Family Box".

In the pre-birth stage, our souls organize their destiny according to the content of these two boxes. The Family Boxes are a consequence of the risk we take when we come to earth.

When the Third Energy is sending negative energies from these two boxes, God has the right to repurpose these energies into beacons for the wife of our soul, the body, to make them follow the spiritual way of evolution.

B) THE SECOND OPTION:

This applies when the Third Energy is sending negative energies that *do not* belong to us and originate from the Personal Boxes of:

- the place where we live
- the country we belong to
- the people with whom we argued

In such cases, God is entitled to warn us so that we can avoid these situations.

I gave a lot of such examples in my first book. In the case of Ramona's accident, God warned me in time to help that woman avoid a serious accident. Also, He warned me that I could have a car accident so that I could keep myself away from it.

C) THE THIRD OPTION

God's third option is actually an obligation. If an overaccumulation of negative energies is reported in the Personal Box, God is *obligated* to help the Third Energy apportion the negative energies on Earth, even though those energies could impact on the innocent. Here are three examples:

Distribution of negative energies worldwide. This category includes the COVID-19 pandemic, which came out of the Personal Box of our civilization and affected so many who didn't deserve it. It affected me too, with various negative energies from June 2019 until late February 2020 (see Examples in Chapter One of this book).

Distribution of negative energies nationwide. This category includes the terrorist act on September 11, 2001, when the two New York City icons were destroyed. In this case, the Personal Box of the United States was overstuffed with untoward international conflicts. The Third Energy decided to use the negative energies from the Personal Box of the United States to raze the World Trade Center to the ground. Thousands of innocent people who had never created any negative energy for the Personal Box of the United States lost their life.

This includes the excessive accumulation of negative energies on a personal level, like Maria's unfortunate accident mentioned at the beginning of this book. In this case, God *had the obligation* to stop me from going to see my friend, just to let the negative energy impact on Maria's life.

Restrictions of the Third Energy

The Third Energy can operate with any negative energy in this Universe, including the negative energies of the Universe itself. But I know that this energy has the right to operate with the negative energies from the Personal Box, provided that we create a certain accomplished energy.

For instance, if we are *fully* convinced that we shouldn't be aggressive, and we make a definitive decision for our future, then our negative energy of aggression in the Personal Box automatically turns into accomplished energy. In this case, the Third Energy of the Universe has no right to send us negative energies of aggression, because we alone have transformed all our energies into accomplished energies.

Supervisory position of the Third Energy

Let me specify a few particularities first:

- The Third Energy finds itself between two worlds, the material world of the Universe and the spiritual world of God our Lord.

- All the Laws of the Universe are located in the Third Energy.

- Our Personal Boxes are placed in the Third Energy during our life on this earth and afterwards.

- During the course of our life, the chakras of our body are part of us as human beings, but after our physical death, they get accumulated in the Third Energy of the Universe.

Therefore, after the physical death of our body and our Personal Box, the chakras are placed in the Third Energy, and the latter is the one that determines what level of evolution we deserve here on earth according to the energies we acquired in our Personal Box. For instance,

if we are going through the stage of our material evolution, convinced that in order to succeed we must fight and judge those who are wrong and oppress others and show them that we're always one step ahead them, the Third Energy will never open her gates for us here on earth.

If we are genuinely convinced that we must love the surrounding world irrespectively of what they think of us and allow our wives to enjoy their supremacy over us and we must live in Harmony and Love with God and the rest of the world, the Third Energy will let us be born on an alien planet, in harmony with our principles.

If we have a higher level of evolution, we're not obligated to go to the maximum level we deserve. This decision is entirely ours. Even if we deserve to be born on an alien planet where the level of evolution is perfectly in line with our principles, we can successfully be born on planet Earth if we want to.

Any soul reincarnated at a lower level than it deserves is not necessarily pursuing carnal pleasures but sacrifices his life to save the people living at inferior levels, and thus saves our whole civilization. One of them was Jesus Christ and many others like Him, who weren't much appreciated here on Earth. In exchange, out there in the spiritual world, they are held in high esteem and are awarded a tremendous value and a level of evolution beyond imagination.

How the negative energies are created and how the Third Energy operates them. In my first book, I wrote extensively about the importance of the Essential Law of the Universe, the Family Law, which stays at the foundation of the entire Universe and all the living forms inside it. We all are made of a soul, which is the representative of the husband, and a human body, which is the representative of the wife of our soul. Our essential role here on earth is to train ourselves to live as a couple, as husband and wife, and learn all the subtleties of this relationship. I will explain here how the negative energies are created in a couple relationship, how the Third Energy operates these energies, and how the negative energies are generated across our entire society.

After she graduated from high school, Lya was admitted to the Faculty of Physiotherapy at the University of Quebec. We bought a two-bedroom condo for our medical business and rented it out to our daughter, who billeted one of her best friends with her to save money on utilities.

Lya and her girlfriend were a perfect match, though in personality they were poles apart. Lya was quiet and introverted, while her friend was active and swift. But they were living together in peace and harmony, and it seemed that nothing would ever separate them.

But in time, their relationship went cold. They weren't arguing, but they gradually grew silent and distant with each other. Lya was obsessed with the cleanliness of her apartment, while her friend was negligent and contemptuous. After a while they developed a tense relationship, and one day they fought so hard that Lya's friend left and never came back.

After Lya told me the whole story, I said to her, "Lya, I understand your frustrations, I truly do, and let me help you get over it, as I am going to explain to you what caused this conflict from a spiritual point of view.

"You were two opposite characters from the very beginning, yet you were a seamless match, presumably for eternity. Notwithstanding the harmony of your relationship, you have ended up in a big argument, which turned you into foes for life. The same thing happens to a husband and wife, two persons who initially love one another desperately and after a while end up in a matrimonial separation.

"What's going on? Why do two people who love one another so much come to a divorce?

Let's see what happened between you and your girlfriend. When we enter a relationship with another person, an energy develops between us, some sort of a Personal Box of a couple, a box where positive and negative energies go. In this case, initially, the Personal Box of your relationship gathered a lot of positive energies, generated by your different personalities and your harmonious bond.

"But let's see what happened later on. Living in the same apartment, you discovered the negative particularities of your characters, and this became a growing irritation for both of you. Your own characters and the arrogance of your own bodies could accept only your own principles and ideas and innermost feelings, which you'd had since you were little. The arrogance of your bodies made you focus on the negative side on your roommate, and you began thinking negatively about her and hating her and passing judgment on her.

"All your negative thoughts and hatred and judgment were ground into negative energies pitching one against the other and getting stuffed in the Personal Box of your relationship. And in time, these energies turned into a huge cloud of negative energies, which the Third Energy turned against you, making you loath one another forever.

"As you can see, the negative energies grew in the Personal Box of your relationship, even though you had never argued before or spoke about your discomfort with each other. Try to imagine this: If the cloud of negative energy between you and your girlfriend was created based only on what you were thinking about one another, what would have happened to a family if the husband and the wife had *verbally* exchanged barbs of sarcasm? How big can the cloud of negative energy grow between husband and wife if they express themselves verbally? Imagine that within a marital couple relationship, save for the propensity of our body to find the negative particularities of our partner, there are other urges that manifest themselves between man and woman."

Conclusion: The obligation of the Third Energy of the Universe is to coordinate with all the energies created in the Universe respecting the Laws of the Universe. One of the laws is the Boomerang Law, which requires that any form of energy be returned to the one who produced it. In the case of Lya and her girlfriend, the Third Energy had to return all the negative energies that had accumulated in the Personal Box of their relationships.

After we get married, one of our body's particularities is to be possessive; our body believes that our life partner belongs to us, and we can do with them whatever we want. Therefore, we try to change the character and demeanor of our partner and remodel it after our principles and ideas. But if we can't change anything within ourselves, and if the way we were in our youth remains unchanged until we get old, how can we make someone else change?

Another particularity of our body is to believe that she is right and he is the most rational and accurate of all. The more we believe in our rationality and correctness, the less often we are right, and according to the Law of the Universe of the Paradox of Life, when we believe we know something, we actually don't know it at all. Why?

We are so strongly convinced that we are the good ones who judge the surrounding world where the bad ones live. This principle wreaks havoc in our relationship with the world, especially with our families, where our ambition and self-centered attitude prevails when we show our correctness and rationality to our life partner and our children. The rationality of our thinking destroys our families and our entire civilization.

When we call ourselves rational and correct:

- we cannot see the signs of God

- we create politics based on rationality, which generates national and international conflicts

- we create religious politics based on rationality, leading to inter-religious and international conflicts

As you can see, our correctness and rationality fuel gigantic clouds of negative energies that precipitate more divorces than marriages and ignite conflicts, wars, and meltdowns. The Third Energy of the Universe is forced to manipulate the immensity of the negative energies created by us, which can't do anything other than lead us to divorce. Only by going through extreme negative experiences can the human being become aware of the true paths we must follow in life.

As you can see, our convictions and persistence to change the world cannot be successful. We grow old, but we don't make much philosophical progress unless we go through extreme negative experiences. So how could we change someone else? The right move in order to change the world would be to start with ourselves.

"Therefore," I continued, "what can we do to avoid dismantling our families and the society we live in? You already know that we shouldn't create negative energies or be hostile to our partner. We should create only positive energies and learn how to accept and love our partner as a mother would her little child who doesn't know much yet.

"We shouldn't let the negative energies sneak into our brains, because once they're in, they will never want to get out when hatred or judgment of our partner flashes through our thought. After that, more negative energies, hatred, and judgment will come. The most important thing for us to realize is that the Third Energy of the Universe cannot pass by even the smallest negative energy of ours. All the negative energies of our thoughts, words, or actions—absolutely everything—the Third Energy will return back to us in such a form or situation until we learn not to create any form of negative energy.

"Most importantly, we should not forget our mission on earth. The most important mission of our soul on earth is to create harmony and love between our soul and body and to create harmony and love between man and Woman. By creating harmony and love between these two couples, we build a spiritual way of evolution for ourselves and a beautiful future for our descendants. By creating positive energies for the Personal Box of our family, we build a sterling future for all our children and grandchildren. And then we generate positive energies for

the place we live in, our country, and our entire civilization. Creating positive energies in our families, we make a legacy for our descendants, for our children and grandchildren, and for our civilization in general.

Practically, the positive energies are the only inheritance our descendants need. Our descendants don't need castles or palaces or our money in the bank. They need a healthy planet and positive energies of love and harmony that we gather over the course of our life and store in the Personal Box of our family and civilization. Our children don't need our achievements, as they came down here to earth to fulfill their dreams, not ours."

This was my speech before Lya.

Lya and her friend could never overcome their taciturnity, which was yet another piece of evidence that when too much negative energy is accumulated in our Personal Boxes, the Third Energy returns this energy to us under destructive forms. In this case, there was an overaccumulation of negative energies in the Personal Box of the relationship between Lya and her girlfriend.

Our Missions on Earth

As you know, we all are God's Messengers on earth and the Guardian Angels for the surrounding world and everyone we may encounter over the course of our life. Let me draw a conclusion on Lya's conflict with her girlfriend, Maria's unfortunate accident, and the COVID-19 pandemic that hit the world. When the Personal Boxes are overstuffed with negative energies, whether they are ours or belong to our civilization, the Third Energy returns all the negative energies to their producer.

In Lya's case, they were returned as an argument.

In Maria's case, they were returned as a tragic accident that left her impaired for life.

As for our civilization, all the negative energies created by our ancestors impacted both the innocent and the guilty.

We continue to think after the old material principles that go back to the dawn of our civilization. This makes the negative energies a burden our society. We continue to behave belligerently and hate and judge other people and whimsically satisfy the pleasures of our flesh. We want more power and wealth and domination over the other ones.

The overaccumulation of the negative energies in our Personal Boxes will never stop unless we take *immediate* measures. But before doing it, we must determine the missions of our souls here on earth. Let's take it step by step.

A) THE MISSION OF OUR SOUL FOR THE RELATIONSHIP BETWEEN OUR SOUL AND OUR BODY

The most important mission of our soul is to make his wife, the body, open her eyes and assess the value of the spiritual evolution. For that purpose, our soul uses several techniques, such as the *consequences* of our actions and the *signs of God*. With these methods, our soul tries to convince his wife, the body, to rid her flesh of temptations like greed, envy, aggressiveness, judgment, the rush for gold and power, deceit, duplicity, theft, offence, murder, etc.

The spiritual evolution shouldn't scare us or make us believe that we'll end up like a monk in a monastery. We shouldn't give up our professions and trades, or our life principles. On the contrary, we must do our best to succeed in the field we cherish.

This means that we must learn how to follow the signs of God each time we find ourselves in a quandary and do as much possible as we can, and even more. The Third Energy of the Universe will always take care to return the negative energies created by us in such a way that we learn to walk in life only on the spiritual path of evolution.

Apart from the temptations of our body, there's another category of negative energies we acquire, especially in adolescence and at maturity when we discover forbidden pleasures and bad habits and try to appropriate them. All these prohibited pleasures and bad habits are nothing else than negative energies, and once they enter our mind, they will stay there and urge us to feed them. For instance:

- Once we taste the pleasure of drinking alcohol, we can't stop and we continue to drink until we become alcoholics.

- Once we kill an enemy, the killing becomes an addiction.

- Once we get the power to control the society, the society is all ours.

No one was born a liar, a killer, an alcoholic, or a thoroughgoing bastard. We become one only because of the society we live in. Like Jean Jacques Rousseau said: <u>"L'homme naît naturellement bon et heureux, c'est la société qui le corrompt et le rend malheureux"</u> (*"The man is born naturally good and happy, it is society that corrupts him and makes him unhappy"* [1712–1778] Bibliography 35).

The negative energies we let into our brains at maturity turn us not only into alcoholics, pompous, and high-handed bullies and murderers but also into political leaders eager to manipulate the masses and wage wars, as if war were just a game. They also create religious leaders and economic moguls who manipulate large bodies of people. For them, money is preferable to the health of the environment and the planet we live on, and they continue to destroy them just to get richer. It's very important to know that when we reach the leadership of the world, we have the opportunity to lead with energies of global dimensions. If the energies we create from this level are negative energies, then the Third Energy of the Universe will be obliged to return all these energies to us. Imagine what can happen to a person on whom a global Negative energy falls.

We all are creators of positive and negative energies. We do it through the mechanism of:

- our thoughts

- our words

- our wishes

- our feelings

- our actions

All these energies get stocked in our Personal Boxes and later, the Third Energy of the Universe will turn them against us in response to the mistake we have made. This is a telling example of negative energies.

Proposal

To solve the problem of the negative energies, whether created or accomplished, I believe that we should explain it to our children from early school years and make them aware of all the extant negative energies and mechanics of their creation so that they can avoid them when they become of age.

B) THE MISSION OF OUR SOUL FOR A MAN AND WOMAN RELATIONSHIP

This mission is in respect to the creation of the Personal Box of our family. All the energies we generate over the course of our life in our interaction with the surrounding world, through our personal achievements, and in our relationships with each member of our family, accumulate in the Personal Box of the family and will be passed over to all our descendants, who will suffer the consequences of our greed, dilapidations, and lawlessness. Or they will take advantage of the love and harmony we build all around.

Our mission for the members of our family. Each of us is a little God with his own age experience acquired here on earth. None of us is the same, and we all are individually unique.

In this Babel of personalities, we must remember that we came down to earth *not* to change the other ones but to change *ourselves.* We should not correct the negative features of our family members but accept them and love them with all our heart. In fact, we should take advantage of the entourage of our family to diagnose *our* negative particularities and change ourselves.

When we decided to be born in this body, we undertook the obligation to be the Guardian Angel for all the members of our family; therefore, we have the duty to protect them and pay attention to their wishes and purposes and help them fulfill their dreams. We should express our opinions to change their mind or the course of their action, since we have our own purpose that is different from that of any other human on earth. We can only smooth the flow of their lives and be at their side when they *need* us, not when *we want to.*

Our mission for our wives. For anyone we meet in life, even those randomly encountered in the street, we have the mission to act as a Guardian Angel. In every human being on Earth there is a God at a stage and with a life experience totally different from ours, and we must approach them with deep respect and love and understanding. We should not try to change them; instead, we should try to learn from them and help them only if they reach out to us. Our mission is to pay attention to their desires and assist them in fulfilling their dreams.

Our Mission for our Spiritual Fathers. In light of Chapter Two, where I explained the relationship between us and the entire Universe, we can say that any energy we create in this life affects us and the entire Universe at the same time. When we do wrong, we suffer, and together with us suffer our spiritual forefathers and God our Father and the whole Universe.

The *enormous* volume of Negative Energies for the Personal Box of our civilization is not our biggest problem. What scares me is that we destroy our Mother Matter, who gave birth to us and took care of us and made sure that we didn't miss anything before we became human beings on earth. It took her a billion years to make us grow and reach the adolescence period of our evolution. Our astounding arrogance and greed are hampering our judgment as we continue to use the resources of our Mother, the earth, to satisfy our thirst for power and gold.

Our mission now is to take all the necessary steps to protect our Mother Matter for the earth on which we live. And we can start this enterprise with our daily routine and save as much as possible of the natural resources of our Mother on earth. Also, we should persuade our colleagues at work to do the same thing and go global with our ideas and suggestions for a sustainable protection of our Mother Nature.

It is very important that we not ignore the negative situations in our lives, because the Third Energy of the Universe is careful to send us a very important message through these situations that we must be aware of and put into practice with holiness. We must take into account not only personal negative situations but all situations at all levels: negative situations at the family level, at the regional level, at the country level, and at the world level.

If on a personal level the Third Energy is trying to send us a personal message, and if on a family level the Third Energy is trying to send us a family message, then on a global level the Third Energy of the Universe is trying to send us a message for our whole civilization, especially for all the leaders. COVID-19, the war of the Russians against Ukraine, and the war in Israel are direct messages for our entire civilization that we must not ignore but analyze from a spiritual point of view through the prism of Spiritual Psychoanalysis. This way we'll make the most just decisions, and let's put them into practice as a matter of urgency, because the future of our civilization depends on the decisions that the leaders of the world make now. We can't wait for other cataclysms to happen to our civilization, because they could be the last.

THE IMPORTANCE OF THE ENERGIES TO THE FUTURE FOR OUR DESCENDANTS

Our most difficult task is to stop the industry that generates negative energies for the Personal Box of our civilization. Each of us has an *enormous* influence not only on his family and society but also on the entire Universe, as each is a would-be God. So imagine the power we harbor in our souls!

To build a future with a continuing evolution of our civilization, we must stop the ongoing material evolution and switch to a spiritual alternative. And we should begin with ourselves. We should abandon material thinking and embrace the spiritual approach to life. In this way, we discontinue our personal production of negative energies and make only positive ones for our Personal Box and that of our family, of everyone we interact with, of our workplace, and of our civilization.

We shouldn't act with fanaticism but simply behave spiritually at home and at work. Even if we can't create positive energies for the Personal Box of the world, at least the energies we make for our entourage have a *tremendous* significance for our civilization. Every positive energy from every Personal Box of everyone is an exceptional benefaction for the positive energies of our civilization.

I remind you that negative energies are created because of materialistic thinking. This form of thinking is a selfish thinking focused only on our own person and does everything for the satisfaction of its pleasures of superiority, wealth, and domination. The more we want to take advantage of the world around us, the more we become poor with an emptiness in our souls. Spiritual thinking, compared to the material one, is focused on the outside world on doing good to everyone around us. It's based on the Boomerang Law of the Universe, that everything we create for someone else will come back to us. In the case of materialistic thinking, we try to take advantage of the surrounding world so that we can have more. As a result, when we take from someone, we take from ourselves, so we remain poor. In the case of spiritual thinking, we try to do good things to those around us, so when we give something to someone, we give it back to ourselves.

We can change the destiny of civilization even through wishes. If every person on this planet wants to live a *pure* life, their wishes will help neutralize a *huge* quantity of negative energies accumulated in the Personal Box of our civilization. But if we continue to wage wars and foster riots and hatred, we will let the negative energies of our civilization continue to accumulate. As a consequence, the Third Energy won't hesitate to turn them back to exact retribution as pandemics, wars, or world catastrophes.

Chapter Four

THE LAST SECRET OF GOD THAT I REALIZED OR THE MEANING OF 12 AND 21 AND THE LENGTHY STEPS THAT TOOK PLACE BEFORE ARRIVING AT THIS CONCLUSION

THIS IS THE ONLY PART THAT I WROTE APPROXIMATELY A YEAR AFTER I FINished my second book, *The Messages and Secrets of the Universe*. I wrote all the other chapters from the beginning of March 2020 until July 2020, but I only started writing this chapter in the summer of 2021.

In the spring of 2020, shortly after I understood God's message about the COVID-19 pandemic, I started to write this book. I was rushing to finish it as fast as possible to send it to the Romanian-English translator for translation. I wanted this book to be published as soon as possible, because I didn't want to miss the opportunity to bring God's message to people's attention as fast as I could.

Even though I had finished the book by July 2020 and hoped that it would reach the publisher by the end of that year, its publication was to be delayed much longer. I will start this chapter with the description of the situations in my life in which the numbers 12 and 21 appeared as some landmark numbers, and then to better understand why the publication of this book has been so long delayed and why I wrote this chapter. I will tell you, step by step, about all the events that happened after I finished writing this book. Even if the situations described by me at the beginning of this chapter seem to have nothing to do with the numbers 12 and 21, they all convinced me about the true meaning of the last and most important number—number 21.

THE SIGNS OF GOD RELATED TO 12 AND 21

Readers who read my first book, *The Destiny and Signs of God*, know the history of my life and the story of God's signs related to numbers 12 and 21. To those who have not read my first book yet and don't know what it's about, I will give a short explanation about the history of my life in relation to these numbers. Here's how these numbers were born.

In Moldova, I was a psychiatrist and was treating adolescents in a region of over 250,000 people. Later on, I moved to Romania, where I worked as the only psychiatrist in a region of over 150,000 people. I loved this job so much, and I was hoping to practice in Canada.

I landed in Canada in 2005, and for the first three years, I worked in construction so that my wife, Nastia, had ample time and financial support to study and earn her degree in family medicine. From 2008 on, after Nastia managed to pass all of her equivalency exams and started her residency training, I began preparations for the equivalency exams too. I managed to pass two exams, and I was supposed to sit another two.

In the meantime, knowing God's/Universe's ways of communication, I was teaching my girls to uncover for themselves the messages God was trying to send them personally. Time passed, and the girls were learning to recognize God's signs better and better, but for me, God hadn't said anything about my chances to get my medical studies validated. I sat my third exam several times and failed. And still, God wasn't making it clear.

At one point I even said to my girls, "What do you think, if I can see the signs that God is sending you, can I also recognize the signs He's attributing to me personally? I think I would, but the problem is that He doesn't tell me anything at all. He says absolutely nothing about my exams and about my future."

God's silence roused my anger, and I remained confused, with no clues about what was going on.

As I was staying at home, shunning the outside world, busying myself with reading and analyzing books from dawn to dusk, God found a way to send me a message that drew my attention to two numbers: 12 and 21. As you know, when you read medical literature, you deal with images, graphics, drawings, numbers, letters, and such. From this quantum of information, the numbers 12 and 21 were the only ones that caught my eyes. These numbers had an inestimable value, and I was letting them slip through my eyelids and permeate deeply into my brain. I didn't understand what was going on, and I was asking myself: "What is the meaning of these numbers? What is God trying to tell me?"

After two unsuccessful years, in the spring of 2012, when I had to sit my exam for the fourth time, I realized that if I didn't pass, there would never be another chance, meaning that I would have to relinquish my job as a psychiatrist and suffer torment. Previously, God had advised us not be obstinate and not to embark on the road of "closed doors," so I wasn't willing to walk down any condemned road.

If I had stayed true to my principles, I would have pursued my career and would have passed that exam and become a doctor in Canada. But even though I knew how painful such a decision could be, I listened to God, not to my whimsical preferences. After I failed my fourth exam again, with my heart ripped apart, I abandoned my medical career, and as God was pressing on me, I dedicated myself to writing my first book.

It happened in May 2012, and the title of that book was *The Destiny and Signs of God*. Time passed by, and I couldn't bring myself to make much progress. I was distressed and had no creativity. Without my medical profession, I had lost all hopes of living. Worse, I had never written anything, and I had no idea how to do it. Emotionally and professionally, I wasn't ready for it, and I had no idea where to start and where to end. I only knew of God's intentions and messages that I was going to reveal in the book, even if in my mind there was no logical coordination of this process.

Little by little, one month after another, by December 2012 I finished the first chapter.

The chapter was only a few pages long, and even if it wasn't big, lest I should lose this information, I printed it on paper.

I went up to my office to connect the computer to the printer, and I pressed the print button. Important! Attention! The moment I pressed print, the date and time on the computer were *precisely* 12:12 on the 12th day of December 2012. Such an exact, perfect, and unique coincidence left me in perplexity. My hair stood on end all over my body, and I couldn't believe that God had organized this accurate situation for me. It was like in the realm of fantasy and imagination, where you can't imagine that such coincidences exist, even more so that it could happen to you.

In those moments, I realized how important my book could be, particularly before God our Lord. And after I learned about the meaning of the number 12, I was so proud that God had chosen me to be His messenger on earth. I was proud to write a book under His guidance.

The number 12 was the confirmation that it was foreordained that I should sacrifice my psychiatric profession for the sake of a new destination: to write a very important book for our civilization, a book that would change not only my destiny but also the destiny of our entire civilization.

I did not know the significance of the number 12.

As I continued to write, I understood that the number 21 would belong to the Law of the Universe of the "Wheel of Life." I considered that writing my first book coincided with a negative period of my life, and in 2021, I was hoping that my book would be on the market and that it would sell like hotcakes. I would become famous and, fingers crossed, would be welcomed in the psychiatrist guild thanks to my Spiritual Psychoanalysis study.

I thought that the psychoanalysis I described would offer new trends and orientations to psychiatry, psychoanalysis, psychology, and psychotherapy. That thought gave me hope for tomorrow, and I was looking forward to 2021 to see the result of my achievements.

THE GIFT FROM A WORLD-RENOWNED FRIEND

In the month of June 2020, my wife and I were planning to take a trip together with our Canadian friends to Romania and Ukraine, and also to spend some time with our parents in Moldova. Due to the COVID-19 pandemic, no one could travel outside the country, and our dream vacation was suspended. We were stuck in Canada.

I was frustrated that I couldn't visit my parents, but what could I do? So I used that time to finish writing this book, which I considered a high priority. And then I sent it to the Romanian-English translator for translation.

In the meantime, many friends of ours from Quebec and Montreal came "storming" our house. That summer, due to the impossibility of traveling outside the country, they rushed to our place. Everyone knew that our town had tourist attractions for Canadians. Here we have the Atlantic Ocean, the mountains and the lakes, and rivers with waterfalls and typical Canadian vistas. Our house is located on a mountain ridge on the shore of the Atlantic Ocean, providing gorgeous views.

Through the large windows of our house, we can watch the sun rise over the vast expanse of the ocean, and we can enjoy the beautiful moonrise. In other words, just staying at our house is a real pleasure, as you can rest or take a tour outside the town to enjoy the real Canadian outdoors. Seeking an escape from the nightmare of their lockdown, our friends rushed to find refuge in our home, in this picturesque corner, and to take pleasure in the scenery.

Many friends came by, but their vacation schedule was so limited that I didn't even have time to breathe before others showed up. Some would leave in the morning, and others would arrive at dinner. Amongst this cluster of guests, a former boxing world champion came to visit us. His name is Lucian Bute, and he came with his wife and two small children. Like anyone else, they brought us a gift. He brought us three beautiful vases of different sizes, colored in a perfect match of blue and green.

It was a big, impressive gift, and I was shocked—not because the gift was expensive and so beautiful, but simply because I do not like gifts. I don't like giving gifts or receiving gifts. By nature, I am very eclectic in my shopping choices, especially when it comes to home interior design, and I need time to roam dozens of stores for months before I find something that *perfectly* matches the interior of my rooms.

I had nothing to complain about those vases. They were of a high quality and probably very expensive, and of good taste. But the problem was *me*, because I didn't know what to do with them or where to put them.

Although I was confused, I managed to conceal my emotional distress and I showed Lucian and his wife my gratitude for their marvellous present.

Usually if someone brings me an important gift, as in the case of Lucian Bute, and I don't find it useful for me, I put it back in the bag and give it to someone else on a special occasion. Now I was hoping to do the same. Thus, on the day Lucian and his family were leaving for Romania, I saw them to the car, and then I came back inside determined to put my thoughts into practice. I had the image of the interior design of my whole house on my mind, and I realized that the colors of the vases didn't match any color of any room. I went looking for the bag in which the gift was brought to prepare it for another person.

Lucian's gift was quite big, and it came in a large bag. You can't find such bags at regular stores, so they must have been available somewhere. Otherwise, I had nothing to wrap up my gift with.

But the bag was nowhere to be found. "Nastia! Where did you put the bag from Bute's gift?" I asked my wife.

"I threw it away," she answered.

I was shocked and helpless. If the bag had vanished, I would remain stuck with the gift. I couldn't wrap it with paper, and I couldn't give it to someone else by carrying it in my arms. The bag was the only solution to give out those vases, and my wife had tossed it away.

When you're forced to do something unexpected, you must turn to Spiritual Psychoanalysis to find the hidden message of God/the Universe. Nothing in this Universe happens by chance; everything has a specific meaning, especially in extreme situations where the probability is low that it will happen. So we have to discover the meaning of the situations by asking questions of Spiritual Psychoanalysis.

In this case, I asked myself: Am I doing it wrong? Does God want to tell me that I should keep these vases? But if I keep them, what can I do with them? Asking myself these questions, I suddenly realized that I had missed to check the design of my basement. I had thought of all the rooms on the ground floor and upstairs too, but I never thought of the interior design of the basement.

Ten years ago, we had barely bought the house and my wife and I hired a professional designer who decorated the entire house, including the basement, in a creative combination of modern and old artistry. In the basement, the main object we wanted to put on display was a carpet woven by my mother. It was the most valued object we had in the house. So in the basement, we rolled down that special carpet, which was an old-style model in perfect harmony with the fireplace. We also placed colorful and modern furniture of the latest trends, in red, white, and purple shades, to match the magic carpet woven by mother. And that was all.

We never thought that apart from furniture and the carpet it would be good to improve the design with more colors or items like vases, bowls, paintings, or something that could bring fresh vim into the room.

Basically, Lucian's vases were a very simple message from God, who wanted to tell me something through the discarded bag and make me think about the design in the basement. My mother's carpet was a harmonious mixture of red, purple, and blue flowers, dotted with green leaves on a dark background. The modern furniture and the curtains were all red and purple, but nothing in the basement was blue or green. The vases we received from Lucian Bute had green and blue colors and seemed perfect for bringing in something new. They were the only ones closely attuned to the interior line, standing out with all the colorful carpet and covering the empty spaces.

I was stunned. What a harmony those vases could create with my mother's carpet! I couldn't believe that God insisted that I make such improvement in the basement, *particularly* with that glassware gift!

The Spiritual Psychoanalysis of Lucian Bute's Gift

After I realized that the circumstances involving the bag for Lucian Bute's gift was such a clear message from God, I said to my wife: "Listen, Nastia, look how God counseled me with regard to the design of our basement. Basically, the arrangement was made in line with the colors of my mother's carpet, and the carpet is what I cherish the most in our house. If someone told me now to take one single object from my house and leave, I would pick up my mother's carpet, because it's the most valuable to me, the symbol of my mother's work and life and love for me and my family; it is invaluable and priceless and represents my childhood with my dear departed mother. I don't need gold or expensive things in my house as they mean nothing to me. There is nothing more expensive than the legacy that her callous hands made through laborious work and dedication."

Let's see what's hidden behind His message. Surely He has much more important things to tell me than just making me think of my mother's carpet design. Here's what I think:

As you know, I am a meticulous person, especially when it comes to interior design, even if I can't hand-pick the items that match my rooms. On top of that, I'm unhappy if someone brings me interior decorations. So far, the gifts from our friends haven't matched anything in my house.

Now, let's ask some questions considering the principles of Spiritual Psychoanalysis—the principles of probability. When there's low probability that an event may happen to us, surely God is trying to send us a message. In the given case:

1) A world-renowned person stepped into my house for the first time: Lucian Bute and his family.

2) I received a gift for my interior design, the only gift I had received in a lifetime that matched the interior arrangement. I alone wouldn't have been able to think of such an association of either colors or objects.

3) Finally, Lucian Bute's gift matched perfectly *only* one invaluable item in my home, the carpet woven by my mother.

In that situation, three factors were involved with very low probability. And when all three unfold at the same time, they lessen the degree of probability even more.

As a result of the Law of Probability in Spiritual Psychoanalysis, we can confirm that God is trying to say something to me. What would be the message? We will figure it out by examining the details of this situation.

To begin, let's ask ourselves: Who is Lucian Bute? Lucian Bute is a boy from the countryside who worked hard and rose to prominence in the world.

What's the connection between him and I? And what is God's message for me? What unites us is that we're both boys from the countryside, even from the same region, and we grew up and were educated by the same principles and values of life. Through this similarity and bond, God certainly wanted to tell me that I would be as famous as Lucian Bute. I believe that through my mother's carpet, God wanted to reconfirm that both Lucian and I have the same ancestral roots, we originate from ordinary people, and we will conquer the world. In other words, I believe that the situation with Lucian Bute's gift is a first step towards my future success. I believe that in 2021, my professional achievements will peak, and I hope that my Spiritual Psychoanalysis will be accepted as a new form of psychoanalysis that will help me return to practicing my profession.

That was what I explained to my wife. Moreover, I was hoping that in 2021, after my Spiritual Psychoanalysis is accepted as a new form of psychoanalysis, I would be invited to various conferences and congresses. I even hoped that a certain university would invite me to deliver explanations about my scientific research.

At the end of this chapter, I will describe the last message God was trying to send me through my mother's carpet, which is the connection with the number 21 and that I would understand much later.

THE SITUATIONS UNFOLDING AFTER LUCIAN BUTE GAVE ME HIS GIFT

THE FIRST SITUATION: I ACQUIRE A NEW CAPACITY

After our friends from Montreal and Quebec were gone, I started to see something that I had never seen before. When I was about to fall asleep, or when I woke up for a minute and then was falling asleep again, I saw a light attempting to break through the dark space that shrouded me. That dark space was dense like pitch, and the light beam was laboring towards me, trying to create a tunnel. But the light could hardly make progress through the black fuel that was clotting the tunnel with its tentacles. The light seemed powerless, and it failed to probe through the darkness. Suddenly, a new ray of light came through.

This scenario was constantly changing. The light found new avenues to penetrate towards me, but the tentacles blocked it, and then again, the light created another tributary and followed it through the darkness. Each time, it took the light between three and five seconds to make its way through. Here's the image I drew, which may be vaguely similar to the one I saw in September 2020:

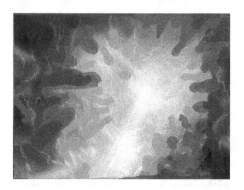

FIG. 9 THE LIGHT SOURCE CROSSING THE DARK SPACE SURROUNDING ME

Initially, this image gave me the creeps, because I realized the world in which we live. Then, for the first time, I understood that the material world in which we presently live is actually the world of darkness, and God can hardly walk through to reach us.

Also, I remembered what my cousin said before she died of cancer. She was so young, and she was terminally ill, and she found herself more in the other world, in the Kingdom of Heaven, than among us. She said, "I want to go out of here as soon as I can. Here, we *all* are hired to do harm. I don't want to stay here anymore. I want to get out of here as soon as possible."

The vision of that dark canopy, as well as my cousin's words, made me realize what kind of life we're living on earth. Practically, I understood that *all of us* are constantly doing harm. We're living under the impression that we're doing the right thing, but our intention is to do harm. Darkness is our shepherd who forcibly drives us into eternal fighting and discord, and we are plunging in it.

Look at our planet, at our civilization, at the daily news. Look at our relationships with our neighbors or our family. We're entangled in eternal conflicts with someone or against something. No one on this planet lives in harmony with the Universe and the surrounding world. We are all maneuvered by the dark forces of this energy; we are all misguided by our selfish bodily temptations, and we are craving to satisfy our own pleasures. Belligerence is in us, and the whole world is our eternal enemy.

In spite of all the bad things we do, and notwithstanding the opaqueness of our world, where the Divine Light can't get through, our good Lord can find the avenues and solutions to reach out to us and give us hope of living and spiritual evolution.

I was anguished and hopeless, and I felt desperate about our world, but after a while I came back to my senses and rejoiced that God had gifted me with the power of seeing the Divine Light streaming through the black fuel of the material world. I was elated and proud, and I was certain that at this rate, pressing ahead with my spiritual evolution, God would lend me strength to get in touch with His Kingdom, just like Jesus Christ used to do (Matthew 19:21).

With this thought in mind, I needled my courage to focus on the light Divine and walk towards it. And each time I saw the Divine Light coming down to me in the middle of the night, I tried to step towards it. I was moving forward, and then I was staying in the light, immobile, while around me a corridor/tunnel of tentacles of the blackened world was taking shape. I continued to train myself, and from three to five seconds, the duration of this process was extended to twenty to thirty seconds.

As I was standing in the beam on the corridor of darkness, surrounded by those tenebrous limbs, I noticed two details:

a) Not only was the Divine Light coming towards me, but I myself had grown into a source of light that would attract it.

b) The black arms of the World of Darkness weren't invading me; they were only on alert, and they were patiently waiting for me to lose focus so they could extinguish the light in which I stayed. And however hard I tried to break the bonds and touch the light, I was outpowered by that black energy.

But even if the forceful dark energy rebuffed me, I knew that my path was the path of the righteous and the only way to connect myself with the spiritual world. Jesus Christ Himself had connected with us in the same way through the corridor of light that I had just found.

CONFIRMATION OF THE ESSENTIAL LAW OF EXISTENCE OF THE UNIVERSE, THE FAMILY LAW

My new experience of seeing the World of Darkness (material) in which we live and the Divine Light that penetrates this darkness confirmed once again what I already knew:

1) the existence of two entities of the Universe, which form a couple between husband and wife

   – the matter of the Universe, which is a World of Darkness and the wife of God
   – the Supreme Consciousness/God, who is the white light and the Husband of the Matter of the Universe.

2) the relationship between these two entities as a relationship between husband and wife

3) negative energies are gathered inside the matter where the chakras live

4) Supreme Consciousness/God means only light and love

SPIRITUAL PSYCHOANALYSIS OF THIS EXPERIENCE

When the penetration of the light lasted three to five seconds, I realized that the energy of darkness was *not* aggressive to the Divine Light. It was negativist in that it wanted to remove the Divine Light from it, but at the same time it didn't want this light to stop approaching it. Their relationship was like a harmonious game of tenderness and love between light and darkness: the light comes through smoothly, pleasantly, and caressingly, and the arms of darkness gently cover it.

I noticed the same thing when I was standing in the beam of light in the corridor created by the tentacles of darkness. Even in that case, the dark energy wasn't aggressive to me. On the contrary, it was quiet, making a harmonious vibration of love, waiting for me to lose my focus and, with its tentacles, block the corridor of the incoming light.

This harmonious love relationship of light penetrating the darkness was exactly the same as the harmonious love relationship between a man and a woman: the man caresses the woman with love and tries to penetrate her continuously, and the woman gently turns him down for a while and then welcomes him inside her, and their relationship is consummated with pleasure and ecstasy for both parties.

From this relationship, it can also be seen:

- The feminine nature, which feels the need to be constantly loved and approached, and to be important and the center of her husband's attention

- The male nature to love his wife with tenderness and harmony permanently and look for permanent solutions so that his wife accepts him and loves him.

In other words, in this relationship we see God's eternal love for His wife, the matter of the Universe, regardless of how His wife feels about Him.

The relationship between the energy of the matter of the Universe and the Supreme Consciousness/God demonstrates that negativism belongs to the feminine nature, the representatives of wives.

While in a relationship at the spiritual level, the feminine negativism generates harmony and love, and harmony between husband and wife, and between the matter of the Universe and God at a material level of evolution. Here in the material world, the feminine negativism manifests itself through a rigidity of bodily temptations, by violating the laws of God our Lord and going against our soul.

The materialist negativism in the material world is arrogant and believes itself to be superior to the spiritual evolution. Under a pretext like "Any way of evolution is the right way" or "We don't know who is right" or "This is who I am, and everyone else must accept me as I am" or "Those around me have to change, but not me," the youth nowadays know only what they want and what they like. They can't see the world around them, and they're unable to observe/ see even the smallest detail happening right in front of their eyes. All this gives our "modern" civilization a sense of arrogance and an egocentric materialistic personality that never existed before.

Some of the humble so far have been trying to change and respond to the requirements of the surrounding world. They had respect for their parents and their friends, and they mutually respect each other. Today, such respect has vanished, and everyone cares about their personal pleasures and principles. Our civilization has become the most selfish of all times. The modern-materialist principles built on materialist thinking advocate no spiritual principle and hold the current generation back from any spiritual development.

The relationship between God and the matter of the Universe, which I began to see with my own eyes, demonstrates that negativism is a normal phenomenon of evolution that must be chiseled and modified. It also shows that from materialistic negativism, we must turn to a spiritual one and create harmony between husband and wife at both soul-body and husband and wife level.

A genuine spiritual thinking is based on the idea of giving priority to the surrounding world, to the people around us, over our own desires and principles. Listening to the wishes of the living world and fulfilling them means heeding the advice of the Universe. And by listening to the Universe, we will fulfill our true wishes. Deciding to follow the principle of the Boomerang Law marks the first steps to the day our dreams come true.

The Boomerang Law says that absolutely everything we do for the world, we do it for ourselves, and everything we do against the world around us, we do it against us. In other words, if we create negative energies for the surrounding world, we create them for ourselves, and everything we do for the surrounding world, we do it for ourselves, not for the people to whom we do good or evil.

Confirmation of the Importance of our Souls Here on Earth

My new vision experience of the dark world opened my mind to the importance of our souls in our material world:

a) Our souls are little lights of the spiritual world, dispatched to blink and bring light into the World of Darkness, the material world.

b) Although we're in the dark and we slowly shine and spread the light around, we can't do it alone. We need the Lord and His Divine Light, which keeps falling down on us.

At the same time
3) God needs us. He needs us to help the spiritual light probe more effectively through this terrible darkness.

In other words, our souls are God's messengers here on earth, and we all are His messengers and contributive factors for extending His light in this darkness. So we all should ask ourselves: What is the mission of my soul here on earth? What should I do to spread His love and Divine Light in the darkness of this material world?

THE AGGRESSIVE NEGATIVE ENERGY THAT AROSE DURING MY EXPERIENCE

Alas, shortly after I started to feel the pleasure of penetrating the corridor of darkness towards the Divine Light, in that image a negative energy appeared, aggressive and devastating, and I felt powerless and vulnerable. The energy grew darker and more invasive, and I could sense its aggressiveness deeply in my bones.

Each time the spiritual light was probing the darkness, a new, aggressive negative energy would congest the entire image of the tunnel of light. I became unable to peek through the beam of light and glimpse the process of the penetration of the Divine Light, as it covered my image completely.

While initially I thought that the World of Darkness in which we live was as dark as pitch, after the new negative energy made its appearance, I noticed that it wasn't really that black. The World of Darkness is a black-gray color, just like the sky during the night, while the negative energy had a truly terrible black color.

This is what the invasion of the negative energy looks like:

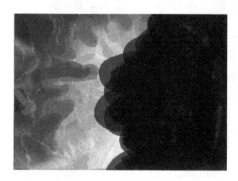

FIG. 10 INVASIVE NEGATIVE ENERGY OF AN ABSOLUTE BLACK COLOR

This black energy returned every evening, and I became its prisoner. I was stuck and scared as it continued to appear for reasons unaccounted for.

You will find the Spiritual Psychoanalysis of these energies under "Spiritual Psychoanalysis of the Situations Related to My Mother's Death."

THE SECOND SITUATION: THE FATE OF MY FIRST BOOK RELEASED ON THE MARKET

My first book, *The Destiny and Signs of God*, was released on September 24, 2020. The book kept my hope high that scientific researchers would accept Spiritual Psychoanalysis as a new form of psychoanalysis and I could revert to my beloved professional field of psychiatry. Also, I was hoping that the proceeds would be enough to help my dear ones and to publish the second book (this book), currently being translated.

I was hoping that the world would avidly enjoy the discoveries I had made with the His help, and I believed that everyone would want to learn how to communication with the Universe and ultimately with Him. I was sure that the examples in my book would leave scientists voiceless, and they would accept the new way of psychoanalysis, the Spiritual Psychoanalysis.

Sadly, my expectations shattered shortly after the book was released on the market. No one was interested in what I wrote.

Spiritualists: I contacted several groups of spiritualists on Facebook, but they didn't want to accept another method of communication with God/ Universe, apart from their method of meditation. They don't believe that any simple person could communicate with the Universe without meditating, that they could live in harmony with the Universe by simply listening to it in every moment of their life. They don't believe that every moment of our life is also a form of meditation.

Religionists: I tried to talk to people from religious groups, but they are indoctrinated by their two-thousand-year-old political religions and don't want to give up so easily their materialistic principles of thought, lending them the power to manipulate the masses and dominate large swathes of the world.

Scientists: I directly contacted psychoanalysts from several European countries, but they too are indoctrinated to the core by the materialistic thought and refuse to accept soul or spirituality in the scientific field.

I understand quite well that the theories I described in my books run counter to all the areas of our civilization. They collide with politics, religion, spirituality, scientific thought for every single person and their concepts and beliefs. But, at the same time, we should be *aware* and agree that absolutely *everything* created on earth has been built on our materialistic thinking. We should all acknowledge the failures of each of us and our civilization deriving from our materialistic principles of evolution. Let's concede that such an evolution does not inspire anything good. We've been struggling in vain with the same problems for thousands of years, but we haven't learned sense from our failures. We are tilting at the windmills we're building ourselves and aren't making progress, yet we're following the same old materialistic principles from our apparition as primates on earth.

Now the time has come to realize the failure of our materialistic evolution and take a radical turn by adopting the spiritual evolution and spiritual thought. We are wise and capable of making a very simple differentiation between evolution and material thinking compared to evolution and spiritual thinking: any desire or temptation or material thought has an end, but the desires, the principles, and the spiritual thinking are on eternal ascent, and they grow stronger and more important and more needful (see *The Destiny and Signs of God*).

The Spiritual Thinking is the thinking of people who realize that the Universe is a form of consciousness, the human being is a form of consciousness too, and the consciousness of the human being is a part of the consciousness of the Universe. In the Universe there are the same laws on which evolution is built; the Universe tries to get in touch with every human being to guide them, to mark their life with beacons so that they can find the best pathway for their universal evolution and learn to listen, to be guided according to the beacons of the Universe, and follow and abide by the Laws of the Universe.

Remark 1: The beacons of the Universe are the signs from God described by me.

Remark 2: The Spiritual Psychoanalysis is the apogee of spiritual thinking. Only people with spiritual thinking will be able to go ahead with a Spiritual Psychoanalysis of their lives and the surrounding world.

Our essential mission on earth is to bring the Divine Light into the darkness of the material world and create a basis of harmony in the relationship between husband and wife. Not only between husband and wife as soul-body, but also as husband-wife between man and woman. Look at the principle of the relationship between man and woman—people who practice yoga and spirituality don't take it into consideration. They are focused only on their spiritual evolution of their soul and their body. For them, the family is insignificant. Any spiritual mind who meditates for hours every day and, at the same time, swaps his sexual partner from one day to the next has entered the path of sophistry and deceit, moving away from the mission of evolution commissioned to us. Sexual freedom should not be our moral principle if we really aspire to a spiritual ascent.

I understand that their meditation technique is an ideal way of ascension for the soul-body relationship, but it is focused *only* on their personal energies, which send their principles against the Essential Law of the Universe, the Family Law, and overrides our purpose on earth.

The sexual relationship and love between a man and a woman are sacred. We must entertain them in faithfulness, fidelity, and respect, because our essential duty here on earth is to learn to live in harmony in the family between husband and wife, like our spiritual parents live, God together with His wife, the matter of the Universe.

As a result, the way of meditation and concentration only on their own person is a selfish way of evolution. To achieve the ultimate goal of our development, we must start from the creation of harmony between husband and wife (man and woman) and meditate through the PRISM of our life partner, of our family. Until then, the individual meditations of the spiritual minds will be no different from the materialistic-egoistic principles of materialistic thought.

On the other hand, I believe that proper spiritual evolution requires a good understanding of the basic construction of the human being. I believe that what God taught me about the construction of the Universe, about us in general, and about the stages we must go through is very important for all those who practice spirituality. Before we cure a disease, for example, we must know the structure of the sick human being and the way the disease manifests itself. The pattern is the same for spiritual evolution: first, we must learn to know who we are and how the negative energies develop and manifest in our life, and then how to move into mindful meditation and spiritual cleansing. Otherwise, just talking about love and God's light without knowing the spiritual "anatomy" means our efforts will be unavailing.

I want to bring to the attention of spiritual people and everyone else that the Spiritual Psychoanalysis described by me in my books is a new way of meditation, a continuous meditation throughout our lives that includes the family relationship between soul and body, between husband and wife, and our relationship with the Universe and our spiritual parents, the Supreme Consciousness of the Universe and the matter of the Universe.

In regular meditation, we focus all our attention on our physical body in the present moment. At the moment of meditation, we live the moment of the relationship between soul and body. I propose the same principle of concentration through the lens of Spiritual Psychoanalysis. When it comes to our relationship between husband and wife, we must focus all our attention to feel our partner exactly as we feel ourselves during meditation, in all aspects, to feel his desires, the suffering, the pain, the joy. By feeling him, we can live in indescribable harmony. Feeling, encouraging, and being a stable support in our partner's life, we ourselves grow in our spiritual evolution.

When it comes to our relationship with our Spiritual parents (Mother and Father Universe), we must focus all our attention on feeling the surrounding world exactly as we feel ourselves during meditation—to feel every movement of nature, to feel any situation, to listen to any person. All the movements around us in which we are involved are the energies of the Universe, the personal advice of the Universe for each of us. Feeling all the energies of the surrounding world coming towards us, we will feel the presence of the Universe (Mother and Father) around us.

When we can feel not only our body but also our life partner, to feel the presence of the Universe in every moment of our life, then we will be able to say that we live in true harmony—harmony for which we came to earth to learn.

At the time when I started giving group meditation classes with the help of Tibetan bowls, one of the women asked me to give her a private message session with the bowls. The woman had been practicing meditation for a long time and had a fairly advanced spiritual level. She had a well-developed sixth sense, and she felt the positive and negative energies around her.

But according to her, she wanted to go to India for a pilgrimage and was afraid. She didn't know whether to go or not. On the one hand, her heart suggested that she leave, and on the other hand, her brain had doubts.

Initially, I thought that she wanted to leave on her own, and I said to her, "Do you see your level of spiritual evolution? The meditations made you trust your senses. This is exactly the same principle I propose to people through the prism Spiritual Psychoanalysis. As we feel the energies of our body, so we must learn to feel the energies of the Universe, of the surrounding world. Your fear is because you don't trust the energies of the surrounding world; you don't trust the energies of our parents, the Universe.

"Here's what I want to tell you about your situation: First of all, when we want something, it means that it's a desire of our body (the wife of our soul), and if we want something, it means that we must satisfy all our desires; otherwise, we'll enter a vicious circle and return to the same situation until we do not satisfy it. Our desire could either be a destiny of ours that we must follow, or it could be a negative energy that has nested in our brain and doesn't want to come out—an energy that wants to do us some harm.

To detect this, we must know that the most important moment is the first step we take when we start on a new path. Exactly at that moment, the Universe is with us and urges us to go on this road or not. If we see that something isn't working, such as we have problems buying tickets, or we can't find the credit card, then we don't have to be afraid to give up. Look at this particular energy, this situation of the first step. We must learn to feel it exactly as we feel the energies of our body."

During the conversation, the woman told me that in reality, the pilgrimage proposal came from her daughter, who organized everything. A group of several spiritual persons had to make this trip through the holy places and monasteries of India.

Then I said, "In this case, I'd like to tell you about another aspect of Spiritual Psychoanalysis. All the situations that come to us and in which we become involved without our initiative are the energies created by the Universe for us. When we're involved in some negative situations, we must ask ourselves the questions: Why is this happening to me in particular? What message does the Universe want to convey to me through this situation? What have I not done, or am I not doing well? What should I change/correct for me?

"And when a positive situation happens to us or is proposed to us, and everything goes flawlessly—as is happening in your case now—we must thank the Universe for who we are; it's the reward for our effort, a direct gift from the Universe that we must accept with the greatest love and joy.

"As you see, the Universe is always with us and waiting for us to see it, to feel and love it exactly as we feel and love ourselves through our meditations. By feeling our life situations, we feel the energies of the Universe that have been distributed to us personally. You have reached a fairly high spiritual level thanks to your meditations, but now the time has come to move to a much higher level—to meditations in harmony with the energies of the Universe. When you feel the energies of the Universe exactly as you feel the energies of your body, then you'll be able to say with confidence that you truly live in harmony with the entire Universe.

"As you can see, we shouldn't be afraid of the world around us but have faith in everything that happens to us; trust all the people with whom we are in contact; trust nature, plants, and animals that are involved in our lives; trust in all situations and events in our life. These are the energies of the Supreme Consciousness of the Universe—energies through which the Universe/God tries to communicate with us, tries to guide us, tries to give us advice. We just have to trust in the surrounding world and treat her with the greatest love and respect. By trusting the world around us, we will have respect for our spiritual parents, Father Universe and Mother Matter."

In my opinion, the concept of "modern" spiritual liberalization resembles the Communist laws of 1917, when the Russians created the first Communist state. For the Communists, the essential principle was that all people should be free and equal, whether Black, White, men, or women. All of these laws seemed to be democratic and convenient for everyone. Along with the "Communist Democracy" and the right of all the people to freedom and equality, the country's leaders decriminalized free sex. In the first years of Communism in Russia, sex was as free as drinking water. Men had the right to have sex with any woman they liked outside of their marriage. Also, though very young, women were wordlessly giving themselves to men in order to pay their dues to the community.

The liberalization of the "feeling of love" in the spiritual mind of our civilization is not different from the Communist laws in early twentieth century.

In the wake of the liberalization of sex, Russia was grappling with syphilis and gonorrhea. If our civilization has already faced the sex liberalization, should we now, in the period of scientific progress, return to the problems of one hundred years ago?

The Spiritual Psychoanalysis I have described is something far superior to spirituality. If spirituality is a limited collaboration between the chakras of the human body and the chakras of the Supreme Consciousness of the

Universe, then Spiritual Psychoanalysis is much more than that. This is a method of researching the Supreme Consciousness of the Universe in its vast extent down to the smallest details and nuances of his activity; this is a method of undetermined and infinite collaboration between the subtle consciousness of the Universe and the consciousness of the human being.

In order for you to better understand what I want to tell you about the visionary ability of Spiritual Psychoanalysis, imagine that:

a) The vision capacity of all religions regarding the Kingdom of God have a volume the size of a planet (Planet Earth);

b) The vision capacity of the spirituals regarding spirituality has a volume the size of a solar system; and

c) Spiritual Psychoanalysis could offer us an *infinite* horizon/capacity of vision of the construction of the Supreme Consciousness. If initially this psychoanalysis could offer us a horizon the size of a galaxy, then with our spiritual evolution, we will be able to expand our horizon of vision to the size of a universe.

The Spiritual Psychoanalysis described by me in both books is part of one of the essential methods of scientific research into the construction of the Supreme Consciousness of the Universe. Through the prism of this psychoanalysis, we can not only discover the laws and the functioning mechanism of the Supreme Consciousness of the Universe, but it helps us to discover ourselves, to discover the purpose for which we came to earth, to discover where we come and where we go, and to discover the ways/ methods of collaboration between the human being and the Supreme Consciousness of the Universe/God.

What is much more important than that is the fact that through the lens of Spiritual Psychoanalysis, each of us is able to discover his unique way of connection with the Supreme Consciousness/God. As each of us is unique in this Universe, so are our connections to the Supreme Consciousness— unique connections that belong only to us.

I was taken aback that the psychiatrist, the psychologists, and the psychoanalysts didn't want to hear about my Spiritual Psychoanalysis. I was disappointed, because after I chose the profession of psychiatry in the 1990s, I was intrigued by the connection between the soul and science.

Translated from Greek, "psychiatrist" means "doctor of souls," and I *eagerly wanted* to find the connection between science and spirituality.

But in the end, I was destined to find this connection, and it became clear that the professionals in these fields would be as curious and intrigued as I was. But I was in shock to see the opposite. I contacted psychiatrists, psychologists, and psychoanalysts from Germany, Sweden, England, the United States, Australia, etc., but no one wanted to hear about spirituality. Their rigidity and lack of interest in anything other than their materialistic thinking disheartened me. I tried all the ways of persuasion, but without any success.

I got angry and I said to some of them, "Scientists resent looking at the abilities of animals and birds to predict danger. They look for different explanations and answers when animals or birds anticipate hurricanes, torrential rains, storms, catastrophes, etc. Entire research institutions have been created in this field, but when it comes to the same scientific research on the human being, *all* scientists, with no exceptions, rebuff such concepts. They barricade themselves behind the Lacanian Psychoanalysis, which is categorically against spirituality; they hide behind the materialist explanations, but they will in no way give in or at least listen to the theory described by me, which is based on personal experience, the experience of a psychiatrist who knows how to differentiate between hallucinations and reality, between illusions and reality, and between a delusion and reality.

"If scientists would think logically, even if they have materialistic thinking, they would easily realize that humans are descended from monkeys. Why do scientists research the monkey's ability to predict the future, and when it comes to the human being, they say that's just superstition? If monkeys can find the antidote to intoxications, for example, or sense the coming rain and the storm, isn't the human being able to do the same thing? If humans come down from the monkey, wouldn't they be able to do the same thing? If a teenager learned to ride a bicycle, then after he grew up he no longer knew how to do it, would you say he can't ride a bike anymore? It's absurd and stupid to insist on saying that the human being is less developed than the monkey, its predecessor, that he can't feel how a monkey feels.

"We are all able to sense and predict the future, and not only through the sixth sense, as birds and animals do, but we are much more advanced than birds and animals. *We are able to communicate directly with the universe!* We communicate personally, without interpreters or brokers, and solve problems, starting from personal ones and ending with world problems.

"To achieve that, we only have to open our hearts and souls and accept to study the human being according to the same principles and criteria we use to study the life of birds and animals."

"My book *The Destiny and Signs of God* is already a start in this direction. The Spiritual Psychoanalysis described by me is a first step that makes the connection between science and spirituality; we should only continue the research in this field."

That was one of the messages I sent to a group of psychiatrists and psychotherapists.

And I said to another group of psychoanalysts who didn't want to hear about my Spiritual Psychoanalysis: "Every tradesman on this planet goes by the rules of their trades. Tractor drivers drive tractors, mechanics deal with mechanics, cooks make bread, but the only craftsmen/professionals who don't fulfill their duties in relation to their jobs/professions are the psychiatrists, the psychologists, the psychoanalysts, and the psychotherapists, because none of them want to hear about the soul and spirituality.

"When the name of the psychiatry profession was invented, all those who practiced this profession believed that there was a correlation between the soul and the body, and then they knew that the answer to psychiatric suffering was hiding behind the disorders of the human *soul*, and a solution ought to be found to the problem of the soul and not the body.

"I understand that over the years and during the long spells of materialistic beliefs of our civilization, scientists have abandoned their spiritual principles. However, we are no longer in the 1970s when the Lacanian theory was written (Lacanian psychoanalysis), which brings arguments against the signs of God. (The initiator of Lacanian Psychoanalysis is Jacques Lacan, who lived between 1950 and 1980. His theory is based on the principles of materialistic thinking to describe the soul, which is radically opposed to the Spiritual Psychoanalysis described by me.)

143

"Since then, several decades have passed, and multiple evidence has been adduced to sustain the connection between science and spirituality:

- Scientific research has been done, including on near-death experiences.

- Many children remember their past lives and find their former families from their former lives.

- Research in quantum physics provides solid arguments for the existence of the Supreme Consciousness of the Universe.

Why should we ignore this evidence and stick to the research of those who are no longer alive?"

I really can't understand that since quantum physics physicists have already discovered that the Universe is a form of consciousness, the same as the human being, why it's so hard to accept these concepts to create a new science—a science of spirituality, a science that would change completely the destiny of our civilization. A science that stops the self-destructive materialistic evolution of our civilization. A science that would set the foundations for a new era of evolution and usher into an ever-prosperous evolution of our civilization.

I'm not talking about God or soul as a form of religious expression. We're not obliged to use religious terms, but we can't ignore that the so-called God in religions is in reality the Supreme Consciousness of the Universe demonstrated by quantum physics, and that the soul described in religious books is as such the consciousness of the human being. If quantum physics discovered these forms of consciousness, is it really so complicated for the scientists in the fields of psychiatry, psychology, and psychoanalysis to accept this form of science as a new form of scientific research?

"If you are hard-headed and unwilling to accept the soul in your scientific research, then why do you hold to be what you are *not*? You *cannot* call yourselves psychiatrists, because psychiatrist means 'doctor of souls,' and you don't fulfill any criteria of this job; in your case, you should call yourselves 'brain doctors.' You cannot call yourselves psychoanalysts, which means 'analysts of the soul,' but you should call yourselves 'analysts of words.'

"Why don't you speak the truth? Recognize your materialistic stubbornness and call yourself what you really are? Why betray the principles of psychiatry conceived when this profession was born?

"If I treated you exactly as you treat the psychoanalysis described by me then, the result would be the following: All the theories of psychoanalysts have no material basis. They are all just inventions, principles, and beliefs of those who invented their theories.

Let's take Sigmund Freud, for example, who assumed that our problems stem from events unfolded in our childhood. Then Lacanian psychoanalysis went completely against spirituality and the signs of God. Modern" psychoanalysts deal with the psychoanalytic research of the toys_that children throw away.

"If I were to treat all these theories exactly as you treat my theory, I could confirm with certainty that they are nothing but personal principles and fantasies of those who invented these theories, because none of them has any material basis:

- No one can prove from a material point of view that Sigmund Freud's theory is valid.

- No one can confirm the veracity of the negativist-spiritual Lacanian.

- No one can confirm that children throw away toys because they are frustrated with their parents.

"Materialistic 'modernism' has changed the mentality of scientists so much that psychoanalysts don't even realize that instead of dealing with the 'analysis of souls,' what they are meant to do, they take care of the 'trash toys.'"

Our civilization is currently at the most important crossroads of its evolution, when it is to choose the path of the future:

- the materialistic path that we have all followed so far, a path that leads us to self-destruction; or

- the spiritual path of evolution, which has a continuous evolution and is in continuous ascent.

The only people who could convince our civilization to choose the spiritual path of evolution are the psychiatrists, the psychologists, the psychotherapists, and the psychoanalysts. The sooner they welcome spirituality into their scientific endeavours, the faster our civilization will take the radical turn of prosperous and continuous evolution; until then, we will go down the material path of self-destruction and tilt at the windmills that we build ourselves.

It's unfortunate that the physicists are much more advanced with their scientific research regarding spirituality than the specialists in this profession. In such conditions, the quantum physics specialists should be called psychiatrists and psychologists, because at least they meet the requirements of our professions. These physicists have every right to call themselves psycho-physicists, which corresponds to the research of the soul and the Supreme Consciousness.

An example of comparison:

The transition of our civilization from the material thinking to a spiritual one is as difficult as emigrating from a poor country to a developed one. Here is an example:

A family of two doctors with a lot of potential, who are our friends from college time, lived in Moldova for many years before migrating to another country. They moved to Romania and, after a few years, to Sweden. During the years they lived in Moldova, I insisted that they should go to another country. So they followed my advice and immigrated to Sweden.

Here's what they told me: "You know, when we were in Moldova, where the economic conditions were so bad, we were still at home, in our motherland, with our parents and our friends. It was like living in a swamp where it is warm and good, but you can't move, and you sink down under. Only after we escaped to Romania did it become easier to move from one country to another. And a few years later, we found ways to immigrate to Sweden, and we made it."

Our civilization is *ENTIRELY* built on the principles of the material thinking, and it takes heart to leave the "swamp" in which one finds himself. No one has the courage to emigrate outside of this material thinking. Most people hesitate to get out of this lethal swampy thinking and adopt a new way—the spiritual and progressive thinking. Only when we have the courage to take the first steps towards a spiritual thinking will we move up our evolution scale like our friends who moved from one country to another.

As you can see, my first book, which appeared on the market in September 2020, was not as successful as I expected. If I initially thought that this book would bring me great success in 2021, and that the fame of my book would be the meaning of the number 21, then I was wrong. I was already convinced that the number 21 couldn't possibly be related to the success of my book in 2021. But what could it be?

THE THIRD SITUATION—LIFE INSURANCE

In September, after all our friends were gone, our life insurance agent called us to renew our contract with his company.

Nastia and I are not proponents of life insurance; however, ten years before we bought the house, we applied for a bank loan, and the bank requested that we sign an insurance policy so they could release that loan. After a few years, we paid off our debt and, unwittingly, continued to pay the insurance policy. We did it for several years without knowing that our insurance was void.

The insurance contract had covered only the period before returning our loan to the bank; it was a reward for the family members in case of death. Basically, we gave money to the insurance agency so they could stuff their pockets. They didn't even bother to inform us that our insurance contract was over.

Nastia and I attended a meeting with the insurance agent, who suggested we accept family protection coverage. Initially, we agreed, though we were unhappy for having paid the insurance for years without knowing that the premiums didn't cover our family members in case of death. We agreed to pass all the medical checks required by the insurance; however, when we saw the insurance agent a second time to sign the papers, he informed us that our insurance didn't cover our death in our country of origin. In other words, if we died on a vacation in Moldova, at our parents' house, the insurance wouldn't pay our death benefit.

We were angry for having contributed to an insurance contract that was worth nothing. When we heard that the new insurance wouldn't be valid if our death occurred in our home country, Nastia said to the agent, "Mister, please excuse us, but all things considered, we refuse your insurance."

The agent was surprised and angry that now, after we had passed all the medical examinations, we gave up their insurance. But he had no choice. That was our adamant decision, and he had to accept it.

A month later, I was having health problems, which were getting worse. From one week to the next, my heath condition rapidly deteriorated. I had excruciating pain in my right testicle and in my prostate, profuse rectal bleeding, terrible right shoulder joint pain, huge lymph nodes, and lymph nodes welded to the skin began developing. All these symptoms were located all over the right side of the body, indicating that I had cancer or a form of cancer of the sexual organs, with abdominal and bone or colon metastases.

At the beginning of November 2020, I was 90 percent sure that it was cancer and that I was going to die. I was afraid that my family members would learn the bad news too soon, and I didn't go see a doctor. I thought that it would be better for them to find out later.

I was scared. I wasn't afraid of death, but I was worried about my children, who would be left without a father prematurely; I was worried about my mother. I was afraid that she would outlive me and she would never recover from this blow. It would have been her worst nightmare.

On the other hand, I didn't understand why God wanted me to go through such a temptation, why He made me sacrifice my life to write spiritual books instead of letting me take advantage of my achievements, why He made me drop my life insurance if He knew that I would die, and why He didn't let my family have at least one benefit from my death.

I didn't understand the meaning of the number 21. If God's message through the gift of Lucian Bute was that I would become famous and make enough profit in the year 2021, then my alleged disease was telling of the end of my life in 2021, for which I was completely unprepared.

(See the continuation further in this chapter).

THE EVENTS THAT RADICALLY CHANGED THE COURSE OF MY LIFE AND PUT ORDER IN ALL MY THEORIES

The Life of My Mother, Anica (Anicuta) Rotaru (Focsa)

Before telling you what happened to me in the fall of 2020, I need to acquaint you with the history of mother's life, such an important source of information for the continuation of my book.

My mother's name as a small child was Anicuta Focsa, and after she got married, she became Anica Rotaru.

She was born and lived poor in Moldova in the aftermath of WWII, at times of famine orchestrated by the Russians and their Communist regime.

Anicuta went to school only two years, because her mother had died and she had no one to take care of the household and her little brother. She was still young when she married Fanase, a boy from her village.

After the marriage, she started working in the Communist Agricultural Association in the village, and she was frustrated with her lack of formal education. Anica worked hard in the collective farm (that was the name of the Communist Agricultural Association), as if inflicting punishment on herself. "Since you didn't want to go to school, you must *WORK* now," she would say inwardly.

My mother worked all her life in tobacco processing. The work was toxic from poisonous dust and required huge physical effort. She would get up at 04:00 in the morning to cook food, go to work at 05:00, and return home after midnight. Sometimes she even arrived at 01:00 or 02:00 in the morning. She'd sleep for two or three hours and go back to work.

My father, Fanase, was jealous and lazy, and he didn't help at all. Usually, the husbands of the women who worked in tobacco processing went several times a week in the evening, around 21:00 or 22:00, to relieve their wives so that they could go home to wash and rest themselves after two long working days. My father never did that. He didn't even know where she worked.

149

Fanase didn't do anything around the house either. My mother had to find time for the domestic chores; she cooked, cleaned, and took care of the household. My sister and I were little, but we used to help her occasionally.

After she retired, my mother continued to work hard. The collective farm was abolished, and the land that belonged to the state during the Communist period was returned to the people living in the country. Like everyone else in the country, my parents received three to four hectares of land, and they had to work with their bare hands, because all the equipment from the Communist Agricultural Associations had been seized and decommissioned by the Communist leader. No one had any tillage equipment. So my parents bought themselves a horse, which became their only farming input.

For self-sufficiency, my parents also had a cow with a calf, two pigs, a few sheep, chickens, and ducks, which needed to be fed and taken care of.

My father used to wake up late, and he expected my mother to cook for him at specific hours four times a day. At noon he'd take a nap, and he went to bed early; in other words, he continued to spend his life in self-satisfaction and pleasure. All this while, my mother was slaving for him. To cope with all that, my mother sped up the pace, running continuously.

I've lived in four countries of the world, but I have never seen anyone work as hard as my mother throughout her life. Continuously sacrificing herself and overwhelmed by fatigue, she had another burden on her shoulders: her husband, who was extremely jealous. She couldn't talk to any man, because my father would suspect her of cheating and would beat her up when she came home. She couldn't even talk to another woman, because he suspected her of speaking ill behind his back and would beat her for that too.

When they were young, Fanase would lock my mother in the house and beat her black and blue. My sister and I grew up, and he couldn't beat her too much, because she would run away from home and sleep in sheds. When my sister and I attained maturity, my father forgot his bad habits and would only punch her in the ribs when we couldn't see him.

My father was narcissistic, negative, lazy, aggressive, and a sociopath. He didn't talk to anyone, not even his children. He was permanently unhappy about what we were doing and was always there for a fight. Hardly a day passed without an argument. Even now, at the age of fifty-four, I can't bring myself to talk to my father like a son to his father, and I never speak to him for more than a minute.

Although she lived all her life with a tyrant and couldn't meet with anyone else, my mother didn't divorce her husband. To her, keeping her children and grandchildren together was more important. She would hate herself if her children and grandchildren suffered because of her divorce. She had gotten so used to her sufferings and buried them so deep in her soul that no one could really probe and see what was lying inside her. No one could know that she was in pain because of her husband and because she never had any support or consolation. Her behaviour would only speak the strength of a woman full of love and desperately eager for life.

In all my life I have never seen anyone who loved people so much and was so loved by the world around her. Her love was contagious, making everyone open their hearts and soul to her. Her love for her children and grandchildren and for the surrounding world helped her find her peace of mind and happiness beyond the tyranny of her husband.

When she was processing tobacco in a collective farm, she was amiable with her workmates, and they, in turn, respected and loved her because she was cheerful, understanding, vivacious, and commonsensical, with a warm, golden heart; she knew how to listen to anyone and understand, support, and comfort everyone and give them wise advice. Her workmates followed her like bees to honey.

When she retired and leased out her land to a private association, my mother started to make cow's milk cheese, which she sold on Thursdays at the local market. She would pour all her heart and soul into preparing the cheese. Her cheese was the best in the whole town. She had her devoted clientele who had befriended her out of respect for her work and special personality. My mother was extremely proud of her achievements: she had found the secret of the tastiest cheese in the region, so everyone loved her, respected her, and wanted to buy that special cheese from her.

The peak of my mother's happiness was in the past ten to fifteen years, when the results of her work were reflected in the achievements of her children and grandchildren. All her life, my mother had worked for her children and grandchildren.

When my sister and I were little children living with our parents, in wintertime, our mother would weave carpets as wedding gifts for us, the essential things in our home after we got married. At our weddings, my mother gave us all the money she had saved in her life so that we could buy our house. She didn't buy clothes and shoes for herself; she saved all the money from her hard work for her children. She only wore hand-me-down robes from her sister.

My sister got married in the 1990s, and I did the same at a time when our country experienced the worst economic crisis. The economy was in free fall, and life was worse than in the aftermath of WWII. Everything built during seventy years of Communism was now being destroyed. Factories were dismantled, and the people in the country were working the land with horses and wooden tools from the nineteenth century. Given the circumstances, my sister and I had to go abroad to make money to help our families survive the sheer poverty.

Going abroad, we left our children in the care of my mother, the only one available for this job. She worked night after night in her household, and for her it was a pleasure. She was proud and happy that she could help out her children and spend more time with her beloved grandchildren. She cooked delicious food for them, massaged them, comforted them, and caressed them.

My mother's love for her children and grandchildren and her help during the most difficult period of our lives made our family united, harmonious, and full of love. Since then, our children can hardly wait for the summer vacation to go on a visit to their beloved grandmother.

Even though Nastia and I changed four countries and lived far from my mother, our children were never absent from their grandmother's place. Starting from their first year of life until the end of their college years, they spent every summer vacation with their grandmother.

From the entire village of my parents, inhabited by some 2,500 people, my family and my sisters have accomplished the most in life.

- My sister built a dream house in her natal village, a fairytale household with all the amenities the likes of which you can't find in Moldovan villages.

- First we moved to Romania, where we lived in the mountains like in paradise, and then we moved to Canada, where again we accomplished more than most Canadians, living in a house on the mountain coast on the shores of the Atlantic Ocean.

- My sister's children have also done very well: my sister's daughter became a doctor in Romania, and her son became a construction foreman in Russia.

- My eldest daughter became a doctor in Canada, and the youngest one graduated from the Faculty of Physiotherapy and became a Canadian physiotherapist.

Along with our achievements, my sister and I have dedicated our last ten years to my mother's comfort. We created all the best conditions for her house: we completely renovated the kitchen, we built a new fence, we rebuilt the enclosures for animals and poultry, and we installed sewerage and water systems in the house, along with indoor toilets, a shower, an automatic laundry machine, and air conditioning. My mother had never seen or dreamed of living in such conditions at her age; she never imagined having the things that most Moldovans don't have.

All the accomplishments of my mother's children and grandchildren were in the fantastic realm. She had never seen, never heard, and never dreamed of such realizations at our place and in her household we had been happy to rebuild.

We were telling her about us, about the family, and we showed her on the Internet via Skype how we lived and what we used to do, and her breath was taken away with happiness; her heart and soul were filled with joy. Her happiness was overflowing, and she couldn't control it. She told the story to all her friends in the village, to every person she encountrered on the road. All day long she talked about it with everyone in the village—about the accomplishments and lives of her children and grandchildren.

For the last ten years, since my mother learned to use the Internet and Skype, I've called her at least once every day. Not a single day passed without calling her. Even if we were away on vacation in other countries, we found ways to speak with her. My mother was sitting in her house, behind the stove, in a forgotten village in Moldova, watching our whole life in reality: we showed her the house where we lived in Canada, along the mountain coast on the ocean shore; when we went on vacation, we showed her the highways; we showed her the shopping centers where we used to shop; she traveled with us on all the vacations around the world; she visited all the Canadian islands we went to; she saw all the countries in Central America where we went to relax in wintertime; she saw all the countries of South America. In short, staying at home by the fireplace, every day, my mother traveled with us all over the world.

She was so happy about the life we lived and about her children and grandchildren. She wouldn't miss a single moment or event of what we showed her through the Internet. When she was with us on Skype, it seemed like she wanted to absorb us with her big soul.

When I was at home talking to her, I'd busy myself with cooking or eating my lunch. When I was cooking, my mother could stay with me for two to three hours until I completed the job. Even though she was tired and it was time to go to bed (the time zone difference is seven hours between Canada and Moldova), she wouldn't abandon me halfway in the process. She guided me and gave me all the instructions any chef might need. Many times I forgot where I had left the knife or the spoon, but she knew exactly where they were. I was pleasantly impressed that she knew much better than me what was in my house. I didn't know so well where things could be found, but her curiosity to see a story-like life of her little boy made her "teleport" with her imagination to my place.

If I was too late with putting the vegetables in the soup, or if I forgot to stir in the pan, my mother was always on the lookout and never let me lose sight of anything. "Make sure you've put in the vegetables," "Take a taste to see if you need more salt," she would say immediately.

In the last ten years, this relationship of love and harmony between mother and son continued to grow, and it can't be expressed in words. You have to feel this kind of love to understand it. My mother's love made me feel extremely happy, full of life, and accomplished. My heart was racing with joy at the thought of having passed the age of fifty years and continuing to feel like Mama's boy with her by my side every day.

Since 2012, I had gone through a rather sad period in my life because I had lost my job as a psychiatrist forever. Losing the hope of becoming a psychiatrist again in this life made me lose my reason for living. During this time of sadness, my mother was always by my side, and through our relationship of love, harmony, and understanding, she made me feel like a child loved and caressed by his mother. Affectionate as she was, she comforted me and helped me overcome the most painful problems of my life.

But years passed and my mother's health condition gradually deteriorated. She suffered from joint pains and had to take a bunch of painkillers. Every year I used to bring her several thousand Tylenol pills from Canada that barely last her for one year.

Although she was in pain, she prayed to God not for her health but for the health and prosperity of her children and grandchildren. Every moment was dedicated to prayers to the Lord for her children and grandchildren.

Her suffering and her devotion to us urged me to pray to God with all my heart. And I was praying more and more, begging the Almighty to ease her predicament. She had suffered enough in her life; she had worked hard and she deserved an easy end. I asked God to alleviate her pain and let her live comfortably until the end.

What scared me the most was that my mother would pass away and I wouldn't have the chance to say goodbye to her. Since 2005, when I'd moved to Canada and lived far from her, I had been afraid that I wouldn't be with her before she died. I couldn't imagine that one day I would be without my beloved mother and would no longer feel like the mother's beloved child.

To spend more time with her, I used to go to Moldova for five to six weeks every year. Although the distance from Canada to Moldova is quite big, for the last twelve years, I've been out there every year to feel like a child once again at Mother's home .

The only time I couldn't go to Moldova was in the year 2020, because flights were cancelled due to COVID-19. I was sad, but I was convinced that I would make it up in 2021.

The Most Painful and Confusing Period of My Life

The beginning of November 2020, for me, was a period of stormy situations. On the one hand, I was anxious due to the worsening symptoms of my disease, and on the other hand, right on November 3, for the first time, my publisher sent me several copies of my book *The Destiny and Signs of God*.

I didn't know what to do—to be happy that my book finally saw the daylight and I would probably be successful, or to be destroyed because I suspected I had cancer.

This dilemma didn't last long: precisely two days after I received the books, on a Thursday, November 5, a fall sunny day, my wife, our older daughter, and I were at home getting ready to have lunch, when my mother called us on Skype.

I let her talk to Nastia and Sara, because I was busy cooking lunch, and my mother's stories didn't interest me very much. I talked to her every day, and I knew almost all the news from her. I knew everything she had to say to us. Nastia and Sara hadn't spoken with her in a long time, and they had more to say and catch up with. They had to reveal their secrets and convey all their love to each other since they had last met.

They were talking on Skype in the kitchen where I was preparing the meal. Passing by the computer at one point, I heard my mother say something about the doctor. She said that Louise, my sister, wanted to take her to the doctor for a check-up.

I couldn't believe my ears! As I told you before, my mother had suffered so much in her life, but she repressed it in the depths of her soul and didn't complain to anyone; she didn't talk about her hardship, her husband, or her illnesses. Even if in recent years she had an excruciating pain in her joints, she would never show it or complain to anyone. She accepted the pain as something coming with the age, and she had to put up with it. So if she was talking about the doctor, it must have been something *very* serious, and lest I should get it wrong, I asked her to say it again.

"Wait, Mom, I didn't hear very well what you said. Did you say doctor?"

"Louise said that she can't stand to see me suffer like this and that on Monday we'll go to the doctor for a check-up. On Sunday, we'll attend the church mess, but we'll go to see the doctor on Monday morning."

"But what happened?" I asked. "Why do you have to go to the doctor?"

As she never complained to anyone, my mother didn't quite know how to answer, and she just said, "I don't know where all this power goes."

I really didn't understand what was happening. I had talked with her every day, but I hadn't noticed anything unusual that would make me suspect that she was sick or frail. She told me that for the last few months she hadn't gone to the market, but I thought she didn't go because she decided not to exhaust herself too much. I was glad that she wasn't going there anymore, but I had never thought she was weak. Through Skype, I didn't see any major change in her, even though I saw her every day.

This news hit me hard. My mother was feeling weak, and I was in shock. I couldn't believe that she was dying, because deep inside I was certain that if something serious happened to her, I would feel it with the help of my sixth sense or in my dreams.

In recent years, I had developed the ability to sense and predict future events or situations. I sensed them with my sixth sense or I had dreams that depicted future events accurately. My dreams had become so real that I was dreaming exactly what was happening in real time somewhere else; I dreamed exactly what was going to happen the next day or within a week. I dreamed of people whose situations, feelings, and emotions were perfectly like in reality.

After all those premonitions in the past years, I was 100 percent convinced that when my mother nears her death or gets sick, I will know everything, because I will be able to foresee absolutely everything regarding her condition. If I can sense when all my close or distant friends, or even my dog, are in pain, or if I can feel Sara's thoughts and messages in her sleep in the middle of the night, telling me that she arrived safely in Montreal, I had no doubt that if something serious happened to my dear mother, the dearest and the most important and most loved person in this world, I would not miss her sufferings. I was convinced that I could foresee not only the stages of her illness, but I would also know the exact moment when she would leave us.

In this case, after hearing the surprising news about mother's weaknesses, I was sure that she would be fine.

I had analyzed not only my premonitions but also the situations unfolding in the last year, 2020, when the COVID-19 pandemic was in full swing. That year was the first time I wasn't at mother's house, and I didn't feel like a child once again at Mother's house.

I understood that in June 2020 the first wave of the pandemic meant that the flights had been cancelled, but I didn't understand why God didn't say that I should go to Moldova in August, or maybe in September? He must have known that my mother was sick. Why didn't I feel anything at all? Why didn't God warn me that I should go to see my mother while she was still healthy, and I could really feel like a child with her again?

Asking myself these questions and analyzing the situations unfolding until then, I concluded that what was happening with my mother was nothing serious. I said to myself: *Probably everything will be fine.* But I remained in a state of anxiety.

Even if I had convinced myself that everything would be fine and I didn't need to go to Moldova on an emergency basis, something inside me urged me to call the travel agency to check for flight availability. The agent said that the only available flights from Canada to Moldova were provided by Turkish Airlines only on Sundays. So even if I wanted to leave sooner, I couldn't because I had to wait until the following Sunday, November 15.

On Monday, November 9, after the church mess, my sister and her husband came to take my mother to a private polyclinic for a check-up. After the examination, the doctor told them that she might have a problem with the aortic valve that could be fixed with a simple surgery. To confirm the diagnosis, she had to come back the next day Tuesday, November 10, for an ultrasound examination.

I learned about the result of the medical test, and I gave a sigh of relief. My guess about her state health was true.

The next day at the private polyclinic, my mother was so weak that she couldn't bear the ultrasound examination until the end. During the examination, it was revealed that her pancreas and all her internal organs had been invaded by cancerous tumors. Basically, she was suffering from terminal pancreatic cancer, and there was absolutely nothing they could do.

My sister called me and told me the results, but I was without words. I felt as if someone had hit me hard on the head and I'd lost consciousness, as if I'd been stabbed in my heart and was bleeding profusely, as if the knife was stuck in me and someone was twisting it in the wound. The pain was deep inside my heart, a terrible pain that can't be expressed in words, a pain that can be felt and understood only by those who live through it and have a relationship of love and harmony with their mother, just like I had with mine.

I didn't understand what was going on and why God hadn't warned me about anything, and why I didn't feel anything. How could I feel everyone, the sufferings of all my friends and enemies, but not feel anything about Mother's predicament? Why didn't He warn me that I should go to see her in the last stage of her life? Why did He keep me bogged down? He didn't even warn me that she was sick, and He didn't warn me that I should go to see her in the last year of her life and feel like a real child at my mother's home for the last time.

The pain in my soul was growing unbearable, but I had to be strong to support Mother. I had to be strong for her to feel safe.

My sister and I didn't tell our mother that she was sick with cancer, because the word "cancer" in Moldova means "crab," a freshwater crustacean like the American lobster, only of a much smaller size. So if I had told mother that she was sick with cancer, she would have imagined that she had a lobster in her belly that was eating her organs.

She was an old woman from the countryside, and lest I should scare her, and to give her a sense of safety and to be a part of her love and peace of mind on this earth, I told her, "Mother, the tests indicate large damage of your internal organs. Because of your hard work during your life, your organs have reached the highest level of exhaustion, and now they're so vulnerable. They lost all power to function, and we can't do anything about it. Such is life. We can't do anything. At some point, we all have to go to God. We all have to bid adieu to our loved ones here on earth and join our parents, friends, and relatives waiting for us with love in the other world. They miss us desperately."

After I found out the painful news about Mother, in the afternoon of the same day, I called the travel agent to buy my ticket to Moldova. All the borders were closed and only a few planes were flying because of COVID. So many travelers had remained stuck in different countries, sick with COVID. This notwithstanding, I called the agency because I had no choice. I had to go home to see my mother. I had to go for the last time and spend my vacation with my dear, beloved mother. I had to go to feel like a child at mother's home for the last time in my life.

In addition to my mental breakdown, I had reached the maximum of my somatic pains that I mentioned earlier: the pains in my genitals had increased, the rectal bleeding had become more abundant, and the axial lymph nodes in my left arm were so large and painful that if it hadn't been for mother's illness, I would have presented myself at the emergency. I was convinced that I had developed a cancer of unknown origin, which had spread to the lymph nodes.

I ignored my condition, indifferent to what could happen to me. I wanted to go home as soon as I could to see my dear and beloved mother and spend her last moments with her. The only comfort was that even if I were sick with cancer and died soon, my mother would die before me, and she wouldn't suffer for outliving her beloved son. Her suffering would have been way more painful, and I didn't want her to go though it. She had suffered enough in her life, and she didn't deserve something like that. I didn't know how long she would live.

But before going to Moldova, I had to consider several facts:

- I wanted to be with my mother before she died, but I didn't want to see her dead because mentally I would collapse, as the pain would be too strong for me and I couldn't imagine myself recovering from such a painful sight.

- The end of the year was approaching, and I had to prepare all the documents to file for our company income tax, so I had to get back to Canada by December 24.

- I was told by the travel agent that a seat was available on Sunday, December 13. But I didn't like to travel on the thirteenth after all the unpleasant things that happened to me in relation with that number. A few years earlier, when I was returning from Europe and had to change planes in Frankfurt, the boarding gate was 13. After I boarded the plane, my nose became itchy and runny, and I was confined in bed by the flu for almost a week.

Now that the COVID thing was spreading out, I didn't want to return on December 13. I was afraid of catching the virus and not being allowed into Canada. At the same time, I didn't want to influence or change the fate of my life and the situations God would organize for me.

To live in harmony with the Universe, we must not influence the situations that must happen to us. If God prepares a sequence of events for us, we don't have to analyze them, discuss them, or try to change them with the help of "intelligence" or through different "cunning" methods. We must let ourselves be carried away by the tide of events and accept the fate meted out to us, the one that God created especially for us. (Caution: We must be very careful and differentiate between the fate built by God for us and the temptations of negative energies that lure us to doom. We must not go headlong into the wall and say, "This is what God told me." NO. I have in mind situations that are already prepared by God for us, such as in the case of going to Moldova.)

For that reason, without calculating or thinking about any details, I told the travel agent that I wanted to go to Moldova and return in four weeks. I had the impression that if I left on November 15 for four weeks, the return date would be on December 20, right before Christmas. I don't know why I thought so, but that was what simply came to my mind.

The agent told me that the return date was December 13. I was scared at first and didn't want to take it. Normally, if I had a materialistic thinking, I would use the "cunning" techniques and would have asked the agent to change my return date, but since it simply happened to me, just like that, I let myself be carried away by the flow. With fear in my heart, I accepted, come what would.

From Thursday, November 5, when my mother informed us that she had to go see a doctor, her condition began worsening. She had no pain, and she didn't feel anything that would make her uncomfortable. The only thing she had were exhaustion and weakness, intensifying from one day to the next.

Before the church mess (the Sunday village feast), my mother could work up to six to seven hours a day. For important holidays in Moldova, people cook a lot of dishes, and they need a few days to complete this traditional work. So my mother pushed herself to cook and finish everything on time. When her guests came over on Sunday, she could hardly sit at the table with them. My father, as usual, didn't help, but insisted that she do the honors.

On Monday, after they returned from the medical examination, my mother slept the whole afternoon, so exhausted after several hours at that private polyclinic. On Tuesday, the same thing happened. She barely made it to the polyclinic, and after she came back, she slept until evening.

In spite of this weariness and need for sleep, my mother was up to prepare my father's meal at specific times so he would not betray his habits. In addition, she called me on Skype every evening at 07:00, when our local time was 12:00 noon. She was there on Skype every evening, and I could see that she was getting weaker.

Thursday then Friday, her frailty became so obvious that when she turned on the computer at 07:00 in the evening to call, she forgot to press the call key.

On Thursday, she called me a little later, but this didn't raise any suspicion for me. On Friday, she didn't call me, so I called her about twenty minutes later than the usual time and asked her why she hadn't called.

She was sitting down, bent over from exhaustion, and looking at me from under her eyebrows, unable to lift her head up.

"Well," she said, "I don't know, I turned it on. I'm sitting here in front of the computer and I forgot to call you. Yesterday it was the same. I turned it on and forgot to call you."

She sounded so weak, and she couldn't sit up to talk via Skype. Hearing her, my heart broke with pain, and I realized that she was melting down like a candle, day by day, faster than I had expected.

While initially I thought that she'd live at least another half a year, now I realized that the situation was much more serious. The sudden worsening of her health scared me, and I thought I wouldn't get to Moldova while she was still alive. A few more days and I would be there with her, and my heart was ripped with a fear impossible to describe. My soul pain had no limits, and from that moment on, the pain in my soul became so great.

My flight to Moldova was booked for Sunday, November 15, with departure from Montreal. The airport was located at seven hundred kilometers from my home, and it took me a whole day to drive there.

I was supposed to take off on Saturday, November 14, and the last day I could speak with my mother via Skype was Friday, November 13.

I realized that again I was sucked in the whirlwind of number 13, and I started to worry about the future these numbers reserved for me. Not only that the date was 13, one of bad omen, but I was scared that it fell on a *Friday*, making it clear that my destiny was way more serious than I imagined. Analyzing the whole situation with number 13 and Friday, and overwhelmed by Mother slimming down rapidly, I knew that I would see her and talk to her for the last time. I was so afraid that she wouldn't make it until I got there in Moldova.

My condition was of a terrible fear and hopelessness, with an indescribable pain in my soul and my heart

For the last ten years, we had talked via Skype every day, with only a few exceptions. That usually happened when my mother had problems with her computer or there was a power outage or other things. Otherwise, *every day*, we talked via Skype, regardless of where I was.

I used to speak with her when I went out shopping.

I spoke with her when I was downtown.

I spoke with her even when I was on vacation.

Normally, I was spoke with my mother at twelve o'clock noon, the local time in Canada, when I was having lunch and it was 7:00 p.m. in Moldova, when she'd finished all the household chores and could spend time with me.

Every two or three days, I had to cook, and my mother was with me and gave me instructions, what and how. She used to tell me when to boil the meat and add the vegetables, and how much rice or potatoes I should use. Practically, she was my *boss*, and I was the subordinate cook who performed the functions. Although she was on Skype watching me on the monitor, she oriented herself better than I did in my own kitchen.

Then on Friday, November 13, I had to cook for Nastia and Sara, because I was going to Moldova and I had to leave them food. Though extremely weak, my mother stayed with me and gave me advice for the last time. She had done it so often in the last ten years!

I asked Sara to take video footage of me while I was cooking and my mother was watching over me. Nastia was there with us, trying to seize all my mother's movements.

I used to make schnitzel from chicken breast, and I showed my mother all the stages of what and how I did it.

Each of us wanted to send our love to my mother, who could hardly look up at us. And in her eyes there was so much love for all of us. We all wanted to be united with her together to the depth of our souls.

In those moments in my kitchen, there was love, harmony, respect, nostalgia, impatience, and a desire for communication. It was a harmony that had never existed at home. We all loved one another, we all shared our love with each other, and we wished that the intensity of those moments never ended.

We talked about how we were together all the time, about the fact that my mother was with me every day and passed on all her culinary knowledge to me.

At one point I said to my mother, "Thank you, Mom, for being with me and teaching me all the recipes for the tastiest meals, the ones that you cooked for me since childhood. Now I know how to make them here in Canada for my children and my family. My children in Canada grew up eating the same food I grew up with. Your granddaughters too; we all were and will remain spoiled by your delicious treats. You taught me absolutely all your recipes, and I cook and will continue to cook only according to yours."

"Yes, yes, you know everything," my mother answered me with a tired voice but lovingly.

Meanwhile, Nastia also wanted to convey to Mother a little attention with love. Nastia used her hobby of taking care of plants. Our house is full of Nastia's plants. Her last success was a coffee tree she planted, and it was quite big. Nastia came to the computer and showed it to my mother.

"Look, Mom, here's a coffee tree. Soon we will have our own coffee at home. I brought these coffee beans from a plantation in Costa Rica. In Costa Rica, I also showed you the hotel where we stayed."

Sara also wanted to say something to her dear grandmother. She also wanted to convey, in a way, her feelings of love, and she asked her, "What did you do today, Mamuca?" ("Mamuca" is a diminutive of "Grandma" in our region.)

"I slept all day," my mother said.

"Yes, today I woke up at five in the morning and I couldn't sleep. It never happens. Usually, I sleep until noon, but today, I don't know what happened," Sara said to her.

"Mom, have you talked to Marina and Ghenadii yet?" I asked her. (Marina and Ghenadii are my sister's children.)

"Yes, I did. And I also spoke with Marina and Ghena, with all my grandchildren. Ghena has no way of coming home, and Marina would like to come over, but because of COVID, she doesn't want to take chances. He's afraid of getting sick," my mother said.

"It doesn't matter," I continued. "The main thing is that they called you, that you saw them. It's very important that before we leave this life, we take the opportunity to ask forgiveness from everyone and say goodbye. Let's say goodbye quietly and with love to everything and everyone who has been with us throughout our life. When people leave this life quickly without saying goodbye to everyone, it's very difficult for all. Look, Mother, how you managed to speak with everyone, to say goodbye to everyone, to your children, grandchildren, and great-grandchildren, to Marina and Ghena, and to Lya and Sara and to Nastia, to everyone."

"Yes, yes, yes," my mother said.

I was frying the schnitzels in a pan, and I continued to speak. "From now on, you have another life, a life with your parents who are waiting for you with love, and with your brother and your dear cousins. They all are waiting impatiently for you to reach them.

"And about us, Mom, don't worry, because we will soon catch up with you. Here on earth, life goes by very quickly, and before you know it, we'll be on the other side. So wait for us there. When we come, welcome us at the gate."

"Is that so?" my mother asked me with a smile.

"Yes," I answered, "and you will welcome us with love." She continued to smile because she liked what I was telling her. She didn't know what was happening in the other world, and she was curious to hear my stories. And I was happy that I had received various accounts from people who had experienced a near-death experience (NDE), and I knew how their souls can be comforted.

"Now, when you're walking onto the other side, your parents will welcome you at the gate, along with your grandparents, your brother, and your cousins. All those who loved you here on earth will be there to welcome you with true love from their hearts."

"Well, as God wishes," my mother said.

"We still have work to do here on earth; we are not done yet. You, you've finished everything; you've worked since you were a small child. You worked for everyone and helped everyone settle in their place in life. Dear mother, so much you have worked and struggled!

"How I wish we lived longer and spent more time together, especially if we lived in love and harmony with our children, grandchildren, and our whole family. But we must move on. We can't live forever in the same life. We came here to earth, we did the duty we have to do, and at some point, we have to accept to move ahead, because we have other things to do, much more important things.

"Life in the other world is beautiful; actually, it's much more beautiful than here on earth."

My mother wanted to say something to me: "Ghena cries and tells me, 'How short this life is, Mom.' And I said to him, 'What can you do to Ghenuta more?'"

I went on. "I told you about the situations I heard on TV about the people who died, and after a little while they were reborn in their family. I don't know if it reminds you of a boy who died and was born as a son to his sister."

"Yes, yes, I remember."

"At first, his sister, who in this life was his mother, didn't understand what was happening, but after her son told her about some situations that only the two of them knew, the sister/mother believed him. So be careful what you're doing there. Don't rush to return to our family. Just stay there and wait for us, stay and rest, because you've worked and struggled too much in this life. So be as it may, but you fully deserve to stay there longer and rest."

"Good, good," my mother answered.

"In your next life, you won't suffer the way you did. Everything you've suffered in this life will not happen again. First of all, now you will go to

God, and you will relax there, far from all the torments you suffered here; and then in the rest of the lives you may have, you won't live these torments anymore. Never ever. Because we all came here to earth to fulfill some functions and be subject to temptations, needs, and hardship, and once we've gone through them, we won't repeat them. The important thing is that what we're given to do here on earth must be done with all our heart, and you are the only person I know on earth who tackled all the difficulties head-on and courageously. You did it all by yourself, without any help or support from anyone. You alone did all the work, as both a woman and a man, and there wasn't anyone to sustain you and understand you. From the moment you were born, you worked continuously from dawn until late at night' you worked hard to succeed in doing them all. Diligent people like you will never live again the painful life you have lived.

"It's worse for those like my father, who come here on earth and think only of how to satisfy their pleasures. They should behold! Because of all the miseries they produced in this life and in the after-life, it will turn against them and they will suffer in loneliness.

"In this life, you didn't have the opportunity to go to school, and you regretted it all your life. But you will see, in your next life, thanks to God, you will be born to a family of smart people who will provide all the conditions for your education and comfort. You will live a happy childhood with your dear parents, and as I told you before, you will become a teacher. You had wished for it since you were a child. For you, teaching students in school was something unattainable. But in the next life, God will be happy to fulfill your sacred desire.

"Secondly, you will no longer live with a man like my father, who isn't interested in you and only cares about himself, his pleasure, his desires, and is indifferent to how you feel and why you suffer. Just as tolerant as you were of your husband and everyone around you, your new husband will be of you, who deserves a man full of love and understanding.

"This is how it's going to be, dear mother. You and I have already talked about it for a couple of years."

(Incidentally, my mother and I had been talking about the spiritual world for several years. I had talked with her dozens of times about the near-death experience, children who can remember their previous lives and God's messages. In short, I talked with my mother about everything I wrote in my first two books.

While I was frying the schnitzels, Sara continued to video and listen to what I was saying to her grandma. Occasionally, she turned the camera towards her grandmother, sometimes towards me.

"From now on, you know all the stories," I said.

I finished frying the schnitzels and I went on, "Look, Mom, this is the last schnitzel that I'll make together with you."

I had picked up the laptop so she could see how the last schnitzels are fried.

"Look, Mom, can you see? Here are the last schnitzels we are frying together for the last time in this life."

The pain in my soul was excruciating, and I felt like crying, but I controlled the flood of my tears with all my might, to hide it from my mother.

In the meantime, there was one schnitzel left to cook, and I again picked up the laptop to show her the last meal we cooked together.

"Look, Mom, this is the last schnitzel in our life, from now on, maybe another time, but I don't think there will be another."

She knew that this was really the last time we'd cook together, and shades of sadness marked her face that I can't express in words. Parting with such a dear and beautiful custom was a loss that one can hardly imagine. It was the end of the beautiful years spent with my mother in the kitchen, the years full of love and understanding, full of happiness from a harmonious relationship between mother and son. It was over now.

I found the strength to control my tears behind my speech, but Sara, who continued to video, couldnt help herself from crying in silence. Only the sound of her deep breathing could be heard against the background of her overflowing emotions.

"Look, now I'm done. Along with the food, I did the dishes, and tomorrow morning, I will travel to you and will feel like a child at Mother's home again."

There was sadness in the kitchen. To defuse the situation, I continued to speak, keeping my tears at bay. My emotions were running wild, and I was pausing to dab my tears away, and then I went on. "I thank the Lord for giving me the opportunity to go to your place to spend a little more time with you. We all wanted to go to your home to see you for the last time, but look how the situation is. With this COVID, you can't go anywhere."

"Yes, yes," Mother said.

"Do you remember when I left for Canada fifteen years ago?"

"Yes. I do."

"Then I thought I would never see you again, because in those days, people who came to the USA and Canada returned to Moldova after ten or fifteen years. Then I really thought that we would be separated forever. But do you see how God worked this? Even though we lived in Canada, He gave us the opportunity to come home every year to be together. In all these years, a wonderful relationship was built between us as a mother and children, and as a grandmother and grandchildren. Every year, we all lived the most beautiful moments together. We lived together; we huddled together. I felt like a child in his mother's house; our children felt loved too, the dearest and the most wanted grandchildren of all. And you felt like the happiest mother and grandmother on earth.

"Since Nastea and I moved with goods and chattels to different countries and different localities, our children didn't have a stable place where they could settle and feel at home. For them, your house was their parental nest, where they spent all their summer breaks from the day they were born until now. There they felt at home; they felt they were with someone/their grandmother who loved them, caressed them, understood them, advised them, and waited for them to come home. Now they've grown up, finished college, started working, and don't have time to come to you anymore. But deep inside them, you remained their source of warmth and love and joy. Thanks to you, they lived their happiest childhood because you waited for them, you kept them warm and coddled them, and you bought them baby chickens every year and made a cemetery of dead baby chickens."

Sara, who continued to record, started to laugh through her tears, which were running profusely from crying. What a beautiful memory for both my mother and Sara! Every year when the girls went to Moldova, they always wanted their grandmother to buy them hatched baby chicks. My mother raised chickens every year and didn't need to buy any, but since her granddaughters wanted baby chickens, she used to buy some for them. Being too small, most of the baby chickens died after a few days, and they buried them in front of the house. Every year, the baby chickens had their own cemetery.

My mother cheered up and asked Sara, "Why are you crying? Are you unhappy about the cemetery?" And they laughed together.

"But did you lay flowers for them, Grandma?" asked Sara, crying and laughing it off.

"Yes, yes, yes. How could I not?" answered Mother.

"Look, Mother," I continued. "You have brought so much happiness and love to our family, for your children and grandchildren. One can't get enough of it. It's true love that comes from your soul for your children and grandchildren. All this love you've spread around here on earth for your children and grandchildren is growing so big. And it will continue to expand in our families with the help of your children and grandchildren and great-grandchildren. You have no idea how much love you've created here on earth and how big this love is growing. Only when you go up there to the Almighty, only from there will you see what you created here on earth in our family, in the family you made."

Sara could no longer contain her emotions. She was sobbing uncontrollably and knew and understood very well what I was saying, and she knew the boundless love her grandmother had for her.

Touched by my words, my mother confirmed, "Yes, yes, yes."

And I went on. "Your love will spread on the face of the earth not only through your children and grandchildren, but through the book I wrote. You've already seen how the book is sold all over the world, on our entire planet.

"What I wrote in it has mostly your merits, because you raised me. You educated me to be a decent, wise, and obedient child, one who knew how to obey our Lord, so this book is due to you. You gave me wisdom and love, and not only when I was a child. You were always by my side during and after my college years; you were by my side and supported me in all the most difficult moments of my life, even over the last years, after I gave up my job to dedicate myself to writing my books.

"Regretfully, God asked me abandon my wonderful job to become a writer of His messages, and I was downhearted and lived the most difficult period of my life. But you were with me every day and comforted me with love from withing yourself. You emboldened me to finish my first book, and you gave me the wisdom to convey all God's messages to the whole world.

"Now, imagine that a part of this book is your love, because if you hadn't educated me and weren't by my side to support me, this book wouldn't exist. So you acted just like the mother of Jesus Christ, who supported her son so that He would become what He is now. So this book is entirely your merit."

My mother had never thought of it that way, and she was so proud of what she heard. She had always regarded herself as a humble woman who didn't deserve anyone's attention. Above all, she didn't think that she deserved any attention from God, as she considered herself a sinner before Him.

"As I told you, on the one hand, your love will spread through your children and grandchildren, and on the other hand, it will be the book I write thanks to you. And the time will come when the right book will reach the ears of people all over the world."

"Yes, yes," my mother said.

"Because this book is the book that will mark a turnaround in people's minds. It will change the entire direction of the evolution of our civilization. As I told you, you don't even imagine your importance here on earth. Imagine this: thanks to your love, your suffering, and your work, the whole planet will change its direction of evolution. Thanks to you, the whole planet will be able to see, realize, and walk down a new path—the path of the spiritual evolution that leads directly to God.

"Only when you reach God will you see how important you were here on earth. These torments of yours, these sufferings of yours, aroused your love and wisdom like no one else on the face of the earth could have."

"Yes, yes, that's right," my mother said.

"That's why God sent you here to earth, namely to be mother and grandmother, to cultivate His love in our hearts, to raise our children with hard work and sincere love. That is your legacy for all of us."

"Yes, yes," she nodded.

"And this is it, dear mother." I ended my speech.

"Well then, good health to you Ionica, Nastia, Sara, Lya, Jee, Adrien."

"Come on, Mom, let's forgive each other, because I don't know if we'll see each other again," I said to her with tears in my eyes.

"Please forgive me. Please forgive me, Sara; please forgive me, Nastia, for being wrong in your eyes. And thank you for everything you did for me, for everything you helped me with, for giving me so much. May the Lord give you strength and help you and your whole family. May you have pure and enlightened thoughts from God," said Mother with sadness in her voice.

"Forgive me, Mother," Nastia said, "and thank you for everything you've done for us."

"Forgive us too, Mamuca," replied Sara, sobbing, "and we thank you for everything you've done for us. And we love you with all our heart."

"I still love you with all my heart," my mother whispered with sadness. "But what can I do? Since I have reached this age. We must accept forgiveness."

"Come to our place sometime," Sara said.

And I made it clear so that our mother could understand: "Come back to us in a dream. Tell us how things are over there."

"Yes, yes," my mother said. Well, good health. Mamuca's beautiful."

"Please forgive me, Mother," I said.

"May the Lord forgive you," she replied. "May He give you clean and enlightened thoughts. And may He give love to the whole family, and your grandchildren and great-grandchildren. And may you love them so much that no one will love ever love them as you do. You are the most patient being, the most precious on the face of the earth."

Sara, Nastia, and I were sitting in front of the computer with tears in our eyes, listening to my mother saying her last words on our computer. How we wished these moments never ended! We didn't want it to happen in our life, not even once, but we had no choice. We tried to take advantage of every moment and make it last as long as possible.

For the last ten years, it had become customary in our family that when we had lunch, my mother was present on Skype. Whether we were at home or on vacation, she was always with us at the table. So she was there to give us the lowdown from the village. But on that day, she was totally exhausted and had collapsed on the couch, unable to sit next to us.

Before we parted, I said to her, "Come on, Mom, let me show you what I cooked today, the last time we cooked together." I was holding up the laptop to show her the schnitzels on the plate.

"See?"

"I see, I see, I see," she said.

She sounded weak and there was sadness in her voice that one must experience to understand.

"Here, Mother, thanks to you, I can cook all the meals like at my mother's home. Let's eat," I said to everyone. "We're going to eat, but I see that you're already too tired and can't stay with us anymore. We will eat without you. Is that okay?"

"Okay, good health," she said, sending us an imaginary kiss by waving her hand.

"Okay, Mom," said Sara through tears and sobs. We love you so much."

"Okay. Good health," we all said together, and we shut off Skype.

It was the most painful separation, as I didn't know if I would find my mother alive in three days when I get there. And Sara and Nastia too didn't know if they would ever see her again on the computer.

I turned off the line and we sat at the table, each one crying for himself, without saying anything. It was a painful lunch, the most painful ever. For the first time in the last ten years, we had lunch without my mother, without her comforting us, praising us, supporting us, and telling us wonderful words of love.

Friday, November 13, was the last time that my mother and I cooked together on the Internet, and the first time that we ate without her. Also, it was the last time she could turn on the computer; her weakness and her exhaustion blocked her memory, and she couldn't remember the procedures. That day was the last day she was able to fulfill her functions as a wife and put food on the table for my father.

My sister, Louise, said to our father: "Daddy, don't you see that Mom cannot do it anymore? Do you really not see that she is totally down? Can't you see she's dying? Why are you pushing her like that? It's over! You need to take care of her." For the first time in his life, our father started to cry. He realized how much his wife meant to him.

In other words, November 13, 2020 was the day of major changes in my life, the day of separation from the daily harmonious relationship I had built with Mother for the last ten years.

My separation from my mother on the thirteenth keeps haunting me. I didn't understand why I had to be involved in so many ways with the number 13. The date of my return from Moldova, and the last time I cooked with my mother, were on the thirteenth. I didn't understand what was happening, and I didn't even have the strength to think about it much. My emotional pain was biting deep, and I had no energy to look for answers to my questions.

My last journey to my parents' house:

On November 14, I loaded my luggage in the trunk of my car. We bought our last gift for my mother. The girls bought her the most expensive and beautiful nightgown in Canada. I bought a lot of 70%-cocoa dark chocolate, a relish for my mother, as well as lots of maple syrup candies, her favorite too.

Because I had to drive more than seven hundred kilometers to Montreal, I woke up early in the morning. I was going to spend the night at one of my friends' houses and take the plane to Moldova the following day, on November 15, with a stopover in Turkey.

I got in the car and drove away without saying goodbye to my wife and daughter. It was my last journey to my mother, and I wanted to reach her as soon as possible. And even if my departure was the next day, my tormented soul was urging me to drive faster and faster.

I was racing along the road and didn't notice that I was speeding at 130–140 km/h on a section where the speed limit was 90 km/h. Only after two hundred kilometers did I realize how fast I was driving. Had the police caught me, my car would have been impounded and my driver's license suspended.

I was reckless, and I said to God: "I'm going to visit my mother!" And I went on. "God takes care of me and protects me. He knows very well how I feel."

And I continued to speed. On the road I saw several police cruise, but they all were busy with someone. I didn't slow down until I arrived at my friend's home in Montreal. I had made it in the shortest possible time.

I looked pale and devastated, all from that distressful race.

"What's happening to you?" they asked me.

They must have quickly understood, because they didn't say anything else.

I was battling with my tears, keeping them at bay. I stepped back and turned my head ninety degrees, then I took a deep breath to calm my nerves. I stood still for a few moments and then turned back to them to continue our conversation. Their question was manifestly out of place, and they knew it, so they changed the subject.

What saved us all was the fact that the friends were repairing the house and had a lot of work to do. So we began talking, and I calmed down a bit.

The next day, even though we were in full quarantine due to the pandemic, I took off without problems. My stopover in Turkey was smooth and without incident. I landed in Chisinau the next day, November 16, at 07:00 in the evening. At the airport, in a country with such an oppressive government, where every passenger has problems at customs, especially during the pandemic quarantine period, I was the only one who entered without customs control. The smoothness of my travel to Chisinau gave me a bit of comfort, and I had the impression that God had taken me in His hands and brought me directly to Moldova to my mother's home.

At the airport, Louise and her husband, Grigore, were waiting for me in the parking lot. None of us knew what to say. I hugged them, and then we got in the car and drove away, overwhelmed by the whole situation. The night had fallen and we had to travel 170 kilometers to my mother's home.

On route, my sister told me that I should sleep at their place because our mother was weak and couldn't manage anything anymore. They told me that she sleeps the whole day and we shouldn't disturb her at this late hour.

It was already 10:00 when I arrived in the village. We went straight to my sister's place without seeing Mother. I couldn't believe that I had arrived in my native village where Mother was a few hundred meters away and I didn't go to see her.

The next day, on November 17, even though I had just arrived from Canada with a seven-hour time zone difference, when people in Canada were just going to bed, we got up early in the morning and hurried to Mother's house.

My father was outside, hanging around the house without doing anything special, as usual. He rushed to embrace me and started to sob like a helpless little boy abandoned by his protectors. We stayed in each other's hug for a few minutes until he calmed down. In those moments, I realized what my mother had liked about him: behind his aggressiveness lived a small, clumsy, helpless child who didn't even know how to speak with people because society scared him. My mother was his only salvation, and she was there for him doing everything in and around the house.

My father could never appreciate my mother's dedication, but now when he saw her so helpless, embarked on her final stage, he realized how important and necessary she was to him. He looked lost, and he would have done anything to keep her with him, but it was so late.

We stepped inside. My mother was up, sitting on the edge of the bed, without strength to stand up on her feet and speak loudly. Seeing me, a tide of happiness flooded her, and she took my face in her hands and kissed me on my cheeks with burning love and softly said to me, "My dearest son."

I hugged her with all my heart and said, "My dear and beloved mother. Thank you, my Lord, for bringing me to my mother."

After we hugged and kissed each other on the cheeks, I said, "Mother, here I came to spend my last vacation with you at home; I came to feel like a little boy for the last time at my dear and beloved mother's home."

I was looking at her, and a burden was lifted off my heart, a burden that had been inside me for more than fifteen years, even before we had immigrated to Canada. Since then, I had always been afraid that my mother would pass away and I wouldn't be there when it happened due to the long distance between Canada and Moldova. I was afraid that I wouldn't be able to get there on time to see her before she dies. This fear and my love for her made me travel to Moldova for a five-to-six-week vacation every year. I was going there to feel like a little boy once more at mother's home.

And now that I had reached my mother, I thanked the Lord for helping me spend my last, though painful, wonderful holiday of my life with my dear and beloved mother. This vacation was so different. Usually my mother cooked all kinds of food for me and took care of the cleaning and the housekeeping. Now it was my turn to do all of that for my dear, beloved mom.

Great moments with my mother while I was doing household chores:

Before I got home, my sister Louise was taking care of my parents. She cooked and cleaned up for them. When I got home, I took all the activities in my own hands: I cooked, I put the food on the table, and I cleaned after them, etc.

To my surprise, my father had become extremely careful about my mother. I had never seen him like that. Previously, not a single day had passed without getting into an argument, but now he was a different man. He was taking care of my mother's moves to assure himself that she was doing well. He was helping her dress and put on her shoes, and he was holding her by the waist so she could walk outside for fresh air. He was helping her sit down. In other words, he would notice every single movement she made and every single breath she took. She was a part of him at every movement and with every breath they had experienced together.

At one point, I said to my mother and Louise, "Look how God makes us all come down to earth. Dad, who never appreciated Mom, look how God made him *aware* of the importance of my mother to him, how he appreciates her, respects her, carefully responds to her wishes. It doesn't matter that he realized it now before her death; the important thing is that he became aware that he must appreciate her. This means that in their future lives he will no longer discount her as he did in the course of this life."

My mother was happy about what I said, and she was *so* proud that my father appreciated her, at least now in the last days of her life. Probably she had been waiting for these moments all her life; she had been waiting so desperately to be appreciated and respected by her husband, and now her dream had come true. She was *extremely* happy and proud of him.

My mother was sleeping all day and night; she woke up five to seven times a day and would lie down without enough strength to speak, or she'd get up to sit at the table. Once or twice a day she managed to sit with me. I tried to take full advantage of the beautiful moments with my loving and caring mother.

Every once_in a while, I put my head in her arms so that she could gently caress the top of my head, like she used to do when I was a little boy and later when I went home on vacation.

Another time, I showed her the pictures and the footage of our family, including those with her and us all. I showed her the pictures from my youth, then from the time when we lived in Moldova, then in Romania, and then in Canada. As I was showing her the pictures and the video footage, I told her about all the events and difficulties and successes we had encountered along the way. My mother was extremely happy when she saw everything with her own eyes once again throughout our life. She was also extremely happy because she could see herself together with us.

I never missed a chance to highlight her important role in all our success in life, because she was the only person who united us all, supported us, understood us, and was with us when we needed help or emotional support.

Other times, when she could stay active, I would show her on the globe (that I had brought from Canada) all the places we had traveled: "Look, Mother, do you see? When I called you and said that I had reached the last frontier of the earth and was calling you from there, you asked me how many frontiers this world has. And I told you that I was there, on the other side of the globe." I showed my mother the different places I called her from, including Central America and South America. Thus, I showed her all the places in the world I had traveled and where she had been with us on Skype.

With a heart full of joy and in a weak voice, my mother said to me, "Bravo, Ionel, I am happy from the depth of my bones that you know how to live your life. I am glad that you have a united family and that you are always together."

On another occasion, she told me, "Love your wife and children. Don't waste your life arguing like I did with your father, because life is very short and it's not worth ruining it with your stubbornness. I know that you are wise with me, and it's good that you care for a united family. You go everywhere together and spend time together. Well done! Mom is happy for you."

When my mother couldn't sit up, I would simply lie down next to her and for a while, and we would be together without saying anything. Usually she was very talkative; she knew how to make up all kinds of stories for us or how to praise us so that we'd enjoy being with her. She would caress our backs or heads and tell us her stories.

This time around, my mother didn't have the strength to concentrate and couldn't speak much, and I tried to fill up the interminable silence by telling her about our life and the role of her life on earth, about her importance to us and to her children and grandchildren. And when I saw that she regained some strength, I quickly put my head in her arms so that she could softly touch me.

Even when exhausted and with no strength left to do anything, my mother didn't want to inconvenience anyone, and she tried to manage everything by herself. She made sure that her husband ate on time and that I ate food that one could only have at Mother's house; she didn't let Louise overstretch herself, who had so much to do with her cows and her own household. At the same time, she adapted herself to all the difficulties that came up due to exhaustion.

In Moldova, there is no social assistance, which is why everyone is forced to stay at home and die alone without any help if they don't have children or if their children don't want to hear from their parents. The health system is overstretched, and going to a hospital produces no results without bribery.

The differences between my father and my mother:

I was on vacation to help my mother, but actually I was taking care of my father. I didn't have much to do for Mom. She was lying down in bed for most of the time. She was eating alone, and she was doing her best to go to the toilet without help. So I had little time to take advantage of being with her, of those moments she was awake or could sit.

But as far as my father was concerned, I had to cook for him three times a day—*different* foods. I had to put the food on the table for him four times a day: in the morning at 07:00 a.m. he needed two or three courses of food; at noon he wanted two to three courses of food, and in the evening at 07 :00 sharp, he'd have the other two have three dishes. And at 05:00 sharp after the meal, I had to bring fruits, candies, and biscuits and put them on the table.

Just cooking the meals and setting the table took me more than half a day. My father was not only eclectic about his food, but he was very careless. When he ate, he would leave a lot of crumbs on the floor, and I had to sweep and mop each time he got up from the table. When he started the fire in the stove, the house would get full of trash and ashes; he'd enter the hallway with his shoes on and bring dirt from outside. In other words, wherever he passed by, I had to go after him with a broom and sweep it up, the floor was so dirty.

He was stubborn and acted like a fickle boy bouncing on a whim.

My father's behavior and demands made me understand the torments my mother had suffered her entire life, and how she had to adapt herself and serve him and satisfy his whims. Basically, my mother was a slave to my father, a servant who never had the right to express herself freely. She had to cook all kinds of food for him every day and clean up after him, and she had the whole household on her shoulders. She was busy inside the house but also outside, tending to their self-sustaining resources: their cow with a calf, their two pigs, their sheep, their chickens and ducks, and their horse.

It was then that I realized the effort she was making for us each time we went to her on vacation. When we woke up in the morning, all the most delicious dishes were already prepared on the table, cooked just like at mother's home. And suddenly I understood how strong my mother was. Only a very strong person could withstand so much physical work and the terrible psychological terror.

When they found out that she was seriously ill, her workmates and friends called her and said to her, "How could such a strong woman lose so much weight?"

I was talking to my sister Louise. "Look, Louise, Mom is like a small, obedient child eager to learn something and adapt to new situations and advance spiritually. Even though she lost her strength, she tries not to bother us, either me or you, and she wants to be independent regardless of her over-exhaustion. Even now before death, when she doesn't have any strength left, she can't abandon her instinct to take care of everyone, and she continues to take care of me, of you, and even of dad.

"She takes care of me so that I eat food like at mother's home; she takes care of you so that you spare yourself efforts, and she takes care of our father, to make sure that after she is gone, we will not abandon him but will continue to care for him as she did all her life."

My mother had no formal education, and she didn't have a mother to teach her. For her, life was her school, and the world around her was a source of counsel and guidance. She listened to everyone in her proximity.

She listened to the strangers who gave her advice about cooking or about various treatment recipes for certain illnesses.

She listened to her children and grandchildren. For instance, if Lya told her that she should exercise every day to heal her back, she would do it without complaining, exactly as Lya said. In addition to that, she was proud when she could do something, and she told all the women in the village what and how to do it. When her brother complained that he had to massage his feet every morning, she told him that she had already been doing massages for fifteen years without lamenting.

She knew how to adapt herself to all situations. She believed that she was never tired and didn't look for reasons to skip the things that she had to do. If something had to be done, she did it, however tired she was or how much effort she had to make.

Cooking for her children and grandchildren was never a problem for her. For example, when we came home, even if she had worked to the point of exhaustion around the house, she would find the time to do what *needed* to be done and *not* what she would have liked to do.

Practically, my mother was an ideal model we all should follow for the sake of our spiritual evolution and ascent: to succeed in life, we don't have to do what *we want* to do but what we *need to do*. By following this rule, we follow all the laws of the Universe, including the Boomerang, which says that everything we do for the surrounding world, we do it for us. By listening to situations and the world around us, we listen to our soul and to

God's advice. We listen to the Universe, which is at every crossroad of our life and shows us which way to go.

By working for all of us all her life and listening to what everyone said, my mother followed the most essential laws of the Universe. She heeded the advice of the Universe and lived in perfect harmony with the whole Universe, adapting herself to all the situations, to all the positive and negative energies. Even if she was mistreated by her husband, she would still find the ability to live in harmony with the aggressive, negative material world. My mother didn't fight back at my father's aggressiveness and his negative energies. On the contrary, she sought the key to a life in harmony with him, and she found the way to calm him down and be appreciated.

This fluidity of positive and negative energies that my mother created together with the Universe gave birth to a harmonious future for this world. As for her future, she created a beautiful end of her life. In the last ten years of her life, my mother felt as happy as ever. It was thanks to the achievements of her children and grandchildren, and to all the amenities we installed in her house, such as the water system, the sewage, the toilet, the shower cabin, and the automatic washing machine, which she had never dreamed of.

I told her numerous times that we didn't create these amenities but that it was God who made them for her to reward her for her unabated work and her torments and sufferings, for the love she dedicated to her family, friends, and workmates.

Look what a beautiful end of life my mother has, I said inwardly. *Although she's dying and has no strength left, she isn't suffering or in pain. She's exhausted and sleeps a lot, and that's it. But because the end of her life is approaching, she has the opportunity to say goodbye to everyone.* I managed to come home to spend the most painful, yet the most beautiful, vacation with my dear and beloved mother. All the grandchildren were with her, and we all had the chance to talk about everything, to reminisce about our whole life and make a summary of all the events experienced together in this life.

Practically, my mother's work and torments and affection, and the fact that she was the most diligent and humble person, helped her achieve the greatest successes in her life and the biggest reward from God. Thank you, God, for taking care of my mother!

But my father is the opposite. He didn't listen to us, and he's still not listening to anyone. All his life he was self-obsessed and self-seeking, only for his pleasures and appetites, and so indifferent to the world around. He blocked all the energies of the Universe, whether positive or negative, and he continued to live in the empty shell of his thoughts, principles, and pleasures without considering the people around him. My mother was the one who listened to God and the advice of the Universe, while my father was as stubborn as a mule and refused to heed to Him.

Our whole civilization is guided by the same principles as my father's, namely that we know everything, we calculate everything, we know damn well what we want from life, and we don't care about anyone or anything; we continue our life from the bondage of our materialistic thoughts." I would have liked the new generation to start thinking spiritually, like my mother did. Unfortunately, the new generation is worse than all the previous generations. While erstwhile people showed you respect and did what had to be done, the new generation considers itself so clever and, alas, so knowledgeable of their purpose in life that they became worse than my father. They don't want to do absolutely anything of what they have to do. They all do what *they want* to do.

The gratifying part is that even if Dad doesn't want to listen to the situations, to anyone at all, especially to God, the Lord makes us all come back to earth. He manages to make us all do what we have to do and not what *we* want to do. Look how God made our father aware of the wrong way he was acting, and realize that he must respect his wife and help support her. Look how he takes care of my mother now. If he had done at least a tenth of what he's doing now for her in his life, Mom would not have suffered as much.

I hope the same thing happens to our civilization, and I hope that one day, God will convince all the Earthlings that they must adopt my mother's behavior, not my father's. I hope that the world won't be as stubborn as my father to let our civilization end its life. I hope it will realize and embrace the importance of the spiritual evolution. I hope that God won't be forced to do to our civilization what He did to my cousin's wife, who fell down the stairs and broke her femur bone.

If we consider it from another point of view and analyze my father's presence in our family, I'd like to tell you that his tyranny was not in vain. My mother wouldn't have gotten so attache to us, and she wouldn't have managed to create such a strong bond and harmony between her children and grandchildren. We also wouldn't have known what to avoid in life.

Basically, if it hadn't been for my father and the way he was, none of us would have managed to get where we are. I wouldn't have managed to find God's way to write books about Him, and Louise wouldn't have reached the spiritual level you have reached either. (My sister developed the ability to heal people of various diseases by means of prayers). "

Another subject I discussed with my sister Louise was that none of us had premonitions regarding our mother's death. We both had the ability to sense the future, to sense what was happening to those close to us, and it was strange that we didn't feel anything about our mother's suffering and her approaching death. Our mother was dying, and we had no premonition of her imminent death, as if it could never happen.

On the one hand, we were surprised by our lack of presentiment, and on the other hand, we were perfectly aware of everything that happened before Mom passed away:

My mother was not in pain; she was just weak, and that was it.

Her children and grandchildren, and her friends, had the opportunity to stay by her and feel those moments of separation. In other words, everything was going perfectly; the only thing that was missing were our premonitions.

My separation from my mother and my return to Canada:

During my four-week vacation, I stayed with my mother without going anywhere else. Even though I stayed at home and wasn't in contact with anyone, I got sick with COVID. My brother-in-law had been to the market, where he got the virus. My sister became infected, and from her, it infected myself, then my mother and my father too.

We all had a mild form of COVID. My sister lost her sense of smell. I had diarrhea and fever, and my mother, father and brother-in-law had just a mild form of disease. We weren't officially diagnosed, because in Moldova there is no functioning health system or country management, but all the symptoms spoke for themselves.

Because of the fever, I was afraid that I couldn't get back to Canada. My body temperature was one degree above the normal limit, and it was persistent and didn't go down. At the airport, everyone was screened and tested, and no one could board the plane if they had fever. I was hoping that my body temperature would go down in two weeks, but the COVID-19 does not give up so easily; it lasts interminably long.

Leaving my mother was the most painful part of my visit, but in spite of the pain, our hearts were at peace, because we had spent the most beautiful vacation in our lives. During the month we were together, we bid adieu to one another every moment.

On the day of our separation, my sister's husband gave me a ride to a friend of mine in the nearest city, who had offered to take me to the airport. I was leaving at 3:00 p.m., and I told my sister's husband not to come before that time, because I wanted to be with my mother as much as possible.

Before my ride arrived at 2:00 p.m., I had finished packing up my stuff, and I lay down next to my dear and beloved mother. We didn't talk much. We just sat there in silence, not uttering anything, and then I was going to leave her with sadness in my heart.

My mother was caressing my back, as she had done all her life. She was caressing me and I was sitting immobile, with excruciating pain inside me, trying not to let my tears overcome me.

At one point I said to her, "Mom, we have said absolutely everything we had to say. Now we have nothing left to talk about. For the last ten years, we've talked every day. We've talked for hours on end, in which we gave our deepest love to each other. Now we don't have to worry about not talking anymore, because we said absolutely everything we had to say to each other in a lifetime."

185

At 02:55 p.m., my sister and her husband arrived. My mother was sitting on a sofa. Her eyes were in sorrow, following my moves, and they were sipping in the moments that were to be our last ones together.

I was dressed and ready to go, and my mother said to me, "Ionel, please forgive me."

I kneeled before her and could feel how weak and sad she was. I started to kiss her whole face, her hands, and I said to her, "May God forgive you, Mother, my dear and beloved one, please forgive me too."

After saying that, I stood up to leave. My mother asked me, "Should I walk you out?"

Knowing that she couldn't walk, I said to her, "No, Mother, you don't have to," and I stepped out and looked back at her, just to impress her image in my brain for the last time in this life. She managed to stand up and get to the door, and I continued to walk away, looking back at her.

I was leaving her and I knew that we were separating forever. I was aware that I was separating from her, but I was also separating myself from my parental home, from my parental nest where I had always found the most precious person of my life: my *mother* who loved me like no one else on this earth, and caressed me and cuddled me like a baby. I was leaving my home and the most beautiful part of my life, but my happiness of a lifetime and my feeling about my dear, beloved mother remained alive.

The date of my return to Canada, as you know, was December 13, and as I had predicted, I was going back sick with COVID. With God's help, I managed to get on the plane without being detected with fever. In Moldova, the person responsible for checking the temperature had gone to the washroom exactly when I boarded the plane. And in Turkey, the one responsible for checking my temperature did it quickly, without noticing that he was checking the wrong part of my hand.

Immediately after I boarded my plane to Montreal, my body temperature went down to normal and my diarrhea stopped. I arrived in Canada without any COVID symptoms or problems at the border.

Spiritual Psychoanalysis of Number 13 on December 13, 2020

December 13 was the day of two important meanings and major changes in my life. First of all, on that day, I left my parental home forever while my parents were still alive. That day was my final separation from my native fields, where my mother was lovingly waiting for me.

Secondly, that day was the day I definitively recovered from COVID-19 and acquired immunity against this aggressively harmful infection.

In other words, December 13, 2020, was for me the day that separated me from the beautiful past with dear mother ushering in a new era—the era of combatting all the difficulties of the world. That day was a day of extreme challenges, and it honed and hardened me.

The period before my mother's death:

After I arrived in Canada, even if I didn't have any COVID symptoms, lest I infect my family, I isolated myself in the basement for a week. Both girls and their boyfriends were there, spending their holidays at home. They would drop food for me down the stairs.

In Moldova, my sister Louise remained in charge of our parents and their house. She was called me on Skype every day, and I talked to my mother when she felt up to it.

A week later, my mother had a stroke and lost her ability to speak. She had no energy left and couldn't stand up and walk unescorted. My sister stayed with her day and night and followed her every movement. She was afraid that our mother would die and not have a candle lit nearby.

In the Christian Orthodox religion, it's said that when someone is about to die, someone else must light a candle for the moribund. They say that the light of the candle will help the dying person see the Divine Light and go up to God easily. Another aspect of the moment of death is that it's better to have a stranger watching the dying person. It shouldn't be a close relative like children, mother, father, husband, or wife. It's assumed that the person who dies can't easily separate from the material world when close relatives are next to them. So when someone dies, a stranger must be there to keep their candle burning.

I was with my sister on Skype and said to her, "Louise, please don't worry about our mother's death. You should sleep peacefully at night because everything will be fine. God takes care of everything. I have talked to you several times, and you know very well that God is with us at every crossroads in our lives. Why would you think that now when our mother reached the most important crossroad in her life, between the material and the spiritual life, God would forsake her and abandon her? Won't He do everything possible to help her depart in harmony and love? Won't He organize a smooth and beautiful transition from this world to the next, just as Mom deserves?"

I knew that Louise could understand what I was telling her, yet she was scared and she was staying up all night long.

Even though my mother couldn't speak, every time Louise called me and Mom could sit and listen to me, I continued to tell her about the beautiful life we had spent together, and the relatives that were waiting for her in the World of God, and we praised her and all her efforts and all her love for her children, grandchildren, and the world around.

The last time I spoke with my mother via Skype was on January 12. To my surprise, she was sitting and she listened to me for almost two hours. Seeing that she could be there for that long, I finished my speech about the love she created for our family, and I showed her our house in Canada. I showed her the carpet she had woven with her own hands, which was now in the most important place in the house. And then I showed her every room so that she could see again the beauty and the comfort in which we lived. I showed her the broad view from our house, the mountain coast on the shore of the Atlantic Ocean and all.

After I spoke with her and showed her everything that could be shown, Sara and Lya and their boyfriends came near me, and so did my wife, and we all stayed together, our whole family remained united with my mother like she always wanted. We sat there and told stories, each one individually unique.

We hadn't sat like that before, and over the past few months when Mother was sick, we had never sat so long with her in front of the computer, because she was getting tired very quickly. This was the first and the last time we talked with my mother, all together, for so long.

After speaking with us, Louise gave our mother a morphine injection so that she wouldn't feel the pain during the night. Our mother never woke up.

The next day, on December 13, Greta came to the village. She was a cousin of mine and a very good friend of the family too. And above all, she was my mother's best friend. She had come from Germany to see her mother only for one day. Louise asked Greta to stay with our mom, because she had to milk the cows.

When Louise went to see her at around 05:00 in the evening, my mother was conscious but she couldn't get up and or speak.

Louise said to her, "Mother, I'm going to milk the cows and I'll be back. Look, Greta has come and is going to stay with you."

My mother had never cried in her life, but at that moment, big tears were running down her cheeks. It was the last time she reacted to the world around her.

Louise came back inside at around 06:00. Greta was with her, holding a burning candle in her hands, until she went to God at 06:05 in the evening.

Immediately after my mother left her body, Greta called me on Facebook and showed me my mother, who had just died.

Thanks to Greta, I managed to see my mother immediately after she left us. In the evening after they washed her, dressed her, and prepared her for the funeral, Greta called me again and showed me my mom one more time, already dressed up and ready for the burial. She also sent me some pictures of my mother as she was making ready to leave the earth.

She was buried two days later.

All this time, I stood next to the picture of her lying in the coffin. I was crying for her from all my heart soul. I was crying loudly because it was the time of separation, and I had to free myself from my emotional anguish.

When she was lowered into the grave, I said goodbye to her and then deleted the picture from my computer, the one of her dead. I said to her, "Mom, now it's time for you to start a new life. All your loved ones are waiting for you up there, together with God. I have to start another life too. So far you have been the parental nest of our family. Now it is my duty to build a united family with my children and grandchildren, exactly as you did with us. Just wait for me, because I will soon come to join you; just wait for me at the gate."

These were my last words to her. I took my head in my hands, determined not to think of my loss anymore and to ignore the thoughts about her and ward off my impending depression. I did that because I didn't want my mother to remain attached to me in this world. I wanted her to break free from it and go to God, relieved of all burdens. If she had seen me sad all the time, she would have been late for the Kingdom of Heaven, and I didn't want her to be late because of me. She had suffered enough in this life, and now she deserved all the good in the world.

After the funeral, I said to my sister, "Louise, do you see how God took care of our mother so that she died in the most beautiful harmony? Do you see how God brought Greta, my mother's dearest friend, all the way from Germany? She brought her to our village just for one day, to stay with mom in the last moments of her life and to hold her hand and hold a burning candle for her. I told you that you don't have to worry about her. God was more careful than anyone else to organize a party for her. Mom was the only person I know who fully deserved such a party. Have you known anyone else who, on the day of her death, was visited by her best friend who came all the way from Germany to witness her departure? No one. Only Mom had such a privilege, a privilege from God for all her efforts that she made in this life."

Attention! Important! The process of the death of our body is a very important process in the stages of spiritual evolution. During this period, we manage to become aware of some nuances of life that we can't be aware of in any other state of our existence. So we must not try to change this period, neither with drugs to prolong the death process nor with drugs to interrupt this process. The only thing we can do for these people is to use drugs to reduce suffering/pain.

My confusion on the day my mother died:

The first situation that left me confused was the day on which my mother died. I had never thought that the one who suffered so much in her life would leave us on a 13. That number has always been a number of negative events for me, as it spells confrontation with evil. Knowing what my mother went through and how she managed to build a relationship of love and harmony in her surroundings and in our family, I had always believed that the moment of her departure from this life would be on a special day. Usually important people leave the living world on their birthday or on a major holiday. I was certain that the same thing would happen to her.

Surprisingly, everything related to my mother's death, like the number 13, was involved in everything:

I had booked the plane ticket back to Canada on December 13.

The day Mother died was again 13, January 13.

We cooked via Skype for the last time in our lives on November 13.

I was trying to find the answer to the question. I realized that not only my mother had to do with number 13, but I myself was also involved, because November 13 and December 13 were important days to me. But I couldn't find any answer. I only understood that January 13, the day my mother died, was a very important holiday in the Eastern European countries. On this day, according to Christian Orthodox tradition, the New Year was celebrated by the Julian calendar. For my parents, November 13 had been a very important holiday since their childhood.

The thought that my mother died on a day of celebration for my parents, and that she would arrive safely in the Kingdom of Heaven, gave me a big relief.

The second situation that left me confused was my mother's coffin. My sister sent me a picture of the coffin she had bought for our mother. It was a beautiful coffin, bedecked with an English Green silk cloth. What struck me was its color. My mother's favorite color was cherry red. I was surprised that my sister bought my mother something that was not her favorite, the English *green*.

In recent years, I had noticed that I really liked the green color. I used to buy green clothes; half a year ago, I had covered the house in English green shingles. Exactly a few days before I found out about my mother's illness, in early November, I had planned to buy a new car and a particular English green watch to give me a sense of accomplishment in this life. For me, the English green watch and the car would have marked the top of my material achievements in my present life.

From the point of view of a Spiritual Psychoanalysis, my mother's coffin was like a car traveling from the material world to the spiritual one. So such a coincidence confused me. *What is going on? If my mother's coffin is the color of the car I'd like to buy, does it mean that I don't need to buy the car I've dreamed of all my life? Does it mean that I don't need to satisfy my last material desires in this life?* As I was thinking about the color of the coffin, I was afraid that I couldn't buy the English green car.

See my Spiritual Psychoanalysis at the end of this chapter.

My dreams about Mom:

Before my mother died, I was sure that I would see her last moments approaching in the distance, and then, in her afterlife, I would develop a tight relationship with her that would help me connect with the spiritual world much better.

To my surprise, I felt absolutely nothing before she left us. Practically, I felt nothing before or after her death, not even in the moment she died. I was shocked that until her death, I had been closer to strangers than to my mother. I couldn't believe that God deprived me of the ability to foresee the future, specifically now when Mom, the most precious person in my life, went to meet Him.

I had dreamed of my mother before she died and on the day of her death and after her death too, but there was nothing of what I had expected in my dreams. But for three days, I dreamt only of the following: It came to pass that Mom was young and beautiful, with velvet-like skin, and her soul came down to me, afraid that it couldn't speak.

The day before my mother died, on January 12, when we spoke to her for the last time, I told her, "Mother, I dreamed of you three nights in a row, and you were coming to me. You were young and beautiful, but you didn't say anything to us. Don't be afraid to give utterance when you come back to us in your dreams, because you can speak, your soul can speak. Your body can't speak now, but your soul can. So next time you come back to us, please speak up. Tell us how you live out there, as we will be waiting for you with our greatest love."

Right on the day she died, I dreamed of her again, and she was young and beautiful. I dreamed that her soul came to me and spoke to me like in the times she could speak; more than that, she spoke to me passionately and with love, as if she had been waited for the moment to explode with happiness, and now she kept talking so eagerly. She was talking because she had regained the ability to talk, and she went on without pause because she was talking specifically to me, her precious son. She told me about all the details and the events that happened to her in the last days, and about her last day of her life. She told me in full detail, starting from early morning until dusk before she died. And she concluded: "I am glad that I had a clear conscience before my death, because up here, it's very important to arrive with a clear mind. I knew everything that happened to me until the last moment—after Louise went to milk the cows and passed by our neighbor's place, and then I went away."

That was my last dream in which she made a real appearance, with her young, beautiful soul. I dreamed of her and I heard her very clearly as if in reality. Since then, I haven't had any contact of this kind. I haven't had a single dream about her, like I saw all my deceased friends and relatives. The only way she appeared to me was like a ghost, a paranormal entity you see in paranormal shows. Between sleep and wakefulness, she made her appearance in the form of the energy of her corpse, silhouetted as a ghost manifesting itself as her own voice before her death. I sensed her presence around me, floating like vapoured paranormal ghosts or entities going after a human being.

The most shocking connection with my mother happened immediately after her funeral. In the evening, I turned off the lights and lay in bed, and I felt that someone was sitting on my back, just like you see in paranormal movies, like a paranormal entity trying to get in touch with a human being. That was how I felt that my mother was pressing on my back. Even though I knew it was my mother's energy, the energy of her body, I was worried and shaking with fear.

Imagine lying in bed at night and a paranormal entity begins pressing on your back. How would you feel? That's exactly how I felt, and I didn't know what to do anymore. I was afraid to sleep face down, and I was sleeping on one side so that the energy of Mother's body couldn't press on my back.

I was fearful for two days, and I said to my mother, "Mom, kindly please stop coming to me like that. Don't press on my back, and don't touch me anymore, because you scare me. If you want to come to me, come in a dream so that I can see and hear you, as you came before your death and on the day that you left us." After that, my mother stopped bothering me in a physical form. In the scheme of things, she continued to manifest her presence near me in the period between sleep and wakefulness in the form of a ghost.

I was so scared by her ghosty presence that I couldn't sleep with the lights off. For that reason, every evening I lit a big candle that would last until morning. At the same time, I hoped that the burning candle would help my mother see the Divine Light and she could ascend to the Kingdom of Heaven.

A few days after she died, she started to appear in my dreams. But the dreams were as bizarre as her physical, energetic presence I just described. She didn't appear with her soul as before her death or when she passed away; she showed herself as a ghost or as some energy of her corpse.

In one of my dreams, I was at home and went to the summer kitchen, where she was sitting with her back to me. I was happy to see her and said, "Mom."

She was happy to see me too, but when she turned to me, she looked like a corpse, as if her old body was drained and she was just an exhausted, dried out cadaver with two hollows instead eyes. Just like a ghost you see in paranormal descriptions.

I saw her come towards me just the way she was, and I got angry and shouted loudly, "Don't come to me in your body! Come to me in your Soul! Do you understand?"

She looked saddened, and with a sunken heart, she said that I was right. And then she went away.

I woke up and I realized that even if she had come to me in her body, she was still my mother, and she loved me and missed me. In her appearance, even if she was shaped like a ghost, nothing was alien to me, and absolutely everything represented my mother and her love for me and her joyfulness to see me, her happiness about me, her precious son. She was my mother of her own genuine kind and with everything I knew about her.

I woke up and couldn't believe that I had offended my dear, beloved mother the way I had, and I started to beg forgiveness for my action: "Forgive me, Mother, for saying those words to you. Please forgive me for upsetting you. I didn't know what I was saying. I didn't want to upset you more. Please forgive me and come to me as soon as you can. If you can only come in your soulless body, please come, because I am waiting for you with the most sincere love."

Even though it took courage and I was happy to see her as a ghost, in the form of her corpse energy, I was still confused. Why did she come to me only with the energy of her body/corpse? Why couldn't she come in her soul? I was afraid that she got lost on her way between these two worlds and didn't know how to get to God in the Kingdom of Heaven. That fear made me pray to the Lord to take care of her and help her reach the Kingdom of Heaven safely, because she was the only person I know on this earth who truly deserves to meet the Almighty.

The next dream surprised me just as much as the first. A few days after my mother's death, I dreamed of her, but I didn't see her as a real person. I only felt her presence next to me and, for a reason unaccounted for, I said in anger, "Why are you still so stupid?" (in the sense that her memory was failing her more than before her death).

I woke up all sweaty with fear and shame for what I'd said to her. I was surprised that I had dared to say such ugly words. I had never had the audacity to think in such terms about her when she was alive. Although in her last years her memory was slowing down, I looked at her with love and understanding for what was happening to her during the aging of her body. I had and I continue to have the greatest respect and love a son can have for his mother. I always spoke to her with the greatest affection and sincerity. But in this situation, I didn't understand why I dared to speak to her the way I did.

Later on, analyzing this situation, I realized that those expressions coming out of my mouth had been delivered by the arrogance of the energy of my body, of the wife of my soul. My soul would not conceive such sinful expressions, and only the energy of my body would do it.

To confirm the above, in another dream, the very next day after the incident described above, my mother came to me and said, "Ionel, here in this world you're at a much higher level than me. People at your level don't even look at the people at my level."

My mother's words made me fall into thought. I was surprised that in the spiritual world, in the Kingdom of God, the arrogance of people from the higher levels to those from lower levels is so evident. For me this was an insoluble dilemma, because the people who had a near-death experience argued that in the Kingdom of God, absolutely all are equal, and even a drop of water is as important as the soul of a man. I didn't understand why my mother was telling me that people at my level don't look at anyone like her.

In the next dream, I dreamed that I was on a high terrace with people of my level, while my parents were standing on a platform lower than our terrace. And there was no connection between these two levels. This dream represented exactly what Mother said: people of my level did not look at those of lower levels.

Months passed by and I continued to see my mother only as a ghost, only the energy of her body without her soul. I continued to worry about her, that she was lost somewhere in the transcendent places and couldn't reach the Divine Kingdom of Heaven. I knew that she left this life with difficulty, that she wanted to stay among us to enjoy being with her children and grandchildren. All this made me think, *Maybe this is why she's not in Heaven yet and she lost her desire to enjoy our presence.* I was afraid that my mother was stuck between the two worlds, and I continued to pray to God to help her find the way to the Kingdom of Heaven.

I truly believed that God had abandoned me. I was haunted by the ghost of my mother, and everything around me was beyond my comprehension. Why did I not feel anything about my mother's sufferings before her death? Why did I not feel anything when she died? And now that months have passed, why did I not have any real contact with her, with her *soul*?

These blocked connections with my mother's soul made me feel that God had forsaken me and didn't want to talk to me anymore. That was abnormal. I had been able to have contact with those who died, to predict the unpleasantness of my friends and relatives, and now I was completely blocked, unable to feel absolutely anything about my mother's sufferings, about the paths she was walking down in the most crucial moments of her life in the period of transition from the material world to the spiritual world.

After a few months, I realized that an identical situation had happened to me almost twenty-five years ago. I was in Moldova at that time and we were experiencing absolute destitution, the worst ever. Right then, in the most difficult times for my family, I lost the ability of my sixth sense.

The sixth sense always gave me an edge, because I could predict all future events and know exactly how to proceed. But then when I needed it the most to predict the upcoming predicaments and know how to get out of dire poverty, right then, God stripped me of the most important gift of my life. I felt abandoned and didn't know what was going on.

Only a few years later, after repeatedly sustaining the biggest losses one could, and after I lost twice the amount of money for a house, I realized that I had not been forsaken. I had the impression that God had turned His back on me, but in reality, during the hardest period of my life, He had been the closest to me. He wanted me to see Him in a different form than how I saw Him with my sixth sense. God used my difficulties to teach me how I should see Him through direct communication, which is more practical, more concrete, and more real. God was there at every crossroads of my life trying to show me the way I should go (see details in my first book, *The Destiny and Signs of God*).

Understanding the new way of communicating with Him—a direct communication without interpreters and brokers—it became much easier to find my true destiny for the rest of my life, to find not only my destiny but also the answer to the essential secrets of the existence of the human being on this earth.

Because I hadn't experienced a relationship with God before and I thought that He had abandoned me, now I knew exactly what we should expect when God confiscates our spiritual abilities. I knew exactly that this is a technique He uses to teach us another way of communicating with Him.

So now God had deprived me of my skills to anticipate the sufferings of my mother, the most important person in my life. He stripped me of my powers to anticipate the moment of her death and left me without any connection with her. But now I knew *for sure* that He was trying to teach me a way of communicating with the spiritual world that is different from the one I knew.

I was happy, and with my mind I was searching for clues that could suggest a new form of communication or connection with the spiritual world.

ADDITIONAL SUBJECTS THAT CONTRIBUTED TO MY CONCLUSION ABOUT THE NUMBER 21

My Illnesses That Have Not Been Proven to Be Related to the Number 21

After my mother's death, I went to see a doctor. I took all the necessary tests and at the end of the day, it turned out that I had various minor pathologies, which "by chance" appeared in the same period:

a) lymph nodes and left shoulder blade pain turned out to be a partial ligament tear, which involved the lymph nodes and had healed over several months;

b) rectal hemorrhages proved to be a rupture of a varicose vein from the sigmoid part of the large intestine, which healed by itself; and

c) the pain in the sexual organs turned out to be a urinary infection, which was easily treated with a course of antibiotics.

Spiritual Psychoanalysis of My Illness

First analysis: When all the symptoms began, I was sure that they were a manifestation of cancer, and I accused God of pressing me to give up the life insurance. He knew that I was sick with cancer and dying, yet He influenced me to give up the life insurance that would have brought a substantial contribution to my family. I didn't understand why He did something like this.

When I gave up the insurance, I saw the situation God had created for me, which suggested to me to give up the insurance. I relied on His guidance because I had full confidence in Him.

In the end, it turned out that God was right. I had wrongly accused Him. God is always right. We just have to listen to Him with full confidence, without second guessing His choices, because whatever He suggests is always the optimal way for us and our spiritual evolution. In this case, I didn't need to pay tons of money to the insurance companies for nothing for years on end. I just had to trust God.

Second analysis: At the same time as the symptoms of the disease appeared, I acquired a new ability—the ability to see the Divine Light, which streamed towards me through the darkness of the material world in which we were living (See Fig. 9).

After a short period of time, I started to see the tunnel of the Divine Light, and a black energy appeared (See Fig. 10), which dissipated my Divine Light and left me helpless. The negative energy was so strong that I remained frozen with fear in the dark.

Initially, I thought it was the energy of the cancer that I suspected in my body. In the end, it turned out that the extremely strong negative energy was my mother's cancer, which precipitated her death. After my mother died, the negative energy vanished and never came back to me in front of the ray of the divine light.

Third analysis:

Nothing is accidental in the Universe. Everything is created according to well-conceived principles and in an absolute order. This is also what the mechanism of the appearance of destructive negative energies is about.

Consider the situations related to the death of my mother and those caused by the COVID-19 pandemic. Even if they manifest themselves in different ways, they are still similar in their appearance and stages of development. So the mechanism of the appearance of the destructive negative energies in the Universe is identical regardless of the extent of its appearance:

In the case of the COVID-19 pandemic, the Universe sent a lot of negative energies to the earth, some of which were the energies that directly involved me too (see the first part of my book). After that, the most destructive energy, the COVID-19 pandemic, arrived.

In the case of my mother's death, the events unfolded in the same order. First, the Universe sent me a lot of negative energies manifested in the form of various diseases, followed by the destructive energy that caused my mother's death.

Conclusion: The number 21 could not be related to my illness or my death. But which one was it?

My Book Was Delayed. Could This Be One of the Clues Related to the Number 21?

From March 2020, when the COVID-19 pandemic began, until mid-summer, I wrote about the topics in the book you're reading now. I wanted to finish the book as soon as possible, because I was convinced that God wanted His message about the COVID-19 pandemic to reach the reader as soon as possible.

I finished writing and sent the manuscript to the English translator so that he could translate it as quickly as possible. It wasn't a voluminous book, and I was sure that the translator would finish translating it in record time. I had hopes high that by the end of 2020, the translated manuscript would reach the publisher. The English translator confirmed that by the end of September, or earlyin October 2020, the book would be translated and ready to go to the publisher.

Unfortunately, the translator had some personal problems and failed to meet the deadline, and he promised me that he would be able to translate it by the end of November or early December. At that time, I had my mother's health problems on my mind, and I wasn't interested in the book. By the way, the book wasn't finished in November or December either, and in January, the translator had lost all the translated material from the Internet and had to start the translation again.

Winter passed and it was spring, but my book still wasn't finished. But I never doubted that these delays were the will of God. I never thought that the translator was to blame, but I was trying to find the answer to the question: Why did God make the translator delay the translation of the book for so long? What is He sending me in this message? What should I do? What should I draw attention to?"

OTHER QUESTIONS FOR MY SPIRITUAL PSYCHOANALYSIS

My mother passed away on January 13, and a period of confusion began. Why did God take away my ability to presage my mother's pain? Why didn't God let me feel the moment of her death? Why did she die and I could only see the energy of her body and not her soul?

All these questions were accompanied by the question: Why did God make my book come out so late?

It was only in May 2021 that the translator finished the book and sent it to me.

A few days later, I found the answer to all my questions, to all the situations God had made for me at that time. The answer was so simple and, at the same time, so complex. It was an answer not only to the questions about the circumstances of my mother's death, but also to all the subjects of my books not clearly explained since 2012; this little nuance that I found now confirmed not only my theories but also responded to all the spiritual philosophies, theories of religions, and the concepts of the existence of human beings created on earth.

See the answer a little later in the book.

Spiritual Psychoanalysis of the Situations Related to My Mother's Death

Before I go on with the story of my mother and answer the questions asked above, I would like to approach and analyze more profoundly the situations that took place before my mother's death. We will reveal the Spiritual Psychoanalysis of the situations step by step:

IONEL ROTARU

A) A SPIRITUAL PSYCHOANALYSIS OF LUCIAN BUTE'S GIFT:

Through the bond of the colors of Lucian Bute's vases with the colors of Mother's carpet, God wanted to say to me that, with help from Bute's vases, I highlighted all the positive features of my mother, who stands out in front of our entire civilization, where everyone can see it in her unmatched beauty. Through her way of life, through her way of being, and through her way of leaving the material world for the spiritual one, my mother will remain eternal in the memory of all those who want to follow the spiritual path of evolution.

B) THE SPIRITUAL PSYCHOANALYSIS OF THE NUMBER 13:

As you know, both my mother and I were connected to the number 13:

- November 13 was the last day of our lives when we cooked together via Skype.
- December 13 was the day when I returned to Canada.
- On January 13, my mother left the material world for the spiritual one.

First conclusion: Both of us were in the graces of the number 13, which indicates that God wanted to send me a very important message in connection with my mother's death.

The second conclusion: Considering that the number 13 relates to radical modifications of conflicts and negative energies, it means that the message God wanted to send me was about an intention for a radical change, one that would upset everyone due to the negative energies.

You will find answer to the question "What is this message?" in the next section.

The third conclusion: Immediately after my mother died, every time I thought of her, talked about her, or was in contact with any object or situation related to her, the number 13 showed up:

- sometimes it was 01:30; 10:30
- or 11:30; 11:31; 11:33

202

- or 13:13; 13:00; 13:10

- or 13:31

These numbers appeared more than once a month; they appeared every day when I talked with my sister about Mother, or at night when I was in bed, with my mother on my mind, or during the night when I was hearing my mother's presence next to me.

Based on these situations, I concluded that the number 13 belongs not only to the major changes in our life, but it is the number of my mother, and at the same time, it is the number of the Mother Matter, of the matter of the Universe. Even if it's the number of the negative energies, it's the number of changes, which my mother uses to urge us to change ourselves in order to progress into the spiritual world.

MY MOTHER'S IMPORTANCE TO THE FUTURE OF OUR CIVILIZATION

The time has come for me to reveal the last and most important message God sent to our entire civilization through my mother.

As I said, God didn't accidentally strip me of my ability to predict the future. When you know that you can dream about or anticipate danger or an event in the future of the people around you, and suddenly you realize that God has taken this gift away from you, when your most precious, dearest, and loved person, your mother, is in pain, you will understand that God wants to send you the most important message He has ever sent.

What is that message?

To find the answer to this question, I needed not only to be stripped of my abilities but also to be haunted by the energy of my mother's corpse for a few good months.

One day in May, shortly after I received my translated book, I woke up, and as if my mind had been clearer than ever before, I understood what God wanted to tell me through my mother.

My mind was illuminated, and I had a revelation like in the fall of 2005, when I had a full and perfect image about the construction of the world.

The difference between these two revelations was that back in 2005, I knew nothing about the construction of the spiritual world, and I had to bring into my consciousness all the information about the construction of the Universe. But now I knew the construction of the spiritual world inside out, and I needed only one simple detail: I needed to become aware of the existence of the last piece of a puzzle that would unite and put in one place all the principles and concepts I knew about the construction of the spiritual world, and that would clarify all the details and subtleties of the subjects that were still vague and unclear at that time.

Spiritual Psychoanalysis

From the point of view of Spiritual Psychoanalysis, when we want to find the answer to the messages coming from God, we must not complicate our minds with different hypotheses and philosophies. We must only look at the essential hidden meaning behind the situation.

In the case of my mother's death, the first thing that struck me was that God stripped me of my ability to anticipate my mom's sufferings; however, God wanted me to discover a considerably more important message.

So the second question is: What other situations struck me in the case of my mother's death? To answer this question, let's see how the circumstances of my mother's death developed.

Before her death, all the events developed smoothly. She passed away easily without suffering or pain, and she said goodbye to everyone. In this case, I had nothing to reproach, because God had made all the preparations for her to leave this life with minimum suffering and maximum effect.

The very process of my mother's departure from the material world to the spiritual one took place in the same way, in a perfect atmosphere, because *right* on the day of her death, guess who came from Germany to help—my mother's best friend, who held her hand until she breathed her last breath.

The only thing I complained about was the period after my mother's death, when she started to come back to me disguised as ghost with her corpse energy, making me afraid of falling asleep in the dark. I was so scared that, for several months, I had to keep a candle burning all night long so I can sleep.

So from a spiritual point of view, the correct question should be: Why was my mother coming to me as a ghost out of her corpse energy? Why did everyone who had died before come to me in the form of a soul, and now the most precious person to me was coming back like a ghost?

The answer is the following: For four months, my mother came to me in this form to bring me the last and most important message of God: Not only our souls are endowed with consciousness, but so are our bodies. And that consciousness continues to live after the death of our body, just as our soul continues to exist!

I couldn't believe how simple yet very important my mother's message was after her departure from the material world. This answer was *my revelation* that illuminated my brain and made me realize that behind this particular small detail was hiding the whole basis of all religious and spiritual philosophies and theories so far described on earth.

Through a simple puzzle sheet, through a simple message from my mother, there was light not only in everything I wrote in my books starting from 2012, but also above all the mistakes that all the religions and religious philosophies had committed with regard to the construction of the Universe.

To the questions: "Why is Mother's message so important to our civilization?" and "Why does her message shed light on all the theories and philosophies of the world regarding the construction of the Universe and the spiritual world?"

I will answer: The awareness that human bodies are endowed with a consciousness that, just as our soul, continues to exist after the death of our body, makes us realize that the consciousness of the matter of the Universe continues to live after the death of the Universe, exactly like God, or the Supreme Consciousness, continues to exist.

In other words, my mother's message confirms to us that both the human body and the Universe are made of two eternally-living entities. These entities are completely opposite to each other. In the case of the human body, the two entities are the consciousness of the human body and the human soul. In the case of the Universe, the two entities are the consciousness of the matter of the Universe and God, or the Supreme Consciousness of the Universe.

The soul of man and God/Supreme Consciousness are the representatives of light, love, and harmony in the Universe; and the consciousness of the human body and the consciousness of the matter of the Universe are the representatives of the World of Darkness, the world of the accumulation of negative energies, the world of upheavals and major changes.

Once again my mother's message proves that the Essential Law of the construction of the Universe is the Family Law, the law of the relationship between husband and wife, a relationship that continues to exist both here in the material world, in the living world of the material world, and after the death of the matter.

My mother's message also helps us understand that the World of Darkness is what I thought it was—something temporary between the material world and the spiritual one. During the four months when the ghost of my mother visited, she was in the World of Darkness, the consciousness of the matter of the Universe, where all the positive and negative energies created by us throughout our lives get accumulated. The negative energies created by us do not reach the Kingdom of Heaven but remain in the World of Darkness of the consciousness of the matter of the Universe.

If we take into consideration that the consciousness of my mother's body was blocked inside the World of Darkness, where all the negative energies get stashed, isn't *this* the "hell" that all religions talk about? I think it is.

And now, considering that the consciousness of my mother's body was blocked in the World of Darkness, the question is: "Who is facing the negative energies we create here on earth? Is it our soul or the consciousness of our body?"

I believe that the consciousness of our body has to face the negative energies created during life.

You will find the detailed answer to these questions in the conclusions at the end of this chapter.

When I look back at my mother's message after her death, I realize that number 21 has a completely different meaning than I thought. I realized that 2021 was not the year in which I was supposed to be successful after selling my book *The Destiny and Signs of God*, but it was the year when God finished sending me absolutely all the messages He wanted to convey to me. And now the last and most important message, which would change our vision about the construction of the whole world, had been sent.

Then I realized that back in 2008, when God started to show me the numbers 12 and 21, He knew that my mother would die on January 13, the date that would make me understand that I am aware of His last and most important message for our civilization. God knew all along that my mother would be the carrier of the most important message for our civilization. My mother knew before she was born that she is the most important messenger of our civilization. She always had an influence on me so that I could become, first of all, the direct messenger of God, and then she could send me the last and the essential of the essentials of all God's messages, of all the world's theories and philosophies related to the good Lord and the spiritual world.

When I was telling my mother about her importance in the life of our family and her role in me writing my first book, I believed in her influence on me, which made me open my soul to God. But now, after seeing the value of her message in reality, I realize how valuable and important my mother was. She was really the basis of my books and of all the theories and philosophies of the world related to God. Without her influence, I wouldn't have become a person with a soul open to God, and even more so, I would never have been truly aware of the construction of the Universe; I would never have realized the importance of our Mother Matter. or seen her the way my mother made me see her.

The message my mother received from God was a crucial message, and sooner or later, it will go around the world and change people's minds so that they can see more clearly the world in which we live. Without this message, my books would have no value; without this message we couldn't understand the mistakes of all religions and religious philosophies in the world.

Even if I insisted on introducing a new form of psychoanalysis, Spiritual Psychoanalysis, it would have no value without the last and most important message of God transmitted through mother.

As you can see, all the stars and circumstances regarding my mother's death lined up to bring knowledge to our entire humanity. It was God's last and the most important message:

- They started to line up even before Mother's birth.

- They continued to line up during and after my birth.

- They continued throughout my life and while God and my mother taught me.

To confirm the truth of my mother's message, I'd like to tell you that shortly after I became aware of God's message sent out through my mother, I began to see her in my dreams exactly as I saw her in my dreams the day she died. I began to see her in all her splendor, and I was dreaming of her together with her soul when she was young and full of life. I was dreaming of her better than all the deceased I ever dreamed of. She would come back in my dreams and speak with me exactly like in the days she was alive. She told me about her life in the spiritual world and about her acts out there.

The most important message she gave me after I became aware of God's words was that she returned to her husband, and she reunited with the soul of her body, and they remained together forever. After that, she started to tell me about the stages she had to go through up there.

Before my mother's body consciousness merged with her soul, I could hear her suffering all the time. She was suffering exactly as she had been with cancer in the last two months. But immediately after she merged with her husband/soul, she became full of life and young and beautiful, and she continued her spiritual evolution.

At the beginning, she said to me, "Here they insist that I brush my teeth and take a bath every day, instead of once a week like I used to." Hearing this, I rejoiced. Then I understood that my mother finally had arrived in the Kingdom of God, where they take care of her so that she continues her evolution.

I retorted, "You see, Mother, I told you that in the next life you would become a teacher."

After I had this dream, I called my sister and said to her, "You see, Louise, since our mother was obedient all her life and always wanted to evolve, she continues to evolve in the spiritual world as well. While here on earth, she didn't have time to brush her teeth every day or take a shower every day. Look how God makes sure that my hardworking and obedient mother evolves from a spiritual point of view and learns how to clean up.

After that dream, my mother continued to evolve. Every week, her knowledge was more and more advanced. First, she learned how to do the petty things. Here on earth, she had to do a lot of things; she had to do all the work in and around the house, because my father was disinclined to exertion. My mother was the one who took care of the food and the cleaning. She did the farming and fed the animals for self-sufficiency. Being so busy, she couldn't do it all meticulously; she didn't have time for minor details, and she considered it important at least to finish the chores before she went to bed. In one of my dreams, my mother showed me how she could remain calm and not hurry, and how to do things slowly, methodically, and perfectly.

Later on, she said to me, "I am smarter here than on earth." I realized that she continued to advance more and more, and I was very happy.

For a period of time, my mother studied to become a teacher, and in her last message regarding her evolution, I understood that she was at my level of knowledge and at Nastia's too, because she could talk to me about some medical terms, a confirmation of her advanced level of knowledge.

Of course, I have no proof for the skeptics who can't believe that what I say is true. Nevertheless, I will give you an example that sustains the truthfulness of what has been said so far. In one of my dreams, my mother told me that Dad's dog was sick. He had lice/fleas and intestinal parasites. She told me that I needed to apply some ointment on his skin and have him swallow some medication.

In Moldova, dogs are just animals chained outside to a pole to defend the house. No one pays any attention to them, and no one takes care of them the way we do in developed countries. So initially, I didn't pay much attention to what she told me, because I had never talked to the people in Moldova about Mom's dog in the yard. I never had such a topic on my mind either, and the people in Moldova weren't interested in it. But to my surprise, the day I dreamt about the dog, my sister in Moldova told me that my father's dog was sick and didn't want to eat, and she didn't know what to do. Hearing this, I was pleasantly surprised that my mother knew about the dog's suffering and had told me exactly the remedy that should be used in this case.

I then called my father and told him what Mother said about the dog. Dad listened to me, but he only gave him the treatment against lice/flea, because he didn't have pills for intestinal parasites. Seeing that the dog wasn't getting better, I insisted that Father give him pills against intestinal parasites. As a result, after antibiotic treatment, the dog recovered.

Spiritual Psychoanalysis

A) THE FIRST PSYCHOANALYSIS

It was not by chance that God left my mother in the World of Darkness exactly until the moment I became aware that the consciousness of the human body continues to exist after the death of the body, exactly as the human soul continues to exist. Then, not by chance, the consciousness of my mother's body reunited with her soul exactly after I understood God's last message.

I believe that these truths are convincing enough for us to realize that my mother was a very important person in the spiritual world who has a very important mission for our civilization—to pass on the last and most important message I had received from God.

B) THE SECOND PSYCHOANALYSIS:

The fact that the consciousness of my mother's body was blocked in the World of Darkness and did not unite with her soul until the moment I became aware of God's message made me conclude that my mother had an important mission and that she should leave him alone. As long as she didn't fulfill that mission, she would have to remain in the World of Darkness.

The same thing happens to each of us. We are all here on earth to bring messages from the spiritual world, and we each have a mission. As long as we haven't fulfilled our mission, our body consciousness, our body after the death of our body, remains stuck in the World of Darkness

Cases of the existence of body consciousness are very well known by scientists who deal with paranormal phenomena. These scientists discover not only cases like my mother's, but also situations where the consciousnesses of bodies are blocked because their bodies were killed by murderers, and they try to tell the material world what happened.

In this part of the book, I'd like to remind you of the importance of each of us here on earth. As I wrote before, we're brought here to learn to live in harmony between husband and wife, between soul and body. Our souls are brought here to bring light to the World of Darkness and make the consciousnesses of our bodies aware of the importance of spiritual evolution and the respect for the Laws of the Universe.

I would like to ask you a simple question: If a woman from the countryside, with very little education, who worked all her life in the countryside without knowing too much about the rest of the world, was the most important messenger of God for our civilization, then who are you? Who are you, the educated people, those with a lot of knowledge, who know the construction of our civilization in its entirety, who are you? Are you less important before God than mother?

Look at her for a bit.

FIG. 11 "MY MOTHER WAS BROKEN DOWN FROM TIREDNESS LONG BEFORE THE DAY'S WORK WAS OVER."

Take a look at my mother. Was she ever a simple and humble woman! Ask yourselves once again: If this woman is so important before God, if she sent such an important message to our civilization, we the wise, those with higher education and clear visions of the surrounding world, are we less important before God? Have we come here simply to satisfy our bodily pleasures and take advantage of the corruption and stupidity of our civilization?

To convince you that my mother is really the messenger of God, look at the date when the photo was taken. It is the date of "13." I want to assure you that I noticed it only after I posted this picture in the manuscript, only after I wrote the above words, only then did I notice the number 13. I was amazed and happy that no matter what I say, no matter what I write about my mother, every day she convinces me more and more of her importance for our civilization.

As you know, I was frustrated because God had deprived me of my ability to anticipate my mother's sufferings before and at the time of her death. I was frustrated because there hadn't been any sign or feeling in my heart to confirm the moment of her death.

To make up for my losses, here is what God organized for me a year after my mother passed away. According to Orthodox tradition, in Moldova, on the first anniversary of someone's death, those close to the deceased organize a wake, a remembrance party. Tables are heaped with lots of food, and relatives, friends, and neighbors are invited to celebrate. Apart from the meal, material gifts are given out. Together with the meal, the gifts are considered as presents made to the deceased so that they will have food and clothes in the afterlife.

A few days before the one-year anniversary of Mother's death, my sister organized a "commemoration" at our parents' house, and I organized a small "commemoration" with our children here in Canada. What surprised me the most was that on the night I was supposed to "commemorate" at our house, I had a dream that manifested itself in my brain more vibrantly than in reality. I dreamed of the ascension of Mother to Heaven. I felt this elevation from the depths of my bones, and I saw it exactly as it had been depicted by those who had a near-death experience.

The ascension process took place in a very strong light that illuminated the entire globe. The light was designed like in the workshop of a professional photographer, who presses the camera button and all the lights from all the sides of the room begin shining in your face without blinding you. That is exactly what happened to me and to the whole world.

The process of the emergence of light had three distinct phases. In the first phase, the light increased its intensity to maximum and lasted approximately one second. The second phase was the period when the light shone with all brightness, and the third phase was the period when the intensity of the light decreased from maximum to minimum, which again lasted approximately one second.

Remarkably, in the second phase, when the whole earth was lit up, time froze, and what should have lasted about a second lasted a few suspenseful seconds. Everyone on earth remained motionless, and my mother was being lifted up to Heaven, silhouetted as an angel.

To facilitate the descriptions, here is the image based on the dream:

FIG. 12 "THE ASCENSION OF MY MOTHER"

As shown in the picture, the upper part of the angel, where the head should normally be, was the brightest part of the light; the rays of light representing the hands had lower intensity than the upper part, and light in the leg area was of the lowest intensity.

I would like to remind you that during the entire journey of Mother's ascension to Heaven, I knew exactly what was happening. I felt the presence of my mother and the Kingdom of Heaven to where she was ascending.

Mom's departure from the material world to the Kingdom of Heaven made me rejoice that finally she had reached the place she deserved; I felt more accomplished by her departure than I could have felt in the moment of the death of her body a year ago, because this time my premonition was that I would get to a higher level than before. While in the past I could only sense the events that took place here on earth, my mother's ascension to the Kingdom of Heaven proved that I was beginning to sense not only what was happening on earth but also in the Kingdom of Heaven, in the relationship between Mother-Matter and Father-God.

Based on everything that happened to my mother after her death, I know that at the moment of her death, her soul and the consciousness of her body took two opposite directions. My mother's soul rose to the Kingdom of Heaven, towards God and on a path similar to the descriptions of people who had a near-death experience, and the consciousness of her body remained in the World of Darkness, inside the consciousness of the matter of the Universe, where all the negative and positive energies we created stay dormant.

Based on the experience and the relationship I had with Mother after the death of her body, I came to the conclusion that the consciousness of her body was separated from her soul and was stuck in the World of Darkness for two reasons: my mother's body consciousness had a very important mission, which was to convey God's message to me, and during her life, my mother created a lot of negative energies. In order for my mother's body consciousness to realize that it should not create negative energies, her body consciousness collided with all the negative energies she had generated during her life.

Once these two missions were accomplished, my mother's body consciousness was entitled to reunite with her soul. But even if the consciousness of her body had fulfilled all its necessary missions and was aware of the mistakes it had made in its life, it still wasn't enough for the consciousness of her body to be admitted to the Kingdom of Heaven and to God. To earn this right, my mother's body consciousness had to learn new things: to wash herself to be clean, to be attentive and enigmatic, to have university-level knowledge. Only by going through all these stages of evolution could she ascend to Heaven as a Holy Angel (See Fig. 12).

After the death of our body, our soul goes up to the Kingdom of Heaven, and the consciousness of our body goes down to the World of the Darkness of consciousness of the matter of the Universe. Currently, there are works of scientists for both the Kingdom of Heaven and the World of Darkness.

Research such as that on near-death experiences has been conducted for the Kingdom of Heaven, and there are children who remember their previous life in the Kingdom of Heaven. There is also Spiritual Psychoanalysis described by me. All these scientific works are based on concrete data with specific cases and evidence.

There is paranormal scientific research one can use to investigate the World of Darkness; there are clairvoyants, who again are based on concrete cases with specific data and concrete results.

The problem is that scientists do *not* want to accept spirituality as a form of science. They accept the same research on animals and birds, but they reject any such research on human beings.

Attention! Important! All the consciousnesses of our bodies after our death are locked in the World of Darkness to face the negative energies that we have created during our life. The consciousnesses of our bodies will continue to be stuck in the World of Darkness as long as we live our life according to materialistic principles and continue to create negative energies.

When we reach the spiritual level of evolution and live life according to spiritual principles and no longer create negative energies, the consciousnesses of our bodies will pass directly into the Kingdom of Heaven, together with their souls, and we will we ascend to Heaven just as Jesus Christ said (Matthew 19:21).

My mother's surprise visit:

As I told you, I organized the commemoration for my mother a few days before the one-year anniversary of her death when she ascended to Heaven together with her soul and body consciousness.

Another surprise my mother made to me on the one-year anniversary of her death was on the night of January 12. As you know, she died on January 13, and on January 12, she was with my family on Skype for almost two hours, in which we sent her all our love and affection.

Exactly a year after her death, on the night of January 12, she came to visit me again. This time she came in my dream. I was in front of my parents' house, and my sister was inside. At one point, my mother opened the gate and walked to the front yard, dressed like a queen in beautiful white clothes. She had a kind of turban on her head. She was young, beautiful, and full of life.

Seeing her, I shouted to my sister Louise, "Look, Mom is coming to us!"

My mother had brought a large bag loaded with food and gifts.

The dreams of the ascension of my mother to the Kingdom of Heaven and the dream of her visit at home gave me great relief. On the one hand, these dreams confirmed that my mother had landed in the Kingdom of Heaven at a level higher than I had expected. On the other hand, these dreams confirmed that I had lost my ability to predict the future and see what was happening in the spiritual world.

In other words, I was so proud of my mother's achievements, and of her visit with me. I was so proud of my abilities to see what was happening in the spiritual world.

Chapter Five

THE IMPORTANCE OF THE SECRET GOD SENT THROUGH MY MOTHER

THE SECRET OF GOD THAT MY MOTHER PASSED ON HAS RADICAL IMPOR-
tance in the vision/awareness of the construction of the human being and
the entire Universe. This secret makes all the puzzle pieces fall into place.
He gives us a vision and helps us understand the reasons why different
messages were written both by the prophets and by all the world religions.

Let's see step by step the importance of my mother's message.

THE MECHANISM OF AWARENESS AND MESSAGES

The consciousnesses of our souls are brought to earth to bring light and
love from the Kingdom of Heaven into the World of Darkness. This light
and love make a new entity grow out from the World of Darkness, from the
first levels of life to the consciousness of human bodies to reach the consciousness of the matter of the Universe. To achieve this, the consciousness
of our bodies must learn to respect all the Laws of the Universe.

It's very difficult for the consciousnesses of our bodies to know the
spiritual paths they must follow because, being in the World of Darkness,
they can't imagine what could happen if they didn't follow the rules. Many
times, even if our bodies consciously know that it's not good to abuse
alcohol and food, to steal, be aggressive, deceive, and lie, they need to go

through extreme situations to become aware of their wrongdoing and change their mindset.

For example, one cannot realize how bad it is to abuse alcohol until he becomes addicted and the alcohol destroys his life; likewise, one cannot realize that it's not good to cheat on his/her spouse until he/she is caught and confronted with the situation.

An obvious example that shows the influence of our soul on the consciousness of our body my ability to see the signs of God: When I was a student at the Faculty of Medicine in Chisinau and not married, God, together with my soul, organized several situations for the consciousness of my body so that it become aware of the communication mechanism with the Universe.

For example, when I met Nastia for the first time, she unwittingly gave me a wrong phone number. The phone number was the only source of contact between us. I called her on this wrong phone number on the first two days of the week, Monday and Tuesday, and each time I could get through. Imagine that in a city of 600,000 inhabitants, you call the wrong phone number twice and each time you get the person you want.

When I called her the second time, Nastia gave me the day and time we could meet. The important thing is that immediately after that, I couldn't contact her at the same number. I called her on Wednesday, Thursday, and Friday, but to no avail.

When I met Nastia on Saturday and she gave me her real phone number, I realized why I couldn't reach her when I'd called her on those days. At the same time, I realized the miracle that God organized for us. He made it possible for us to keep in touch with the wrong phone number until we agreed on the exact date and time of the meeting. This miracle suggested to me only one conclusion—*this* was the girl I should marry.

The most important thing in this situation is the fact that although I knew that my situation was a message from God, I was not aware that this was really a situation He had organized for me and a way of communication with the Universe. I didn't know how to delineate this situation or how to analyze what happened to my brain, and I didn't know how to appreciate it according to its true value.

Even if I knew that God suggestedthat I marry Nastia, I still needed extreme circumstances to become aware and be able to explain the phenomenon of communication with God.

Arrogance and alcoholism follow exactly the same awareness mechanism. All of them are aware that they're doing wrong, but they are unaware of the negative impact on their lives and their evolution in this Universe. When the consciousness of our body is aware that it's wrong to produce negative energies, or that it must listen to the signs of God and live in harmony with the Universe, accomplished energies" will be created for our Personal Box.

Another obvious example that shows the mechanism of consciousness is the awareness of the existence of the consciousness of the human body. When I started writing my spiritual books, I knew that the human body was provided with Consciousness. I wrote quite thoroughly about this form of consciousness in my first book, and in this book too, but I have not considered that this consciousness continues to exist after the death of our body. For this reason, for the consciousness of the human body after death, I created the term Personal Box. So, what I have coined in the book so far as the "Personal Box" is an important part of the human body consciousness.

Everything I have written so far is true, though I was not aware that the consciousness of our body continues to exist after the death of our body.

HOW I REALIZED THE PHENOMENON OF THE EXISTENCE OF THE CONSCIOUSNESS OF MATTER AFTER ITS DEATH

In my first book, *The Destiny and Signs of God*, I described a lot of situations that God gave me over the years so that I would understand how our Universe is structured, the way of existence of the spiritual world, and the way of communication with the Universe. I described every situation in detail. The only detail I failed to interpret correctly was not understanding that just like the consciousness of our soul, the consciousness of the human body continues to exist.

A) THE REVELATION I HAD IN THE FALL OF 2005:

When I had the revelation in the fall of 2005, and I was at the height of desperation, God made me aware of the construction of the world down to the last details, and He taught me about the importance of the Essential Law of the Universe, the Family Law. Since then, I understand the importance of the wife of God, and of the wife of our soul, and of the man's wife in the family.

Even though I knew all the details and how the consciousness of the Human Body works, I was unaware of a simple thing—the existence of this consciousness after the death of our body.

In my books, I describe the wife of our soul as a Personal Box with three departments: a) the department of unfulfilled energies of negative energies b) the department of unfulfilled positive energies and c) the department of accomplished energies, the energies that make us advance in the spiritual world.

B) THE FIRST DREAM ABOUT HOW GOD WAS TAKING US TO HIS HOME:

A few months after my revelation, I had a dream about God, who came to our place and took all four of us for a feast at His home. He told me that after two and a half years, my family and I would move to another region where there the are rivers and lakes and a beautiful ocean.

At the same time, He wanted to send me another message. He wanted me to realize that His wife has a consciousness, because in His home lived His wife, who was also like a mother to Him. I realized that His wife was endowed with a consciousness, but I didn't realize that such consciousness was present both here in the material world and in the spiritual world.

The wife of God is also the mother of God, because the material world is completely different from the spiritual world. For that reason, God's wife is like a mother to Him and teaches Him to collaborate and to live in harmony with the World of Darkness.

C) THE DREAM ABOUT THE MOTHER MATTER, GOD'S WIFE:

At one point, I dreamed about our spiritual mother, the matter of the Universe. She appeared to me in a dream so clearly and earnestly that it was imprinted in my memory better than any major event of the day.

She was clad in black, and her hair was dark and devastatingly beautiful. She had blue eyes, a bright spectacular shade that one won't find in material life. When I saw her, I recognized her immediately and knew exactly who she was. I knew that she was our Mother Earth.

In the first chapter of this book, "Secrets of God," I talked about the fact that at some point, our souls will evolve in the form of planets, then solar systems, then galaxies, etc. The Mother Matter I dreamed about was the consciousness of the planet Earth, which means that if our mother is the planet Earth:

- the consciousness of the solar system is our grandmother

- the consciousness of our galaxy is our great-grandmother

- the consciousness of the Universe is our great-great-grandmother

Although when I was dreaming of our spiritual mother she was very calm and quiet and showed empathy and love to me, I feared her as much as I feared the negative energies and the World of Darkness. Then I feared the spiritual mother exactly as I had feared Mother Anica when she died and her ghost started to come back to me in the form of the consciousness of her corpse.

As soon as I woke up, I tried to forget that dream and the existence of my spiritual mother.

D) THE DREAM ABOUT THE HOUSE OF GOD:

In my first book, I mentioned my dream about the House of God, and in this book, I am using the same details to explain the stages of our evolution in the Universe.

In that dream, my whole family was there on that land: Nastia, Sarah, Lya, and I were on a hilltop and, at a certain moment, the end of the world began. Everyone was sucked into the underground, including the houses and everything that exists on the face of the earth. The only people left were the four of us.

In front of us appeared a tall white house, rising up through the clouds to the Kingdom of Heaven and connecting with it.

Everyone who had gone in the underground all started to come out scared, dressed in white clothes similar to the clothes worn by Jesus. They looked scared of what had happened to them down there, and they were desperately seeking refuge in the House of God. They were not interested in anything around them; they just wanted to get into the House of God.

Then I understood that the people who had been in the underground had faced their negative energies from their Personal Boxes. I was sure that they had gone through the Hell of the World of Darkness, which made them aware of how important it was to respect the spiritual Laws of Evolution.

Although I understood that there was a "Hell" in the World of Darkness, I wasn't aware of the existence of the consciousness of matter, which is the World of Darkness and it exists eternally just like the Divine Consciousness.

Important: In retrospect, if I ask myself why I didn't realize Hell existed, the following reasons coming up:

The first reason: I was too influenced by the new spiritual direction described by people who had a near-death experience, and I was ultimately influenced by the books of Neale Donald Walsch, who described the spiritual world in the Kingdom of Heaven considering only God's Kingdom of Heaven. without saying anything about the subject of the existence of the World of Darkness.

The second reason: I feared the Dark World. I was aware of the negative energies, and that there was a material world of darkness, but I was afraid to admit that there was a form of consciousness that belonged to the material world—the World of Darkness.

Psychoanalysis of My Dream

I am now firmly convinced that our souls have always had the same wife, a unique wife since the beginning of their appearance as a life form on Earth.

In the Chapter Two, "The Secrets of God," I explained step by step the evolution of our soul in the material world. Everything I wrote is true except one thing, namely that instead of a Personal Box there is the wife of our soul herself with her consciousness both in a material life and in life after the death of the human body. From the first appearance of our soul in the material world in the form of algae, our soul began to build its wife as an eternal life form.

On the one hand, our soul was like a father to his wife, like a husband and like a son. It was like a father because he showed her the light and love of the Kingdom of Heaven; it showed her the beauty of the spiritual world and recommended to her the spiritual paths she must follow to be enlightened and build her chakras in order to become a human being.

It was like a husband because he had to show to his wife eternal love; they had to live in harmony and love as husband and wife to successfully evolve together.

It was like a son because the consciousness of the matter itself had to teach him the particularities of the material world and of Negative Energies, so that our soul learned to live in harmony with the World of Darkness.

On the other hand, the consciousness of the wife of our soul is like a mother to her husband, as a wife, and as a daughter too. She is like a mother because she had to teach the soul to accept the negative energies, to live in harmony with them, because the evolution of our soul has always depended on the accomplished energies from the Personal Box, energies that only the wife of the soul can build.

She is like a wife because the consciousness of the Wife of our Soul had to live in harmony and love with her husband.

She was like a daughter because she had to listen to the soul, or like to a father to understand the path of spiritual evolution.

Respecting this harmony between husband and wife, our soul has evolved with its unique wife since the beginning of its evolution in the World of Darkness, the Material World. Together they managed to build chakra after chakra, from the level of plants to the level of animals, then to the level of human beings. Thanks to their tireless work and harmonious love, we are human beings on the face of the earth today.

Only by keeping this relationship united, by maintaining love and harmony between the soul and the body, will we be able to build our eternal and continuous future that will help the wives of our souls develop and become whole Universes, and our souls become a God-made one.

Our soul has the same wife when it comes to the material world for the first time, when its wife is only the consciousness of the algae on the earth. Our soul has the same wife, who is the consciousness of the human body, and it will be the same wife when our souls become Gods and their wives become the consciousnesses of the matter of the Universe.

The Soul's Mission in the World of Darkness

The mission of our soul here in the material world is to bring the Divine light and love for his wife, the consciousness of his body. Our souls have almost everything in the Kingdom of Heaven; they live in love and harmony with the whole Universe. The only thing they miss is their achievements and experience in the World of Darkness. For this reason, our souls learn to light up the World of Darkness, starting from the smallest amounts (algae), and continuing to grow this light more and more at the level of plants, fish, animals, humans, the Universe.

Of essence in this whole procedure is that the success of the soul in the World of Darkness depends on the wishes of their wives, the consciousnesses of the matter. Without the wishes of their wives, our souls have no success or possibility of evolution in the World of Darkness.

That's why our souls must be very careful and meticulous in their relationship with their spouses. They must take into consideration all the negative factors of their wives to convince them that the only continuous evolution in this Universe is the spiritual evolution, where all the Laws of the Universe must be followed.

Though the wife of our souls is negativistic, aggressive, and disobedient, and she refuses to heed the advice of those around her, our souls must look for solutions to make her open her eyes to the way she is going. Our soul must love her continuously, accept her as she is, and accept all her negative and positive peculiarities; most importantly, the Soul must *not* force his wife to do anything; it must only create favorable conditions for making her aware of the path she must follow in life. Only by loving them and creating a harmonious relationship between husband and wife will our souls succeed in making their wives aware of the path of their destiny.

The Human Body as a Material Form of Existence

After I realized that our soul has one and only wife for eternity, the consciousness of the matter, I asked myself: "But what is the human body as a physical/material form of existence? If the wives of our souls gather the experience of our bodies and transform it into the consciousness of our bodies, what is the human body as a physical form of existence?"

Based on my life experience, God insisted that my family and I change our place of residence several times, and we did it in eleven towns in four countries. By nature, my wife and I were irresistibly attached to our maternal home, to the places of our heritage, and none of us wanted to make a change by relocating from here to there. But we had no choice. We had to follow the path recommended by God so that we should evolve higher and higher. It is precisely these changes, moving from one house to another and from one place to another, that helped us have such a good life, from the poorest on this planet to the richest.

Each place we lived gave us warmth and stability; in every house, we had many beautiful moments, and we felt the love and warmth of the soul. In addition, in each environment, Nastia and I could meet strong people eager for evolution, and each of them emboldened us to move higher and higher.

Initially, I didn't understand. Why did God insist that we move from one locality to another, and from one country to another? I can now answer this with the greatest confidence. God has trained us so that the souls and consciousnesses of our bodies get used to the continuous changes in this Universe, and He taught us to gather love from every house we lived in and to enjoy the process of change, because only by moving from one house to another could we get a complex vision of the life we live and build ourselves eternally continuous evolution.

Now I can answer with conviction that the human body is the house of the soul and of the consciousness of our body; it is the house of their successes so far, the house that they have built cell by cell, from one life to another. Both of them, husband and wife together, began to build their house starting from the first forms of life. Passing into another form of house, they began to reincarnate into plants, then into animals, and finally they reached the house called the human body. Thus, the soul together with the consciousness of our body will continue to build other forms of houses, much more complex and with more chakras than the human body, and they will first exist as planets, then as solar systems, until they end up together as husband and wife and the house becomes an entire Universe, in which our soul is a God and the consciousness of our bodies becomes the consciousness of the matter of the Universe.

Each time the soul with matter consciousness was reincarnated, it was faced with new challenges in life and in the relationship between husband and wife, that they had to solve and turn into accomplished energies for their Personal Box so that their evolution can go on.

The Suggestion of My Friend Eugen

Eugen is a friend with whom I talk almost every day about the signs of God and the spiritual world. What surprised me in our conversation was that the second day after I wrote about the subject described above, for no specific reason, without addressing our subject, he said to me, "If we stay in the same place, if we live in the same house, or if we do the same thing over and over, at some point everything becomes a routine and we begin idling. The energies of our life slow down and we stop evolving spiritually. We must be aware of that and try to avoid it, try to avoid the stagnant mode and routine in our life. "

In the depths of my soul, I sensed that Eugen's message was a message from God and I must analyze it profoundly. Here is my conclusion:

I would adamantly state that the principle of our evolution is based precisely on the change of our houses and bodies, because:

1) if we live in the same house all our lives, the routine takes over our family and prevents us from evolving or seeing other sides of life;

2) if we work in the same place in the same conditions all our life, and there is nothing new to discover, we stagnate and don't see other particularities of life.

3) if our soul and the consciousness of our body were in an immortal physical body, at a certain moment nothing would be interesting anymore, nothing would appeal to us anymore, and nothing would inspire us to progress and evolve.

But here is what happens to us if we change our house and our workplace, and if we change our bodies from one life to another:

1) By changing houses, we change neighbors, we change our spatial positioning, we change all the previous energies for new ones. In such conditions, we start new relationships and walk down new roads with new destinations. Practically, we discover another corner of the Universe with other people, places, energies, and targets.

   When the energies of our body come into contact with other energies—the energies of people, places, and relationships—they create other new energies, positive energies of experience, knowledge, and understanding.

   Once we have explored all the roads and know all the people around us, and we have created all the positive energies described above, there is nothing left to discover and we no longer have the possibility to create new energies; therefore, we start to reuse our surroundings and the already created energies that become a routine of life. In its turn, this routine becomes dull, as it no longer meets other new energies of life, and the ways/energies are *reused* to idleness. Stagnation of energies leads to decay, and decay leads to the creation of negative energies.

2) When it comes to the routine of the workplace, the same thing happens. The energies around the workplace become stagnant, precipitating the creation of negative energies.

3) If the soul together with the consciousness of our body were not reincarnated tens of thousands of times, and if they didn't pass through all the forms of life, they wouldn't manage to accumulate so much energy and knowledge and experience as they have now.

Compared with the previous forms of life, the soul and the consciousness of our body have to face a new form of energy that is way more complex and difficult to control. They have to face the psychic part of the human being, with social and interpersonal relationships, and they must face the relationship alone with themselves, that is with the soul-body relationship, which highlights and makes them aware of the Laws of the Universe that start from the Essential Law, Family Law, or the law of the relationship between soul-body, between husband-wife, and between the matter of the Universe and God.

When we become aware of all these relationships and we face all the energies of the human being, we will be able to move on to a new way of life. But until then, we have to face the positive and negative energies of the form of the human life.

Quite often while we are reincarnated in a new body, the environment of our society and our education lure us to doom along the road to crime and generations of negative energies. But we don't have to worry about what has happened or is happening to us, because even if we are walking down the wrong path of life, it doesn't mean that we'll do it forever. No, we must realize that what happened to us now is just an untoward experience, and that's all. What we have to do is focus and not repeat the same mistakes over and over.

In other words, any life experience, whether positive or negative, is an experience from which we learn to continue our spiritual evolution. If we do not learn from our mistakes, then we will remain dormant at the same stage of evolution for many lifetimes. We will stagnate until we learn to discard our bad habits and our negative energies for the sake of our spiritual evolution.

As a result, in this World of Darkness, our Soul together with the desires of its wife have succeeded and will succeed in making the light of their ever-growing house brighter. I have managed to evolve from a small primitive algae to the light, love, and harmony of the human body, and they will continue to make this light more intense and brighter each time they reincarnate in their material houses.

E) DREAMS ABOUT HEAVEN, HELL, AND MY BODILY TEMPTATIONS RELATED TO ALCOHOL:

In my book *The Destiny and Signs of God*, I described a series of theories related to "Heaven" and "Hell." I had many dreams and I explained them, but my explanations weren't complete because I didn't understand what was happening. On the one hand, I understood that in the Kingdom of Heaven there is a form of punishment for those who commit serious crimes here on earth, but the examples of those who had a near-death experience, and the descriptions of Neale Donald Walsch, confused me.

Although God showed me exactly what was going on, I couldn't understand what He wanted to tell me. I don't wish to accuse Neale Donald Walsch or those who had a near-death experience. No, I want the reader to understand the phenomenon of awareness, which is quite difficult.

The human being is composed not only of the soul and matter but of the soul and the consciousness of the human body. The consciousness of our body, is extremely difficult to be convinced of. To realize that the consciousness of the body continues to exist after the death of our body, it was necessary that God sacrifice my mother so I could take courage to face the reality.

After my mother died and showed me the beautiful side of the World of Darkness, I had the courage to say that a World of Darkness exists. It's the world of our mother, which isn't as terrible as it may seem. Imagine the World of Darkness as a beautiful, tender, and attractive girl, or imagine her as a mother. Both a girl and a mother are beautiful, gentle, delicate, fragile, and equipped with seven chakras in which positive and negative energies are traveling.

When we look at a beautiful girl or at our mother, we see their beauty, we see their love, their desire for evolution and prosperity; we don't see them as malicious, aggressive, or envious, but we are looking at their beautiful side, because in every person the energies are predominantly positive. The negative energies manifest themselves only in extreme cases and make things change radically.

Imagine that our soul, coming from light and love, enters the human body, which is the World of Darkness. Yes! Really! Our body itself is the World of Darkness. This begs the questions: "Are we so terrible? Is our body so terrible that we must be afraid of it? Should we be afraid of ourselves?" I don't think so. Of course, each of us has a negative part, but at the same time, we have a lot of positive qualities.

Now imagine that the human body is at the primitive level of evolution compared with our mother, the consciousness of the Universal matter; we are more evil and aggressive than our mother, the Universe. Should we be afraid of the Universe?

When it comes to the World of Darkness, we must focus on it as well as on our loving mother, who wishes us all the best in the Universe and is ready to sacrifice herself for each of us so we can be well.

We shouldn't be afraid of our Mother the Universe, just like I learned not to be afraid of my mother's ghost, because no matter how terrible they may seem, they are our real mothers who would do anything for us to be well.

To love our spiritual mother and the World of Darkness does not mean that we must accept evil and negative energies as our way of life. No, we must accept their negative energies from the World of Darkness because they're part of our life, but we must not accept them to build our lives according to their preferences. We must take into account that these negative energies exist in the material world so that we can see the difference between good and evil and realize that the only direction of evolution is towards the Divine Light. The Spiritual Evolution is the only way to continue to evolve in this Universe.

In this part of my book, I will give you an example from my personal life that proves that the negative energies are ready to take possession of us at any cost and at any level of our evolution. I will tell you about my physical temptations related to alcohol consumption.

In my first book, I described the ways in which God tried to make me realize that alcohol abuse was harmful to my spiritual evolution. I was at a party, and I got so drunk that I lost my senses. The next morning, God made me see the Devil himself. He was the height of a man, without a tail or horns, unlike in the books, but his eyes were very large and red from the inner fire, a fire that burned inside his body. He sat and looked at me motionless, with a fixed gaze, which gave me the understanding that he was sitting and waiting for me to make another wrong step, or to continue drinking alcohol, so that he had the right to take me with him. This dream scared me and made me cut down on drinking. But I was still drinking, though not too much.

Seeing that, God created a second situation for me. A barrel of wine fell on the calf of my leg and fractured my muscle. After that I drank less, but I was still drinking.

Some other time, after a drinking binge, I dreamed that I would end up in Hell, where my brain would shrink to a nut size and I would lose my intellectual abilities and become a disgrace.

Although God was sending me important messages about how I was jeopardizing my future, and even though I knew that drinking wasn't good for my spiritual evolution, deep in my soul and in the marrow of my bones there was no clear perception of the harmful impact of this bad habit and why the temptations of my flesh were more powerful than my spiritual principles.

To become aware of the true messages of God, it was necessary that I feel the upcoming spiritual fall if I continued to drink. Look what happened:

Coming home from a party where I had drunken a lot, I felt the need to have a couple more shots. Practically, I couldn't control myself or my bodily desires, and after tossing up one glass after another, I became a zombie.

The next morning, I could hardly understand what had happened. Like a Bermuda Triangle or an enormous vortex from a huge funnel of water, my body was craving for alcohol, starting at the level of the brain, going through my whole organism, and reaching down into the depths of Hell. This vortex was absorbing all the energy of my life, all my powers as a human being, sucking up all my mental and spiritual strengths and all the knowledge I had acquired. It was tossing them into the darkness of the ravenous, bottomless Hell.

Only by realizing and feeling firsthand the infernal process of what happens to me if I consume alcohol was I able to realize the impact of drinking on the future of my spiritual evolution, and I was able to make the final decision to give up the alcohol. Even though God gave me a lot of hints and showed me exactly what was going to happen to me, it was necessary that I reached the extreme boundaries and the depth of disaster to experience firsthand the destructive impact my corporal temptations could cause.

As you can see, we all have to be alert when it comes to material bodily temptations and be aware of the impact of the negative energies on the future of our lives before the disaster hits, before we find ourselves on the brink, because regardless of our current level of evolution, we can descend into Hell at any moment. We all know that what we're doing is wrong, but we're not aware of where our bodily temptations can take us. To convince ourselves, we need to experience firsthand the disaster that befalls us.

Since it's difficult for a single person to realize the impact of the negative energies, imagine how difficult it is for our entire civilization to realize that what it's doing is wrong. It's very difficult for an entire civilization, developed by materialistic principles of existence from the beginning of its existence on earth, to suddenly give up its conservative thoughts. It needs extreme situations to make new, democratic inroads to the spiritual evolution.

To successfully respond to this challenge, we all must join forces to convince everyone about the importance of our spiritual evolution, because one single person can't do anything against the materialist monster steering the minds of our entire civilization.

THE CREATION OF THE SUPREME CONSCIENCE OF THE UNIVERSE

Before I proceed, I'd like to apologize to the reader for not breathing a word about one of the messages of the Universe that I received from God during my revelation in Montreal in the fall of 2005. I didn't want to unveil this secret, since I feared being misunderstood. But as you know, there are no secrets in the spiritual world, and the time has come to describe what I saw during my revelation.

In a distant past where the memory can't reach, when neither Universe nor Supreme Conscience (God) existed, there was only a dark matter under its primeval form of life, a timeless one, boundless, incorporeal, consciousness and lawless, shrouded in a horrendous void.

Slowly and casually, this boundless void was set in motion, and its movements in themselves started to generate energies. The first energies were the most primeval, and they lacked coordination and laws. As the void was moving along, the energies needed synchronization in order to operate smoothly and controllably. And so the first personal vault of the Universe was born, as I recounted in my books. Practically, they started to create the first accomplished energies, which turned into the first laws of the Universe and its first consciousness. This consciousness grew up to the level of a Universe and gave birth to the first Universe before making the human being.

To understand what I mean, I invite you to watch the feature *The Guardians of the Galaxy 2* (2007), in which they deal with the evolution of Ego (Kurt Russel). In this film, the father of the main hero, who is a kind of God, tells the story of his origin, saying that he came from the dust of the Universe that acquired consciousness, then turned into a planet, and later the consciousness could take the form of a human being.

As you can see, what the Universe/God showed me during my revelation in 2005 is in total contradiction with any theories of religion. The first-born child in this Universe is not the Supreme Consciousness or God but the matter. It is she who created the first energies and the first form of consciousness. So the matter is the mother of the Supreme Consciousness of the Universe (of God).

In other words, when we deal with the relationship of husband-wife and soul-body, we must become fully aware of it. Hence, we have to pay careful attention to our wives and bodies, because they laid the basis for the construction of our consciousness, soul, and family. Only a satisfied body and a satisfied wife can generate accomplished energies in anticipation of a continuous and prosperous evolution. As long as we keep oppressing our wives and our bodies, our life and our future will remain in agony.

If we go for a deeper analysis of the creation of the Universe and the Supreme Consciousness/God, we can say that the matter of the Universe is, on the one side, like the mother of God, because with her maternal feelings, she kept for herself all the negative energies of the Universe and bequeathed her best unto her beloved son, the Lord. She handed down to Him her utmost achievements, all her accomplished energies," all her light and love. God is the light, the love, and the wisdom of the Universe because His Mother Matter has endowed Him with all these things.

On the other side, the matter of the Universe is God's wife because only together with a healthy family can they achieve a brighter future. The negative energies of the Universe make God's wife change her mood unaccountably and indulge in profligate desires and wasteful temptations. Even if these desires and temptations are based on negative energies, they initiate the construction of new accomplished energies" of the Universe that help God and the Universe grow and evolve as a whole.

Therefore, God should treat the Matter of the Universe as His own loving mother and, at the same time, His capricious wife, and address all her expectations. Only by satisfying His wife, the matter of the Universe, will He manage to evolve in the spiritual world.

God is the light, the love, and the wisdom of the Universe, and this is what the matter of the Universe is expecting from Him. This is what our body is expecting from our soul. This is what the wives are expecting from their husbands.

THE CONSTRUCTION OF THE UNIVERSE

After I realized the message that my mother had received from God, I understood that our Universe is made up of two entities:

- God our Father and the Supreme Consciousness of the Universe, the light and the love of this Universe

- Our mother, the consciousness of the matter of the Universe, which is the World of Darkness with all the positive and negative energies of this Universe

Although the two entities of the Universe are completely different, they still live together in perfect harmony. Nothing in this Universe is accidental, absolutely nothing of what moves around and is created or gets destroyed and has a well-structured meaning and a purpose.

The consciousness of our Universe is so well structured at all levels—physical, chemical, mathematical, physiological, psychic, psychological, energetic—that every entity and form of life in this Universe receives everything it needs and develops under all the necessary conditions for their evolution. No one and nothing are abandoned, ignored, or humiliated; everyone has equal rights, and everyone has all the necessary conditions of evolution.

The love and the harmony of our spiritual parents is distributed into every cell, every chemical element, every form of life or death in this Universe and give us hope, courage, and zest for life.

A) GOD OUR FATHER:

Analyzing our spiritual parents separately, I'd like to tell you that we know absolutely everything we need to know about God our Father. Neale Donald Walsch spoke more explicitly about Him; the people who had a near-death experience have spoken about Him and so have the religionists.

It's no secret that after the death of our body, our soul mounts up to God in the Kingdom of Heaven, where there is light, love, and harmony. In the Kingdom of Heaven, no one is judged or humiliated, and no one is superior to anyone. All our souls reach the Kingdom of Heaven, whether they made mistakes, killed, were immaculate monks.

Judging from the words of the people who had a near-eeath experience, in the Kingdom of Heaven everyone is equal, even a drop of water has the same value in the Kingdom of Heaven as a person's soul.

B) OUR MOTHER—CONSCIOUSNESS OF THE MATTER OF THE UNIVERSE:

After my mother's death, I was sure that the consciousnesses of our bodies do not have the same destination as our souls. While our souls go up to the Kingdom of Heaven and receive love and harmony from our Lord, the consciousnesses of our bodies are treated completely differently, temporarily stuck in the World of Darkness.

Based on my mother's messages after her death, I'd like to tell you that in the World of Darkness, in the consciousness of the matter of the Universe, the principles of construction and operation are similar to those on earth. Each consciousness of the body is placed, depending on its level of evolution, on the positive or negative energies the body has built on earth during its material life.

Here on earth, people from higher levels of evolution don't look at those from lower levels, and precisely the same thing happens with the consciousnesses of our bodies in the World of Darkness, except that there, those at the higher levels are not those who made the most money or held leadership positions here on earth. No, at the higher levels are those who created the most positive energies for the world.

Here on earth live the lost, the homeless, and the hopeless—people with different special characteristics, and it's the same in the World of Darkness, where people who created negative energies in abundance on earth become lost, without a home, or end up in the so-called Hell.

Here on earth there is the police, justice, prisons, and psychiatric hospitals, just like in the Dark World.

To better understand the harmony between God's Light and the World of Darkness, look one more time at Fig. 9. According to this drawing and considering our reality here on earth, we all live in the World of Darkness. Basically, in this darkness we are in the "womb" of our mother, the matter of the Universe. We are now in the World of Darkness, together with our soul.

The World of Darkness is abundant in negative energies. Just as any human body, the matter of the Universe is equipped with negative and positive energies, but even if the World of Darkness is overflowing with negative energies, let's ask ourselves the following question: "Will a mother harm her child? Especially when the child is inside her?"

Of course, the matter of the Universe will not do us any harm. We're all in her belly, and she feels and understands each of us better than anyone else. She can sense all our motions, every feeling, and every breath we take. Like any mother, she doesn't offend us. On the contrary, she protects us from all the drudgeries, and she provides us with absolutely everything she has for us.

In my first book, I wrote about the importance of the wife's wishes in the family and about her power over the entire family. My mother, for example, considered me a saint in her life, and she wanted with all her heart and soul that I succeed as a holy person. She prayed and paid church services to help my family become successful. I have never known any other mother to pray as much for her children and grandchildren as she did. Thanks to her prayers, my family lives a happy life full of accomplishments.

Just like any mother, the Mother Matter of the Universe wishes with all her heart that her children be spared suffering, and even if her children don't obey the Laws of the Universe Spiritual Evolution, she is still a mother and accepts them as such. She accepts us all the way we are, even if we take drugs and drink, are aggressive, commit murderer, are greedy or belligerent, or are ready to wage wars. Mother Matter understands and feels our suffering, and she lets us satisfy our bodily desires here on earth, hoping that one day we will realize that we must do things in the proper way.

But if children are ungrateful to their mothers and become aggressive and disregard their mother's gifts and possessions, the mothers will turn aggressively against them. If the children show hostility and malevolence to their mothers, their mothers will become their dreaded enemies.

While a mother can be the most understanding and loving person to her children, she can also become their most dreaded enemy. She can become aggressive to her children when they are aggressive to her and can be extremely dangerous when her children attempt to destroy her. When children create huge amounts of negative energy against their mother, she turns aggressively against them by sending back to them all the negative energy they created. In these cases, the mother's aggression becomes so violent that her children have no escape. From the mother's aggressiveness, children will understand that they have to do what they have to do and not what they want to do.

An obvious example of the aggressiveness of the mother of the Universe towards her children is the COVID-19 pandemic. By means of this virus, Mother Matter has visited her children and our ungrateful civilization with all her wrath. Our mother, the matter of our Earth, no longer accepts our mocking of her; she can no longer stand the fact that we disparage all the work she did for us and our civilization for hundreds of millions of years. We are destroying everything she has experienced so far—not only our nature and plants, animals, and forests but also the resources of our Mother Earth that we're using to wage wars and get rich.

God our Father has a different attitude towards His children. He is more gentle and less aggressive than the Mother Matter. He anticipates *exactly* what's in stock for us, and He constantly gives us the most concrete and accurate instructions:

When it comes to choosing the paths of life or making a decision, God makes His presence known at every crossroad in our life and gives us advice to help us make the best choice of a potentially prosperous road.

When any negative energy comes towards us and we don't deserve it, God will be standing in support and will tell us how to avoid such energies/situations.

When we create an abundance of negative energies and have to face them, God doesn't stand in their way, but He lets them get into our lives as situations, showing us how to stop creating such negative energies.

When Mother Matter is angry at us because we disregarded her and continued to generate negative energies in excess, God will certainly do everything possible to let these aggressive energies reach us.

The first situation involves my friend's wife, who fell down the stairs in the basement and fractured her femur bone. The second situation is COVID-19, when God had to organize a strategy to leave us at the mercy of these energies.

Based on the above, I insist that we *all* should learn to heed God's advice. God is at every crossroad in our life, and He is guiding us and shows us the best path for our future. If we *all* listen to what He says, our destiny with have an eternal evolution both personally and globally.

Next, I would like to reveal step by step what happens inside the World of Darkness of our Mother Universe.

THE NEGATIVE ENERGIES IN THE WORLD OF DARKNESS

a) What happens to the people who fail to fulfill the tasks they came for here on earth?

You already know the stages through which my mother's body consciousness went after the death of her body. The conclusion is that these stages are the essential principles by which all the consciousnesses of our bodies are guided.

We all go through exactly the same stages! But the difference from one case to another depends on:

- our level of evolution/the level we deserve after the death of our body

- the negative or positive energies we manage to create during our lifetime

Normally, all the consciousnesses of our bodies will be locked in the World of Darkness as long as we conduct ourselves according to the materialistic principles of evolution and as long as we create negative energies. The consciousnesses of our bodies have the right to ascend to the Kingdom of Heaven together with their souls *immediately* after the death of their body, when the spiritual evolution begins and we don't create negative energy anymore. Only then will the words of Jesus Christ be fulfilled: a day will come when we all ascend to the Kingdom of Heaven with our soul and body together (Matthew 19:21).

Important: What Jesus Christ said regarding the raising of our souls together with our bodies to the Kingdom of Heaven means that in the Kingdom of Heaven, the soul will not arrive with our physical body but with the consciousness of our body.

Let's look at other examples that demonstrate the course of the consciousnesses of our bodies after death.

An obvious example of people who come to earth to satisfy their bodily pleasures is that of my alcohol addiction. If I hadn't stopped drinking in time, surely the consciousness of my body wouldn't have had the same fate as the consciousness of my mother's body. It would have been separated from my soul and would have remained in the World of Darkness for a much longer period of time, and there would not have been enough time to realize that I must I stop drinking;

My body's consciousness would have reached a much lower level than its true level, and of course it would have been haunted by the negative energy of alcohol until it became aware of the truth that it must stop drinking.

Another example is my cousin Lucas, who worked as a psychiatrist in Romania and consumed alcohol in huge quantities; he used his position and disregarded his patients and squeezed them of money. At the age of forty-eight, his alcohol abuse killed him.

All the negative energies he created during his life caught up with him after the death of his body. I dreamed of him for seven or eight years, that the consciousness of his body was in a prison in the Dark World. Later, I dreamed several times that he was divorced and lived alone in the house with absolutely no contact with anyone, just him.

Attention: The loneliness or the "divorce" of my cousin in my dream means that the consciousness of his body is separated from his soul and is not yet worth reuniting with him to continue his evolution from the spiritual world.

More than fifteen years have passed since my cousin died, and I never dreamed of him reuniting with his Soul.

The last example of people who made a lot of mistakes here on earth and about whom I dreamed many times after their death is Aunt Nora, the mother of my cousin Lucas. Aunt Nora was a mean, unscrupulous woman who took advantage of other people's work all her life and made dishonest profits whenever she could.

After her death, I dreamed several times that she was locked in a room where people could only enter with extreme difficulty. To get to her, I had to go through several closed doors. She was alone in the room and had no contact with anyone or access anywhere. In other words, based on the evolutionary stages of my mother's body consciousness, which stayed in the World of Darkness for only one year, Aunt Nora's body consciousness and Lucas's body consciousness remained stuck in the Dark World for much longer, and they will remain stranded until they manage to exhaust all the negative energies they created themselves during their life here on earth.

b) The Hell

The Hell in the World of Darkness is not as terrible as described in the religious literature. It's not a form of punishment for the negative energies we have created here on earth; it is a *confrontation* of our body consciousness with the energies we alone have made. Emerging from the Law of the Universe—the Law of the Boomerang, all that we have made on earth appears before us in the World of Darkness. All the negative energies resurface in front of us so that we realize what we have done and that we should heed the Laws of the Universe and not repeat the same mistakes when we're born again in the material world.

Just as I was trying to understand the construction of Hell, God sent me a dream in which I was only visiting it. Arriving in Hell, I knew that I was only a visitor, and I wanted to pass unnoticed so that those living there wouldn't know that I had come to visit them.

The Hell was shaped like a warehouse of undetermined size, and there were streets with houses and people in it. It resembled a huge, roofed town, like a hall stretching endlessly. In the streets lived people who had made identical mistakes:

On the first street, for example, lived the murderers. Their houses were built from the bones of the people and animals they had killed. There had been killers on this street since the primitive era when people used to hunt mammoths.

On the second street lived the aggressive people who did a lot of harm around them.

On the third street lived the manipulators, the political and the religionists, who manipulated the masses into committing serious crimes, such as war crimes, hatred between nations, or between nations and religions.

The other streets were too far to see what kind of people lived there.

The first aspect that shocked me the most inside the Hell was that these people had no contact with the outside world; they had no television or radios, and there was nothing they could use to be contacted by other people, not even by their own souls.

Important note: On the second day after I had the Hell in my dream, I dreamed about my mother. She told me that she/her body's consciousness reunited with the soul in togetherness. My mother's dream made me realize that in Hell there were only the consciousnesses of the bodies of the people who lived on earth. The fact that they were alone meant that they were divorced or temporarily separated from their souls. If the consciousnesses of the bodies hadn't been so hostile during their life on earth, they wouldn't have been separated from their souls for such a long period of time.

The culprits for the separation of the souls from the consciousnesses of their bodies are not only the whimsical consciousnesses of the bodies but also the souls, because they didn't love their wives enough and they failed to create harmony between the soul and the body. They couldn't convince their wives that they must obey the Laws of the Universe and refrain from satisfying their bodily temptations.

As you can see, in the spiritual world there are unacceptable divorces, as they are a disaster for the consciousnesses of our bodies, for the representatives of women. These divorces are also disastrous for the souls who have reached some level of evolution and remain stuck in the Kingdom of Heaven without having the possibility of evolution in the World of Darkness.

The second aspect that shocked me during my visit to Hell was a strong stench of decaying corpse, spread out by the unbearable smell of chlorine. The stench woke me up from my sleep. I was up, yet the smell had stayed in my nostrils. It was familiar to me. I had felt it here in the material world, and no smell is more disgusting than in Hell. The corpses' consciousnesses were decaying because they had no evolution, and there was no way to exchange and renew their energies in order to stay alive. Thus, the consciousnesses of the bodies became stagnant energies, disguised in a process of eternal putrefaction.

To remain intact and not decompose, the consciousness of their bodies needed huge quantities of chlorine for disinfection. Thus, the smell of a decomposing corpse mixed with the disinfecting chlorine created the horrible smell of Hell.

The third aspect that shocked me was that the consciousnesses of the bodies imprisoned for aggressiveness and murder didn't emanate any danger from within them; they were just like zombies ignorant about the world around, like small children who were lost and scared, with no support or information from anywhere.

This aspect of the people from Hell helped me clarify my dream of the House of God, where the earth was coming to an end and everyone had gone underground. They were coming out from the underground, scared by what they had seen in Hell, and they were running erratically towards the house of God (See Fig. 7).

The fourth aspect that shocked me was that in Hell, even if the people were like innocent little children, scared and lost, the energies of aggression, murder, and manipulation were all present. These aggressively negative energies weren't emanated by people but by the houses themselves.

The walls of the houses where the people from Hell lived were built from the negative energies generated by the people during their life. Arriving in Hell, the consciousnesses of the bodies were distributed to the houses they had built; they lived in an atmosphere of violence, hatred, and misery, which they had built themselves during their lifetime. In my opinion, the people from Hell had to stay in their houses until the energies they had made were completely exhausted. Only by exhausting all the energies from the walls of their houses would they probably regain the right to reunite with their souls.

In my first book, I wrote about the political and religious manipulators who sow hatred between people and create conflicts and make wars; I said that they will end up mentally ill in their next life. Based on what I saw in Hell, I want to tell you what was happening to the politicians and the religionists. I can tell you for sure that in their next life, these people will definitely end up mentally sick. There are numerous negative energies to fool the world, and they are so strong, invasive, and aggressive that no one can fight them. The power of the negative energies that have upset an entire country, or an entire religious group, is such that a single person can't resist without becoming mentally sick.

The next aspect that drew my attention was that in Hell, most of the people were men and only a few women were among them. This made me realize that here on earth, men are the ones who commit the worst crimes. They are the killers, the aggressors, the manipulators, and the creators of conflicts and wars.

As a result, we mustn't ignore the importance of women in our personal evolution and the evolution of our civilization. It is high time we turned our face to our wives, our mothers, and our daughters, because the destiny of the spiritual evolution depends entirely on the desires of femininity on earth, on their capacity of being aware of the importance of the Laws of the Universe and spiritual evolution.

GENERAL CONCLUSIONS

First Conclusion:

In the period of the material evolution of our civilization, if each of us creates negative energies during his life, after death we'll be forced to separate/divorce from our souls and remain stuck in the World of Darkness to face the energies we alone have created. The duration of the separation/ divorce depends on the number of negative energies we have made.

The Second Conclusion—Divorce and Homosexuality

Coming from the first conclusion that the consciousnesses of the bodies are periodically divorced from their souls, we can say that the divorce exists in the spiritual world, which means that the divorce is a normal process of the evolution of the soul together with its wife, the consciousness of the body.

Another divorce process we can call the process of the death of the human body, or the process of separating the soul from the human body.

We don't have to judge those who divorce because it's a normal process of evolution. Our souls and the consciousnesses of our bodies cannot realize that a divorce is not the way we should go until they actually face the divorce and feel firsthand its impact on their spiritual evolution.

If the consciousnesses of our bodies are stuck in the World of Darkness accompanied by other consciousnesses of other bodies, their relationship becomes a homosexual relationship. The longer the consciousnesses of our bodies remain stuck with other consciousnesses of the bodies, the more intense the homosexual relationship becomes.

So even in the case of homosexuals, we must not judge, because this is a normal cycle of our evolution in the spiritual world. We all go through a period of homosexual relationships, and we can't move forward, we can't become aware of the impact that homosexuality brings in the process of our evolution as soul-body until we go through these trials ourselves.

The Third Conclusion—the Sacrifice:

Our body consciousness must take this path after the death of our body, and those who make mistakes, who walk the materialistic path of evolution, don't know what they're doing. They don't realize that they don't do the right thing, and they have no idea of what awaits them. We feel sorry for them, and our soul is in pain to hear about the torments they have to go through.

Knowing these details, we begin to ask ourselves the question: "Is it really necessary to torture these people? Is it really necessary to send them through Hell?"

I don't know. But I think that even if they have to go through the Hell of the Dark World, these people do us a favor, because at one stage or another of our evolution or transitions from a material world to a spiritual one, we see this domain of the Universe where Hell is located, and we see the sufferings of those in Hell. By going through Hell, these consciousnesses of bodies show us an example of what awaits us if we indulge all our bodily pleasures to the extreme. They are an example for all of us so that we can see the advantage of abiding by the Laws of the Universe and the spiritual evolution, and we see where it can take us if we keep on satisfying our bodily pleasures and create wars, destroy the environment, and oppress the poor so that we get rich.

We shouldn't care about the problems of other people. We don't have to judge anyone. To get real spiritual thinking, we have to focus on our personal issues alone, because here in the material world we all have our problems to solve. Some have aggressiveness issues, others self -doubt ones, and others have issues about their bodily temptations. We all have come here to Earth to solve *our* problems and not the problems of homosexuals, of our family members, or our neighbors.

We need to be aware of our own mistakes It's very difficult for us to be aware of how important it is to observe the Laws of the Universe and the spiritual evolution. I told you about the fate of people in the Dark World

245

after they die: some of us have to stay in Hell for thousands or tens of thousands of years until we start to realize that it's not good to do harm.

We all know that our path is not the right one, and we're aware that the evil shouldn't be treated with evil, yet we continue to do this both personally and internationally.

On a personal level, to become aware of the importance of the connection with the Universe and of listening to God's signs, God had to put me through extreme poverty and make me lose huge amounts of money.

On the international level, God gave several examples to the leaders of the democratic countries, because they should not interfere with the domestic affairs of another country. He showed them an obvious example of Iraq, and more recently, He showed them an irreproachable example of Afghanistan, where war was fought for decades and, in the end, the Taliban were the victors.

Have the leaders of the democratic countries drawn any conclusions? Have they become aware of the importance of following the basic Laws of the Universe, that they shouldn't interfere with the domestic affairs of another country? That they shouldn't use aggressiveness against aggressiveness? I don't think so. I am sure that they'll try to send the army into countries like Iraq or Afghanistan again.

Do the voters in democratic countries realize who they voted for? Do they do anything to change their arrogant and selfish leaders with materialistic principles? I don't think they do.

I believe that our civilization needs pandemics back-to-back to understand the importance of the signs of God and living in harmony with the Universe.

Along with the emergence of the human being on earth, various theories regarding the spiritual world appeared. Initially, people believed in spirits and in gods, like the God of wind, fire, water, earth, the sun, etc. Although in time people became skeptical about gods and spirits, I want to assure you that they were right in what they said. Just as there is a consciousness of the human body, so is there consciousness of animals and plants. And if there is a consciousness of plants, there is a consciousness of water, air, fire, etc. There is a consciousness of the sun and a of the earth. I spoke about these forms of consciousness at the beginning of this book.

Later, different theories appeared along with numerous practices concerning the connection with the Universe. The strongest and most imposing theory about the construction of the spiritual world was the theory of the existence of a single God. These concepts gave birth to a series of religious theories that have driven people's minds to this day. The prophets/apostles who wrote these theories saw the construction of the Universe exactly as I saw it. They saw the Kingdom of Heaven where the true God lives, and they also saw the Kingdom of Darkness with all the positive and negative energies from the material world.

The prophets/apostles who created the religions, and all those who came into contact with the spiritual world, are all right, as they all described two opposite forces of the Universe:

- Yin and Yang

- good and bad

- Heaven and Hell

Everyone knows that the spiritual ascension is the only way of ascending in this Universe. In other words, everyone speaks only about God our Father but avoids speaking about the second part, about our mother, who created us and keeps us in her womb during the entire course of our life in the material world.

The only people I've seen worship Mother Earth are the remnants of the Inca civilization in South America, where they genuinely believe in the power of Mother Earth and make sacrifices for her to take care of their harvest. Although these people worship the earth, they don't not have a clear picture of the importance of the earth and Mother Earth in the Universe.

Why is everyone avoiding talking about our Mother Matter? And why would it be wrong if we thought more about this subject? The answer is: Fear of the World of Darkness of the prophets/apostles and of all those who invented religions. Fear of the negative energies in the chakras of the matter of the Universe. Fear of confrontation with negative energies. Fear of thinking about them. They all led to the deformation of the theories regarding the construction of the Universe.

IONEL ROTARU

A) OUR FEAR OF THE DARK WORLD:

I was always afraid of the negative energies; I always avoided the color black and the words describing the evil and the bad. I never wanted to have anything to do with such a form of existence.

I am not the only one who's scared. Everyone is. The religionists were the first ones who struck deep fear among us. If we dig more deeply, what I have seen so far, and I describe in my books, is that the prophets/apostles who wrote the Bible, the Quran, and other religious books saw it too. What He showed me through all the stages of our evolution and the Universe as a whole, God showed to all the prophets/apostles who invented the religions and the spiritual theories. However, we all made the same mistake: we were afraid to face the World of Darkness, and we did everything possible to distance ourselves from such forms of existence, from our mother who created us and keeps us in its womb so we can grow and develop freely.

I haven't changed anything of what I wrote in my books, just to help the reader realize the error I made by avoiding our spiritual mother. After you see the difference between reality and the error I committed, it will be easier for you to spot the errors made by the prophets/apostles and their own religious theories. Their fear of the energies of the Dark World caused them to turn the representatives of women into slaves and treat them like animals and remove them from the list of human beings. Some religions suppressed women's rights until the last century; others suppress their rights to this day. Even today there are women locked in the house, without education rights, dressed in all kinds of clothes that even hide their faces.

Now let's see the importance of the Dark World.

I will start from a simple magnet. If the magnet didn't have two different poles, the magnetic attraction wouldn't exist. The principle of the magnetic attraction is attributed not only to a simple magnet but also to all forms of existence in this Universe: plants, animals, birds, planets, galaxies, etc. If a man and a woman didn't have different characteristics, they wouldn't be of different sexes. They wouldn't be attracted to each other, and they wouldn't be interested in their partnership.

Now, let's dive a little deeper into this topic.

For the Big Bang to initiate the creation of the Universe, two forms of particles were needed: matter and anti-matter. Only the interaction of these two completely opposite forms made the creation of the Universe possible. The chemical reaction between these two completely opposite forms of particles sparked the most energetic explosion ever known, an energy that produced an entire Universe. Only because of their radical differences was the creation of the Universe possible.

In order for the Universe to continue to exist, two completely opposite negative parts are needed: the black matter of the Universe and black holes. Precisely due to these two forces of contradictory negative energies, it's possible for the energies of light and heat of the Universe to exist. Only because of these negative energies is the existence of matter and light possible in this Universe.

As you can see, any form of existence or form of life needs two completely different entities, because only the elements in opposition to one another can make possible the creation of the energies of life and of evolution in the Universe. This rule is attributed to the creation of the human beings and the generation of the energies for the creation and evolution of human beings in the Universe.

The connection between two opposite energies—the energy of the soul and the energy of the consciousness of our body—creates some unimaginable energies, some eternal and continuously evolving energies. At some point, the connection between the soul and the consciousness of the body will get as big as God and the matter of the Universe, and they will be able to create Big Bangs by themselves.

For the evolution between the spirit and the matter to be successful, it's necessary for both entities to have full and equal rights. In other words, both God and the matter of the Universe are our parents, and we must love them equally; we must pray to them both as two equal entities. Even if in the material world, Mother Earth of the Universe makes us face all kinds of negative energies, we must be aware that no negative energy is sent to us to harm us. All the negative energies are sent to do us good, so that we realize that we must choose the path of spiritual evolution and not of stagnation, conservatism, or decomposition.

Imagine that you are addressing your parents. You know that both parents love you and wish you all the best in the world. However, many times our parents give us a slap in the ass. Do you think they're punishing us to make us feel bad, or do they want us to realize that we have to make an effort to evolve?

B) THE MASCULINIZED SOCIETY SUPPORTED BY RELIGIONS AND POLITICIANS:

I have spoken several times about the masculinity of our civilization and the fact that we continue to ignore women's opinions and give priority to men, who lead the world according to the materialist-conservative principle. Compared to the behavior of animals, our society isn't at all different from them. We claim to be intelligent, but our behavior betrays us.

- Just like animals, want to occupy as large a personal territory as possible.

- Just like animals, humans behave according to the Law of the Jungle. The stronger wins.

- Just like male animals lead their herd, so do human males.

- Just like the male animals are the most aggressive and abusive, so are human males. The strongest, toughest, trickiest, and most aggressive dictates to our civilization what and how to do things.

C) FEMININITY AND MASCULINITY OF OUR CIVILIZATION:

Countless times I have spoken about the importance of women in the spiritual evolution, and now I would like to draw the reader's attention to a new aspect of the femininity. All the negative energies of the Universe and of human beings are in their material part, their feminine part, but let's see the differences between men and women.

Who are the most diligent, obedient, and eager to succeed in school, the girls or the boys? The answer is definitely that more girls than boys are the most diligent! And now let's think: While more girls than boys are the most diligent, why are the men in our society the ones who lead the world?

The girls are the representatives of the feminine gender, which has a world of darkness. As a result, coming from a world overloaded with negative energies, where there is competition and superiority of one over the other, their survival instinct is embedded in their subconsciousness. They must survive and get out of their darkness and go to the spiritual light. Their desire for success is so great that it's branded deeply into their subconsciousness, and they can't help wishing for perfectionism and evolutionary success. They are the ones who want the most to evolve and reach God and the spiritual world full of love, harmony, and spiritual light as quickly as possible.

The boys, being the representatives of masculinity, have it deep in their subconsciousness that they are the representatives of the spiritual world, where there is love and harmony and everyone has equal rights, and they don't have to worry about the evolution, because they're already well off where they find themselves. The boys have it in their instinct that they don't need to work because they are already a part of the spiritual world and of the Kingdom of Heaven; they are already a part of God.

The fact that they consider themselves safe and confident of going with impunity for their crimes makes them indifferent to their fate, and they become aggressive and capable of transgressing and committing crimes. Men's "security" instinct is an illusion, because here in the material world, we all pay for our mistakes, and men are the ones who end up in Hell, because they commit the most horrendous crimes on earth.

Unfortunately, some men in their subconsciousness believe that they're superior to women. This is a very big illusion, because in the relationship between soul and body/husband and wife, there must be equal rights for both male and female representatives. We also must consider that both women and men are made of the same component. They are composed of the soul, which is the representative of men and of human bodies, which are the representatives of wives. In other words, both men and women are made the same and have the same rights.

Final Conclusion:

What conclusion can we draw from the last secret that God sent out through my mother?

First of all, I believe that we should be aware of the importance of women in our society and the importance of their desires for our spiritual evolution. To create conditions that make people aware of the reality in which they live, let's make men aware of their dictatorial errors and let women enter the harmonious relationship of society.

The problem of our society is, on the one hand, masculinity at the political and economic level, which is governed by the materialist-conservative principle of aggression, dictatorship, manipulation, etc. On the other hand, there are the religions, which are designed according to the principle of masculinity, where women have no rights but are the representatives of evil and must stay locked inside.

Realizing the principle on which our society is built, let's ask ourselves the following question: What do we need to do to change the way of thinking of our civilization and the conservatist way of the masculinity of our civilization? It's not easy to convince the politicians and the religionists of the importance of observing the Laws of the Universe. They will never give up their insatiable lust for power and domination.

That's why, to convince them, we must get to the root/basis of their thinking principles. The politicians believe that to run the world, a great deal of mysticism and deep and rational thinking are needed. In other words, masculinized thinking is needed, thinking that only men are endowed with. Women, in their mind, aren't able to face such masculine rationality for the family.

The religionists believe that their religion is superior to other religions and ways of life, because at the basis of their religion stands the family. Even if they suppress women's rights, even if they treat them like sheep without a shepherd, they still care a lot about their families. Under the pretext that other nations, religions, and politics don't respect the concept of the family, they consider everyone inferior to their way of thinking.

Consequently, to convince both the politicians and the religionists to renounce their masculinized and materialistic way of thinking, we must come up with solid arguments to contradict them. These arguments could be presented if the scientists in our society accepted spirituality as a form of science. I'm not talking about the spirituality that doesn't have a solid basis of interpretations, or about the interpretations of my dreams. I'm talking about the Spiritual Psychoanalysis I did in my books based on specific examples, with concrete characters, situations, and conclusions.

The Spiritual Psychoanalysis described by me fully meets all the criteria of scientific research, exactly as it meets any other psychoanalysis described on this earth.

Apart from my Spiritual Psychoanalysis, there are a lot of scientific theories about the Kingdom of Heaven and the World of Darkness. Unfortunately, scientists don't want to hear about my research, and they do not want to accept it, although it meets all the criteria of a scientific work.

Here are these two categories of research:

1) CATEGORY OF SCIENTIFIC RESEARCH OF THE KINGDOM OF GOD:

This category includes:

Research of people who have had near-death experiences, This has existed for decades and meets all the criteria of a scientific work. This research deals 100 percent with examining the Kingdom of Heaven/the Kingdom of God.

In the same category falls the research about the children who remember their previous life and stayed in the Kingdom of Heaven together with God Himself. This is irrefutable evidence, because scientists can find the families in which these children once lived.

Just like scientists deal with detecting the abilities of birds and animals to predict dangers, so they could investigate the abilities of the human beings to detect the dangers. The Spiritual Psychoanalysis described by me is part of this research category.

2) CATEGORY OF THE SCIENTIFIC RESEARCH OF THE WORLD OF DARKNESS:

The following scientific research belongs to this category:

- The scientific research of the paranormal. This research is based on undeniable data of various devices for detecting energies and entities from the World of Darkness.

- Shamanism, which could be used as scientific research.

- Clairvoyant people, who can also come up with a lot of information related to the lost spirits and the aggressive spirits from the World of Darkness.

All three fields of scientific research come into contact with the entities of the material world, with the consciousnesses of our bodies that are blocked in the World of Darkness. None of these people can contact the Kingdom of Heaven or our souls, and their only connection is the constituent entities of our bodies.

By accepting all these ways of scientific research, we will be able to demonstrate that it's the politicians, not their aggressive masculinity, who should rule the world; however, the feminine desires for spiritual evolution should get us out of the conservative and self-destructive materialism stand-off.

We will be able to prove to the religious leaders from a scientific point of view that the Universe is not built according to their principle of the family, in which women have no rights, but according to the principle of a democratic family, where women have the same rights as men; even more, in this Universe, Women's desires are much higher than men's desires.

Only then we will be able to convince the world and the religious leaders to become aware of the truth in this Universe based on scientific and accurate data. Only then we will be able to break free and move away from our materialist-conservative and self-destructive era.

But if we don't accept the spirituality as a science in our life, if we don't learn to live in harmony with the Universe, or to listen to the advice of the Universe, which is at every crossroads of our existence, then situations such as COVID-19 will stalk us until we accept the awareness of the reality in which we live.

Psychoanalysis of the Behavior of the Young Generation of Our Civilization

Earlier, I said that the young generation is too focused on their own person, that they're too focused on their bodily pleasures and don't want to listen to the world around them. While the previous generations did what they had to do and what the world around them asked them to do, the current generation doesn't want to listen to anyone, and they only do what they like and not what they *should* do.

Considering their behaviour from a spiritual point of view, the new generation is less advanced than the previous generations, because they don't want to do anything they should do, but they only do what they please: they divorce; they don't want to accept commitments or any kind of suffering; they don't want to struggle; they don't want to get involved; they just want an easy life without stress and torment.

To listen to the advice of the Universe and of our soul, we must learn to listen to the surrounding situations/world and do what we *must* do, not what *we want* to do, because both our soul and the Universe communicate with us through the people around us and through all the situations created around us. By listening to them, we will manage to find the correct path that we must follow in life, and we'll build our destiny based on a continuous and progressive evolution.

Not listening to the surrounding world and situations, we only listen to the whims of our body, and any bodily pleasure begins with a maximum pleasure. But after a while, it ends up in abuse and terrible suffering (example: alcoholism).

The new generation has chosen a path so far unknown to our civilization—they have chosen the path of not suffering. They divorce every time there's a problem in the relationship between husband and wife. They don't want to respect the essential Law of the Universe, the Family Law, which tells us that a man and woman must learn to go together through all the stages and trials of family life, being with the same person throughout their entire lives.

This begs the question: Are they even more backward than the previous generations, like the generations that respected most of the spiritual principles? I think not. The current generation, although they've given up on the principles of the previous generations, don't keep their family united and don't want to do what they have to do. They still managed to take the most important steps that no generation has been able to take until now:

- They managed to listen to their soul wives.
- They managed to eliminate the aggressiveness against the wives of their souls.

This means that the new generation has started a new era—the era of building the harmonious relationship between the soul and their body, the first relationship between husband and wife, which is the most important relationship for which we come to earth.

Of course, their most important mistake is that they don't observe the Family Law of the Universe from the point of view of the relationship between man and woman, but in my opinion, the current generation has a greater chance to build a harmonious relationship between man and woman than previous generations.

Once the new generation has found the harmony of the relationship between their soul and body, once they have become aware of this form of relationship, and once they have eliminated the aggressive factors from their interpersonal relationships, they can move on to the next stage, where they realize how important it is to create a healthy family from the relationship between a man and a woman.

But for that purpose, the current generation should know the Family Law that I mention in my books. Once they are aware of it, they will build not only a new generation based on the Family Law of the Universe, but also a society and a civilization with spiritual thinking, where all forms of political and religious manipulation will be eliminated.

The new generation will have succeeded in the two most important aspects of spiritual evolution. They will have brought out the wife of our soul, the lusts and desires of our body, which is crucial in the relationship between husband and wife at all levels. They also will have managed to eliminate the aggressiveness from the interpersonal relationship, which makes it possible to build a healthy society based on positive reinforcement.

I hope that the new generation succeeds in building a non-violent society, one built on positive reinforcement, similar to Mohandas Karamchand Gandhi's proposals, where interpersonal and interstate relations are harmonious, non-violent relations, and aggressiveness is uprooted.

Chapter Six

GOD IS SENDING OUT MESSAGES THROUGH THE COVID-19 PANDEMIC

THE SIGNS OF GOD AND THEIR INTERPRETATION

Every locality, community, country, race, and contingent has its own Personal Box containing the positive and negative energies they create. When the negative energies exceed a certain level, they burst out and destroy the entire community/race.

First Example: Termination of Humanoid Races

Until the appearance of Homo sapiens, the earth was populated with a multitude of Humanoid races who had the potential of developing into human beings (Grimaud-Herve, Serre, Bahain, 2015, see Bibliography 24). What made these races vanish?

Each race had its own Personal Box. To evolve in the Universe, they were supposed to follow the rules drawn by the Third Energy and the signs of the Lord and thus create positive energies, which get stuffed in the Personal Box of the human being who produced this box, and the human race to which it belongs. But if we don't follow the Laws of the Universe, like Homo erectus and Homo habilis did, and instead create huge negative energies in the Personal Boxes of their races, total meltdown will follow.

IONEL ROTARU

Second Example: Abolishing a Superpower

In 1917, Russia commenced her big communist project, and after World War II, she became the USSR by extending her boundaries over fifteen different countries. Also, she imposed her governing system over half of the European states. The USSR was then one of the biggest economies of the world, with technologically advanced agriculture, metallurgy, and light industry. She started space programs, sending shuttles and satellites into the outer space. And she made her army one of the most sophisticated of the time.

In the USSR, the entire population was indoctrinated with communist propaganda and had the impression that everything was fine in their country. Everyone believed that the stability of their country was so strong that it would never fail.

The economic crisis that plagued the country in 1992 led to the destruction of the entire economic and political system, with many enterprises torn down and their bricks ending up in the hands of the population. The country looked like Britain after the German bombing during World War II. The unemployment rate was high, and only teachers and doctors could find a job. In agriculture, peasants reverted to the old style of harnessing horses to churn their land. Wages were minimal, not enough for a loaf of bread.

Spiritual Analysis

The Personal Box of this country was overloaded with negative energies she had created since birth. It was a dictatorial country that oppressed her people with drastic laws. The USSR was built based on lies, dilapidation, and brutality against her own people and the surrounding world. Her leaders heinously killed hundreds of thousands of people to mind their own interests.

When a country, family, or civilization is built on such criteria, it can't last forever, and at a certain point it will fall apart. Nothing of what has been constructed on negative energies holds for good, and it will crumble down at one time or another. A couple will divorce and a country will collapse.

The overaccumulation of negative energies in the Personal Box of the former USSR caused the biggest economy of the world to go down, together with everything the communist system had built. The citizen of this country returned to the same standard of life as in 1945.

Attention! Important! Imagine that everything built by the USSR from 1945 until 1992 was practically demolished down to the last brick. Now imagine that our civilization was built step by step after the material principle of our thinking. People nowadays think exactly as they did five thousand years ago, and all this while, especially in the past century, our civilization overstuffed its Personal Box with negative energies.

If the negative energies stashed in the Personal Box of the former USSR could destroy so much, what would happen to our civilization if its negative energies are suddenly set free from its Personal Box? Unless we immediately change our demeanor and thinking, all the negative energies of our civilization will destroy everything that our civilization has built, and we will use stone axes and wooden tools again. The Third Energy will send the negative energies back to their producers, and she will destroy everything they built based on their greed for wealth.

This process has already started with the COVID-19 pandemic, which is seriously warning every citizen of this planet that if we don't keep the negative energies at bay, the Third Energy will let all the negative energies from the Personal Box of our civilization run over us.

HOW CAN WE INTERPRET THE SIGNS OF GOD?

Let me elaborate on the ways of interpreting the signs of God, just to give you more insight into the complexity of the message our Lord is sending out through the pandemic. First, I'll tell you what happened to my sister Louise in the spring of 2019.

Those who read my first book know my sister, who is faithful, devoted, and fully conscientious of the power of God. Louise was craving a modern house fitted with all the necessary amenities and services.

She and her husband worked hard abroad, and they used the money they earned with sweat and blood to give a face-lift to their house in their natal village. The investment paid off: the new house had all the amenities a man could dream of. And it was fenced by a concrete wall closed with a metal gate. But Louise had never invested a single cent in her pension plan. Her only savings was the amount of 10,000.00 USD she'd received from her last employer in Spain.

At one point, they bought four cows to support themselves. But Louise continued to spend the money earned in Italy and Spain on improving their house. In the winter of 2018–2019, she decided to insulate the exterior walls to save heating fuel for the season. In spring came a storm with gusty winds and heavy rains that knocked down more than ten meters of their fence. It was the most solid fence in the village and the only one that was knocked down.

(See the image below)

FIG. 13 LOUISE'S FENCE

(On the right is Louisa's concrete fence, and on the left is a wooden fence like all the fences in the village.)

Spiritual Psychoanalysis

After the storm, my sister Louise, who is familiar with the signs of God but which, sadly, she can't interpret very well, believed that the event happened because her husband thinks negatively and badly about everything. I found out about my sister's conclusion from my mother.

"Mom, when you interpret any sign of God, you must take into consideration several fundamental principles," I said.

When a negative or positive situation is coming from outside, it was definitively created by God to teach us what we did good or bad and what exactly we should change in ourselves. And we should ask ourselves:

- What did God want to tell me through this event?
- What did I do wrong in the past?
- What do I have to do?
- What should I change in myself now?

Secondly, in order to prove that this situation wasn't just an accident, we must proceed with the calculus of probability. In Louise's case, we should ask ourselves:

- Was any other material damaged in the village?
- Why was only the most reliable fence pulled down?

Thirdly, now that we know this was a sign of God, we must seek the essential of this message, which we can't find in our brains or in our way of viewing the surrounding world. No, what we should know is that God is speaking with us in a very simple way, only through specific situations.

In Louise's case, God's message is not hidden, nor is it an intricate philosophical riddle, like my sister believes. It is totally stupid to think that way!

A STRUCTURE was demolished when Louise was about to start building another one, which means that God was trying to tell her something.

- Why did God let the strongest fence in the village to be pulled down?
- Why did this happen to the family that invested so much money and effort in the renovation of their house?
- Why weren't the constructions of the other people destroyed?
- And most importantly, why was that fence partially destroyed when Louise was ready to proceed with another project?

The negative energies that made the fence crumble down are the very energies *created* by Louise through her obsession with renovations. All her life she worked in foreign countries and invested all the money in renovating her houses. Her obsession with the "ideal house" had exceeded the limit of normality and turned into negative energies, which made her not see the reality of life or realize that she no longer had money to invest in construction.

She didn't pay into the pension fund. Retirement age was approaching, but she had no pension and no spare money. The last repair of the house would have meant that she spent the last spare money she had left. In this case, God had the obligation to let the Third Energy return the negative energies to my sister, and He did it disguised in a message. Therefore, God found it appropriate to guide those energies to her fence when she was ready to start a new project for her house. God exhausted Louise's negative energies and made her cancel her project of heat insulation and understand she should abandon the construction and the renovation of her homestead. All the more so as Louise was nearing her retirement age and she found herself in a bad financial situation.

Who authored the pandemic? God or us?

One day I was speaking with my mother on Skype about the COVID-19 pandemic and what the future holds for us.

"Everything is in God's hands. We are at His mercy, since we transgressed against Him numerous times," she said to me.

And I said to her, "Mom, God doesn't want to punish us for our mistakes. He doesn't judge or punish anyone. Everything that happens to us and our whole civilization is because of us and only us. The COVID-19 pandemic is a negative energy taking hold of our planet due to the negative energies our civilization has created and continues to create. When the Personal Box gets overloaded with negative energies, the Third Energy returns them to the producer, and God can't do anything against her decision except turn our negative energies into individual messages to help us choose the right path of life. Through this pandemic, God orders us to stop generating negative energies and change our thinking and demeanor in order to avoid the nothingness.

"God tried to send us other messages through the tornadoes in Florida and the stricken poverty in Africa and all the wars and terrorism and international conflicts, which are negative energies created by our civilization and repurposed by God into summons for a change. Unless we listen to these direct messages and stop making negative energies for the Personal Box of our civilization, God will have no other choice than to turn the energies into powerful messages sent out through destructive pandemics and catastrophes. Our future and that of our civilization too utterly depend on us and the decisions we make today and the energies we create from now on.

If we follow the signs of our Lord and do what He orders us to do, all the negative energies from the Personal Box of our civilization will die out, and the destiny of our civilization will be one of love and harmony. But if we continue to destroy the environment and our families and satisfy our carnal pleasures, our future will be a record of pandemics, catastrophes, and conflicts, bringing our civilization to collapse and disappearance."

THE SIGNS OF GOD ARE NOT A JOKE

We all are future Gods, but we should not play like ones. We shouldn't do anything we want without bearing the consequences of our actions. First off, to become God, we must learn to respect the Laws of the Universe.

God is God because He fully observes all the Laws of the Universe, and we should do the same. We should observe the Laws of the Universe like He does. We must train ourselves to follow His signs, which are not a joke but guide us safely and securely during our journey to a spiritual evolution. God is always trying to tell us something, and His suggestions are well-founded, unique, and meaningful with regard to our future. Here are just a few simple examples.

A discussion with my friend:

In the summer of 2010, when the translation of my first book was almost complete, a strange thing happened. As I had nothing to do, I went out to a neighboring village to fish for mackerel. I was driving to the nearest station to buy gas, when a car veered off ahead of me and continued its way at a very low speed. After a few minutes, I got to a bottleneck, where all the vehicles in the street were running slowly. It was strange to see so many cars there at that time of the day.

I realized this was sign of God urging me to go back and call it the day. But I continued my way, promising myself that I would return if the pumps were busy. When I got there, all the gas pumps were taken. I had never seen so many cars at the same time at that station. Definitively, it was a sign that I should go home. I called a friend of mine and told him what happened.

"I understand you," he said. "Listen to what happened to me yesterday. I'm renovating my basement, and yesterday I decided to take a break and go out fishing. As I was collecting my gear, God began telling me that I should stay home. But I said to myself that nothing could happen to me, and I hit the road. I arrived at my spot and cast the line. Boy, the hook got caught in the undergrowth, and the rod broke into three pieces. It was a short fishing party, buddy, and in less than a minute all my gear was gone."

"You see," I said to him, "we both know the signs of God, but we stubbornly continue on our way, hoping that we can go by. But nothing goes as we plan, and we must trust the Lord more than anyone else, since only He knows what the future holds for us. So only He can give us appropriate advice.

"Imagine how hard it is for Him to deal with our reluctance. It took Him more than ten years to make me go through three financial crises and lose huge amounts of money, or the equivalent of two houses, and begin my life from square one several times. So if He needed some fifteen years to teach me see His signs, how long does it take Him to make everyone and the entire civilization turn their face towards Him?"

I hope our civilization will learn how to follow God's signs like I explained in my first book, *The Destiny and Signs of God*, and won't bear the excruciating burden like I did. Imagine how much negative energy He may need to make the entire civilization believe in His signs? And how much suffering will be on this planet if our civilization continues to ignore His signs, such as I did when I was ignorant?

"We shouldn't play with the signs of God, for they are priceless. God is working hard to maintain them and keep us away from the perils. Therefore, we should follow His signs seriously, whether big or small. His signs are the beacons that guide us to the path of the spiritual evolution. They are the holiest connections between us and the Lord and the spiritual world. There is no religion in the Universe holier than the direct signs of God for everyone in the entire civilization."

WE MUST HELP OUR LORD

It's very difficult for the Lord to convince all of us of the truthfulness of His signs. If He wasted more than a decade to make me take the spiritual way, He should make titanic efforts to convince our entire civilization, led by corrupted politicians and conservatory clerics, to do the same.

In Chapter Two, I wrote about the secrets of God and what we truly are. We are the children of God. We are God's messengers here on earth to tell the material world how important the spiritual evolution can be. Therefore, we should rush to help the Lord help us and convince the material world of how essential the harmony between the two worlds is.

God finds it difficult to send His messages directly to the earthbound. He can't communicate through words but only through the situations of life and the negative or positive energies we produced in the past. When I was young and had no knowledge of His signs, the Lord had a hard time sending me a simple message, and He hustled me through a series of difficult situations.

Now our civilization is facing the same perils I faced when I was young, and I believe we should pay attention to His signs like I did. All of you who read my books should know how to proceed. If you genuinely commit yourselves to helping God support us, we will be successful! All of you should apply yourselves to the task of waking up our civilization and assisting the Lord in helping us switch to the spiritual stage of evolution.

God is sending messages through the COVID-19 pandemic. If we approach the pandemic with our material philosophy of life, we'll find the guilty outright. Tucked in our metabolism, our material thinking shows only someone else's guilt, and instead of being introspective, we are quick to put the blame on the surrounding world, arguing that we are never wrong.

As for the pandemic, we found the wrong-doers immediately: we put the blame on China and the heads of a laboratory in Wuhan, and we all want revenge and to take the Chinese to the international court and make a profit from their carelessness. We desperately want someone to pay for what is now happening to us (The Thought, February 28, 2020), (Nehring, May 7, 2020).

I didn't write this book to seek the guilty ones outside of us or to pursue undeserved profits but to look for the wrong inside ourselves and spiritually psychoanalyze the impact of the pandemic and explain how the spiritual thinking should be applied to our civilization.

"Who was involved in the Pandemic?" should be the first question.

"Absolutely everyone from all over the world," should be the answer.

If someone becomes the target of something bad, or if a country becomes the subject of a catastrophe or a terrorist act, God must have sent a direct message to our entire civilization. Therefore I believe that the COVID-19 pandemic that impacted the entire world is a *direct* message that our Lord is now sending across.

Now that we understood that God is speaking to the entire civilization, let's see what messages He was trying to send to us.

WE ARE EQUAL BEFORE THE VIRUS COVID-19

It may sound preposterous. It's absurd, since we all have been impacted, rich or poor, homosexuals or bisexuals, White or Blacks and all the other skin colors. In other words, the whole population became helpless before the contamination. The only ones who could find my question relevant would be the White supremacists, the dictators, the religious fundamentalists, and all the leaders who consider themselves above everyone else. In spite of this, we all know that COVID-19 does not discriminate between races or walks of life, good people or bad ones, God-fearing or unfaithful. For this virus, we all are the same. We all are equal before the virus and in the face of God and the entire Universe.

This is the first message sent by our Lord to our civilization: We all are equal, and we all are brothers and sisters; we all are the future gods. Hence, we must take all the measures to abolish dictatorship and racism and stop oppressing other people for their political and social opinions. We must discard our superiority over other human beings and other societies and give support to the countries in dire straits. In other words, our civilization has come to the point where it desperately needs a true harmony throughout the globe.

We must help the disadvantaged through the stage of their spiritual evolution; we must help them the way we help the little children. I'm not talking only about certain persons or layers of our society, but of all the poor countries of the planet;

We must listen and learn from our peers.

We must treat with kindness and respect those who are better than us, like children should treat their parents.

Who took responsibility for getting our civilization out of the worst disaster on the planet? In normal times, our leaders are the politicians, but now the whole population turned to scientists and experts in the economy and health. These specialists did their best to help us swim across the muddy waters and safely get to the shore. Their priorities were people's lives and health, while the finances came second.

This means that the second message of our Lord is that our civilization should adopt a new form of leadership based on the ideas of scientists, who can resolve the essential issues of the survival of our civilization when environment and moral destruction can hardly be contained.

WHAT ARE THE SPECIALISTS TALKING ABOUT?

During the pandemic, a number of industries shut down for a time, and there was a significant reduction in air travel. Car traffic was also significantly reduced. All this led to a drop in air pollution. For the first time in a hundred years, our planet could breathe freely and normally. We know that our civilization is gradually damaging the planet, and soon we'll get to the point where there will be nothing left on earth.

Spiritually, the planet Earth is our mother, as she created us and the environment around us. So by destroying the planet, we destroy our biological mother, the one who educated us and maintained us to grow up. And now we put a pillow on her face and kill her. Polluting the air and cutting the trees is tantamount to stifling her with a pillow. God's third message is to choose those leaders who can protect our planet, our spiritual mother, the earth.

A NEW WAY TO CHOOSE LEADERS

Everyone on this planet is unhappy with their leaders. We know that once at the helm, politicians will continue to destroy the environment, wage wars that kill innocent people, and concoct dirty schemes on the voters' ticket and taxpayers' money. We vote for them and then we take to the streets and burn them in effigy. If leaders fall short of expectations, we must find new ways of electing them.

The problem is that every country has had the same political parties for dozens of years, and those parties are made of the same people with the same principles and ideas. It means that a country with only three or four parties has only three or four possibilities of evolution, since their parties use the same governing ideas over and over again. Even if the three or four political parties take governance turns, they aren't promoting a continuing evolution because they only bring back the previous principles again and again, just like a hamster spins the wheel in front of the circus audience. Under the circumstances, no one can change anything, since the country is under the perpetual leadership of the same material principles and characters with the same self-centered material mindset.

I believe this situation can be improved if at least one new political party with new, clean candidates makes an appearance at every new election. This new party or parties should come up with new programs focusing particularly on the protection of our planet and the integration of the spiritual development at all the level of society.

WHY DID GOD LET A DEADLY VIRUS COME OVER US?

Man is the only species on earth that destroys his own habitat. He is the only one who upsets the balanced scale of the environment that Mother Nature has created and entertained for hundreds of thousands of years. God made a species of killing viruses similar to the behavior of the human species to make us realize what we really are, what we're doing with our habitat, and what will be left of us after we wholly destroy Mother Nature.

Let's think of the most serious factors affecting Mother Nature:

a) Our material thinking, our greed, and our rush for wealth and domination of the surrounding world goes from a personal level up to the top leaders of the world: economic, political, and religious.

The leaders in charge of the economy destroy the planet to make more money.

The political leaders wage wars to get richer and dominate other people.

The religious leaders have an immeasurable thirst for domination and confuse people about traditions and rituals that have nothing to do with the spiritual evolution.

b) We multiply like rats or hungry parasites in disregard of our habitat and the consequences of our actions.

We know that people in poor countries multiply because they can't afford a minimal standard of living and birth control methods. If the economic and political leaders used spiritual thinking and thought not only about their personal profit, and if everyone on the planet looked for solutions to live in harmony with all people, then we could find a solution to the problems of the entire planet, both from the economic point of view, the birth rate, and the protection of our planet.

Instead of generating conflicts and wars in their countries and spending tremendous amounts of money on weaponry and military forces, we should change our material thinking to a spiritual one and start investing in harmony between people, because from a spiritual point of view, we are one whole family on this earth, and we need to learn how to live in love and harmony.

It has been well-known for centuries that the greed and unquenched thirst for power and domination of the religious leaders produced strategies for conquering and seizing new territories. One of these strategies is to make the faithful hate other denominations so that their "clientele" go on sparking wars, conflicts, and terrorist acts.

Another strategy is inordinate multiplication. Let's see what God says with regard to multiplication.

The first aspect is the multiplication of our spiritual forefathers: our spiritual mother, the Mother of the Universe, together with God.

The second aspect is the direct messages of the Lord for our civilization, our life, and the environment we live in.

The first aspect: It's easy to understand the way in which God and the matter of the Universe multiply. We only have to look at the concentration of human beings in space or consider how many other civilizations there are in this Universe.

If the religions of the world invaded the whole planet and our habitat, God and the matter of the Universe should do the same thing: invade and fill the whole Universe with human beings and create a civilization for each individual star in the sky. Unfortunately (actually, fortunately), the astronomers who studied hundreds of thousands of stars didn't find any other neighboring planet inhabited by humans.

As a result, we can't acknowledge that the theory of religions about the multiplication is true. On the contrary, we can definitively say that their theory is abusive and is used to dominate and destroy our civilization.

For an appropriate Spiritual Evolution, people need time to meditate, analyze, and find their inner-selves, and they need space to find harmony and love between us and the Universe and between us and our spiritual forefathers.

For example, during the pandemic, the city population, especially those who live in blocks of apartments, realized they needed more space to breathe, and a large number of them living in Montreal and Quebec bought properties in the extremities of the province. This is another piece of evidence that God urges us to lower the number of inhabitants on the planet. In other words, we should keep in control the irrational number of our births.

The second aspect: Let's think of the number of women who can't become pregnant on this planet. Why did God order them to be infertile? Why do those women have to go through this ordeal? The answer is very simple: God wants us to get used to the idea of not having children in the future.

The earth's capacity does not have unlimited possibilities to produce the necessary food for a population that can't stop multiplying. We can't multiply without taking this into account. One doesn't need to be an expert in spiritual analysis to realize that something is going wrong. So what is God's message with regard to this situation?

God is telling us in a clarion voice that we should take all the necessary measures to protect our environment and stop multiplying like parasites. I believe that all those theories developed by the religious leaders of the world are in conflict with God's messages. God is telling us through the pandemic that we are parasites willing to destroy our environment, just like the COVID-19 virus is doing to us, and we must discontinue our irrational multiplication and stop any industrial craze that could impact us.

What was the first measure we took to stop the COVID-19 virus? First, people were stopped from traveling from one country to another. Why did God push us to the point where we couldn't travel anymore? God left people stuck in their countries of origin to stop the infestation of our planet and to make us aware of our carnal temptation by seeking beauty and happiness outside our country or place of birth. This kind of temptation makes us forget our personal values and identity.

By leaving the people stranded in their own country, God blocked the import and export operations, arguing that we shouldn't use labor from outside our country but concentrate on our own economy and resources. We should stop using the surrounding world for our own profit. Instead, we should develop our own economy at home. Otherwise, come the new blockages, we will fall into pauperism and starvation. By satisfying their carnal temptations and seeking beauty and happiness outside their country, this generation totally forsook their personal values and the charm of their homeland. This temptation has become uncontrollable.

To better understand this subject, I invite you to see the feature movie *Lucy in the Sky*, directed by Noah Hawey (2019) and starring Natalie Portman as Luci Cola. The movie is about a young girl who became a cosmonaut and went into outer space. For the first time in her life, she saw so much beauty. Coming back to earth, she realized she had lost the purpose of life and found herself in total disarray. She had no interest in family life, society, or any activity on earth anymore. She only wanted to fly back to outer space and live amid its unimaginable beauty.

Luci was romantically involved with one of her workmates, and she told him everything about her new experience. Sadly, the guy betrayed her, and crime charges were laid against her and she had to serve several years in prison.

In this movie, the main character can't see anything interesting on earth and believes that beauty and happiness can be found only outside our planet. Only in prison did she realize that beauty and happiness were actually all around us. So when she was released, she became a beekeeper, a perfect occupation that helped her see the construction of the whole Universe. The Universe is like a beehive: it's made of a large, united family where everything works like clockwork. And there is more than harmony inside a beehive; there is also love and respect for one another, and the soul and the intelligence of the material being.

Spiritual Psychoanalysis

In the past decades, we all started to look for happiness and beauty of life outside our country or the place we came from. In Luci's case, the cosmonaut went through the torments of life and realized that beauty and happiness were not outside around us inside the surrounding people in our family, our profession, and the natural environment.

In the case of our civilization, the people stranded in their own homes must tame and rid their carnal temptation and stop seeking beauty and happiness outside their own selves. Like Luci the cosmonaut, we must learn how to search for beauty and happiness inside ourselves and in our own entourage. By searching for beauty and happiness inside of us, we will certainly find ourselves and our soul too. We need to learn how to meditate and see the signs of God, because our soul is talking to us through meditations and the signs of Divinity.

To live in harmony with the surrounding world, we must learn how to live in the moment and seek beauty in nature and reach out eagerly to anyone in our entourage. It's the only way we can find God, since He is present in all the things and beings around us: in the birds that fly, the wind that blows, the people we meet, and in whatever catches our eyes or we can hear.

Imagine how the young cosmonaut Luci was feeling when she was looking inside the beehives. Imagine how she was admiring the whole Universe inside her beehives. We should do exactly the same and train ourselves to see anything that happens with the same eyes.

Regarding our trips, God wants us to cease being addicted to the exterior world and concentrate on the inner part of our body in order to discover our soul; He says that we should stay focused on the surrounding world every second of our life in order to find Him, because by discovering our soul within ourselves, and the Lord our Father in our entourage, we can understand the essential phenomena of the construction of the Universe. Otherwise, we will continue to satisfy our carnal temptations by looking at the beauty of nature without understanding it.

What was the second measure we took to stop the COVID-19 virus. The second measure was to ask people to stay home. In other words, the best solution to protect ourselves from the global pandemic was to stay home with our families. To lay the basis for a Spiritual Analysis, we should ask ourselves the following question: "What were the challenges of staying home for too long?"

We felt lonely and had to face off with the other ones. Obviously, without our previous social life, we forgot about ourselves and our own souls and how to live in love, harmony, and understanding with the members of their own family.

Spiritual Analysis

From a spiritual point of view, the Essential Law of the Construction of the Universe is the Family Law that I described in my first book. In other words, the primary goal of our souls here on earth is to train ourselves to live in harmony with our family:

- in the relationship between body and soul

- in the relationship between man and wife

- in the relationship between children and parents

- in the relationship between parents and children

To find love and harmony between body and soul, we must spend as much time as possible with ourselves in calm and tranquility and analyze all the developing situations that are true signs of God. We need more time for ourselves to meditate because certain meditations are the best way to discover our soul and his intentions.

To find love and harmony within our family, we must spend as much time as possible with all our family members. We must spend time with our life partner, our husband or wife, in order to understand, accept, love, and support them in their pursuits. And we should do the same with our children and assist them in fulfilling their dreams. Also, we must try to forget the cares and vexations of life and dedicate more time to our parents and love and respect them for everything they did for us. Unfortunately, our society is currently busy making the rich richer and has no time for their own families.

In my first book, I wrote about the importance of cutting down the work hours so that people have time to meditate, analyze their life, and dedicate more time, love, and harmony to their families, as the Essential Law of the Universe, the Family Law requests.

Therefore, with regard to our presence in our own family, God wants us to reorganize the structure of our civilization in such a way that we spend more time with our family and forge love and harmony bonds with our partner, children, and parents, as the Essential Law of the Universe, the Family Law requests.

The third measure we took to stop the COVID-19 virus was to cease non-essential industry. To lay the basis of a spiritual analysis, we should ask ourselves: "What is hiding behind this message? What did God want to tell us by putting the entire non-essential industry on hold?"

It does not take a wise man or a scientist to answer this question and realize that the essential issue of our civilization is the environmental con- tamination of our planet. So God's next message for our civilization is to stop the destruction of our planet by bringing non-essential industries to a halt.

What are the non-essential industries? On what do we waste our money in a reckless and foolish manner? The answer is very simple: Our civilization wastes astronomic amounts on weaponry, military, warfare, and terrorism. And we must stop this craze. Of course, there are fields in which money is being invested for enormous returns, such as the pharmaceutical industry, which holds the monopoly in all the democratic countries.

Other specific measures taken to protect our planet:

First: Other than repurposing the money invested in weapons and military, our civilization should stop any form of fossil industry that pollutes the planet excessively. Any international conflict, war, or terrorist act is the equivalent of a negative energy worldwide, an energy created against our whole civilization.

Second: Our civilization should stop cutting the forests and destroying the wildlife ecosystems.

Third: We should stop manufacturing single-use instruments, such as razors, that can work only during the warranty period. In other words, we must stop polluting our planet with cheap defects and instead produce high technology goods that run for a lifetime. Of course, the human being needs changes, but the technological inventions should work for a lifetime, and only the design should change.

Fourth: One of our major issues is the fast rate of our multiplication, about which I already wrote. For a hundred years, our civilization grew threefold to 7.5 billion people, up from approximately two billion (Wikipedia 1, 18, June 2020). At this rate, the perspective of the next one hundred years is gruesome.

To slow down the birth rate, we should invest less in weapons and the military and more in health and people's comfort in the poor states so they can control their birth rate. We should bring to the attention of the religious people who believe they must multiply in excess God's message to all of us and the ways we should go. We had enough people following the laws written by our religious leaders and our prophets/apostles several hundreds or thousands of years ago. It's time everyone started to communicate with God directly, because God's messages are totally different from those of the traditional church.

THE WORLD LEADERS' MISTAKES AND THEIR NEW FORM OF DICTATORSHIP

When God is sending us a message through a certain situation, we shouldn't turn the situation into our interest, whether personal or political, and make a profit from it. When the pandemic hit the world, politicians around the world tried to make gains from the misfortune that has visited our civilization. The Russians flexed their muscles and showed the "intelligence" of their leader, who settled at the helm like a true dictator for the rest of his life. At the outset of the pandemic, the Russian Parliament voted unanimously to keep him in power until 2036 (Robyn Dixon, June 21, 2020). In the European countries and North America, politicians had a taste of mass manipulation by striking deep fear into the public of living a normal social life.

Practically, politicians made a big mistake by manipulating the masses by the use of fear. From a spiritual viewpoint, fear is a form of negative energy, and by striking fear into the population of the whole planet, we create enormous amounts of negative energy that accumulates in the Personal Box of our civilization.

We should not be afraid of any pandemic whatsoever; we should make a Spiritual Psychoanalysis of all the events that help us understand the messages of God and follow His recommendation to promote changes on a personal social and political level. Also, we should try to adapt to all the perils accordingly. In the case of the COVID-19 pandemic, most of the fatalities were recorded within long-term facilities and elderly homes. It means that we should continue our social activity and protect the elderly as much as we can. If the pandemic wave receded, it doesn't mean that our leaders should keep manipulating us as they did through mass media but leave us in peace.

FINAL CONCLUSION

All the undeserved negative situations I described in this book were created by God so that I could pass them on to my reader and help everyone on this planet get an image of the negative energies as they accumulate to the limit worldwide. The correlation between what happened to me and the COVID-19 pandemic gives us a global picture of God's prominent messages for our entire civilization.

God is urging us to change our thinking and demeanor as He has prescribed. The pandemic was His last warning and the last possibility to convey a direct message about the future of our civilization. If we fail Him, our civilization will suffer a terrible fate, just like my friend's wife did when she fell in the basement.

Due to the overaccumulation of negative energies in the Personal Box of our civilization, God can't protect us or warn us of the upcoming catastrophes, because the Third Energy will force Him to help the negative energies hit their target, like they did in Maria's life.

Stop looking for someone to blame. Our human nature and our materialistic thinking makes each of us look for somonee to blame:

- On a personal level, we blame the people around us for our failures.

- Worldwide, all countries blame their neighbors for inappropriate behavior.

- On a religious level, clerics blame the other religions.

- Politicians point accusatory fingers at the politicians in other countries.

As a result of these accusations, we are creating unending conflicts and wars. Although the politicians and the religionists see that their fight against other countries or other religions doesn't yield positive results, despite their insistence to change the mindset of other faiths or other policies, we still continue the same policy—blaming the world around us and fighting to change it.

I don't need to go too far. Look at the war in Afghanistan that lasted decades, and nobody managed to do anything against the religious invasion of this country. Through this example, God and Mother Matter are trying to send us a very important message: "Stop trying to change the world around you, because no one will ever change when someone from the outside tries to change them." We will change only when we become aware that we have to change. In the case of religious believers, people have to realize, on their own account, the disaster they live in, and the disaster their religion brings around them.

Personally, I tried to forcefully change the behavior of my children and my wife, but I failed. Not only did I fail, but I made my children and my wife move away from the spiritual paths I had urged them to take. It was only after I started to respect their decisions that they managed to realize the harmful effect of some of their behaviour, and they accepted the spiritual ways I was dictating for them. In the case of international affairs, every country, regardless of its level of democracy, must learn to respect the decisions of the countries on this planet.

I understand that the Russian, Chinese, and Arab governments have completely different concepts from the Western countries, where democracy is at home; I understand that it's unacceptable for the democratic countries to condone the aggressive behavior of dictatorial countries, but let's see what the Universe wants from us and what the Laws of the Universe say about our international affairs.

First of all, the Laws of the Universe urge us to stop creating negative energies, conflicts, and wars; these are negative energies made by the democratic countries. Even if these wars and conflicts have all the justification in this Universe, they are destructive energies. In other words, if we really consider ourselves democratic, we must *stop* creating negative energies in the first place.

The second Law of the Universe says that we have to stop looking for someone else to blame; instead, we should blame ourselves. The problem with democratic countries is that they don't respect the decisions of their neighbors, and they insist on forcibly changing the mentality of their neighboring countries. The very policy of these countries is not to tolerate aggressiveness within their countries, but when it comes to foreign policies, these countries call, first of all, to solve problems by force.

278

As you can see, the democratic countries follow this principle: although they recognize and know that force should not be used, they definitely don't realize the importance of this behavior, because internationally, they continue to behave aggressively.

I understand that it's very difficult to tolerate the aggressive behavior of our neighbors, but unfortunately, we have no choice. We must learn to accept them as they are and have the patience until they themselves realize the harmful impact of their behavior. Positive reinforcement is the only thing we can do about it.

A very obvious example is my mother's behavior towards her aggressive husband. By overlooking her husband's aggressiveness and the fact that he didn't appreciate her or help her in anyway, she did her duty to her family and to the Laws of the Universe. She tolerated her husband's brutality for years and looked for peaceful solutions to solve this problem. She looked for ways to use positive reinforcement. Only time, life situations, and my mother's unabated patience made my father respect her, love her, and appreciate her at her true value. Even though it took my mother her whole life, she was triumphant in the mission for which she had come here on earth.

We should learn the same thing, and every political or religious leader should do the same: Become aware that the most effective solution to get out of the self-destruction of our civilization is the spiritual path of evolution with spiritual thinking and with positive reinforcement.

To achieve this goal, I don't think we need to tolerate the aggressiveness against us as my mother did. No. In this day and age, we all should look for solutions to make all the aggressive minds aware of the harmful materialistic ways that lead us to self-destruction, and the importance of the spiritual way of evolution and spiritual thinking.

The essential message sent through the COVID-19 pandemic to our civilization is to start living in harmony with the Universe. First of all, we must learn to live in harmony with our Mother Earth instead of destroying it. For that purpose, we must learn to think spiritually. And the first thing we should do to think spiritually and heed the advice of the Universe is not to behave like the coronavirus, which destroys its habitat.

So we must do everything possible to reduce the multiplication of human beings on earth, like the coronavirus. We have to stop the destruction of our Mother Earth and let Mother Nature take over the earth. We must do everything possible for our planet to become a Planetary National Park again, where plants and animals regain priority. We must let the human beings become children of Mother Earth again—obedient, polite, respectful children who listen to their mother Earth, to their Mother Universe, and live in a perfect harmony all together and become a component of the earth, of the Universe, and not dictators and destroyers, as they presently are.

NEXT BOOK:

THE MESSAGES OF THE UNIVERSE THROUGH THE RUSSIAN WAR AGAINST UKRAINE: SPIRITUAL PSYCHOANALYSIS

Introduction

FIRST OF ALL, I'D LIKE TO APOLOGIZE TO THE READER, BECAUSE BEFORE publishing this book, I bounced back to write about other topics. It's the second time I've done this, and I am so sorry that I had no choice. Only two weeks after I gave the finishing touches to the manuscript to be translated from Romanian into English, the Russian Army invaded Ukraine, and a bloody war broke out.

The subject of the war waged by Russia against Ukraine is of paramount importance, and I don't want to mention it casually, as it carries prominent messages and deserves that a Spiritual Psychoanalysis be done. Russia's forceful action against Ukraine demonstrates the extreme impact on our civilization caused by the gratifications of the bodily pleasures of domination, power, and manipulation of the masses. This heinous war is a perfect indication that at the base of all forms of mass manipulation, both political and religious, stays our materialistic thinking that has guided our civilization from its genesis on the face of the earth.

Chapter One

SPIRITUAL PSYCHOANALYSIS OF THE RUSSIAN WAR

BODILY TEMPTATIONS

Before starting the Spiritual Psychoanalysis of the war between Russia and Ukraine, I would like to dwell a little on the bodily temptations to make the reader aware of the impact our materialistic thinking and extreme and insatiable bodily temptations may cause. I want to use as an example Vladimir Putin, the President of Russia. This character is the ideal representative who demonstrates the meaning of the satisfaction of *extreme* bodily pleasures that a human being could obtain here on earth.

From the beginning of his career, this character started with materialistic bodily satisfactions of wealth. Being the President of Russia, the country with the largest natural resources in the world, he started his career with the most sophisticated techniques to plunder the country's wealth for his personal benefit. He gave the Russian oligarchs the freedom to steal, on the condition that they give back to Putin a large part of their loot. Putin's lust for wealth grew in line with his wealth, which has already reached unfathomable sums of money and richness. As the lust for wealth grew, being a narcissistic personality, so did the Russian President's lust to be the center of attention using the techniques of manipulating the masses.

Availed by all the levers of manipulating the masses, Putin created a "spider web" around himself that covered the whole country. He killed the journalists who opposed his regime, he killed the politicians from his opposition who spoke against him, and he became the person with the most powerful technique of manipulating the masses in the world. All the Russians have become his zombified slaves, who believe absolutely everything that comes out of his mouth. Even if they knew very well that their leader was lying, that he was stealing huge amounts, the Russians became his zombified fanatics.

Reaching the peak of the bodily pleasures of wealth and domination in his country and in the countries of the ex-USSR, Vladimir Putin was no longer satisfied with these pleasures, and he decided to go further and beyond.

Being the ruler with the greatest natural resources in the world and having an army that everyone feared, he decided to start satisfying his other bodily pleasures—the narcissistic bodily pleasures of being in everyone's center of attention. For this purpose, Putin decided to terrify the entire planet with his nuclear weapons, thus showing off his power and dominance over the entire planet and our entire civilization. Putin began to feel the insatiable need for his bodily pleasures that all the countries of the world should kneel before him. Threatening all the democratic countries on the planet, he started the war in Ukraine.

In the mind/consciousness of this unappeasable character was the idea that all the people on the planet would be afraid of him and would worship him as a god. In his subconsciousness was the idea that, finally, the bodily pleasures of his body would receive the extreme pleasure of success, which would make him throw his head back in ecstasy. Fortunately, that did not happen.

According to the Law of the Paradox of Life that I mentioned in my first book, when we have a materialistic mindset and are convinced that we're the most powerful and are superior above all, precisely then we realize that in reality, everything is completely opposite to what we thought.

In Putin's case, who considers himself to be the most powerful person in the world, it turned out that in reality he is the weakest person. In fact, not only Putin considered himself the most powerful on the planet, but everyone on the planet believed that he really is the most powerful. But as the war in Ukraine shows, the behavior of this character proves to us that he is as mentally fragile as Hitler. Both Hitler and Putin were born weak, and they had a childish-infantile way of thinking, yet they managed to ascend to power.

Normally, strong people won't even try to prove how strong they are, because in their subconsciousness, they know that they are strong and it makes no sense for them to prove it. These people are normally people of a calm nature and healthy psyche. But when someone has a weak nature and puerile-infantile thinking, that person wants with all his heart to prove to the whole world that he is very powerful. In the subconsciousness of weak characters there is the frustration of the weak, one that makes them volatile characters, aggressive towards the world around them. They want to prove to the whole world that they are what they are not, that they are stronger and superior to others.

It's extremely dangerous for such people to ascend to power, especially in a country with a huge military arsenal, so it was a huge error of our civilization to let these two puerile-infantile people, Hitler and Putin, rise to prominence.

The war in Ukraine has demonstrated to the whole world that Putin is not only of a childish, unstable, and aggressive nature because of his weakness, but that he is also the worst head of a country that has ever existed: it is because of him that Russia ended up failing from an economic point of view and being despised by the whole world.

Returning to the Law of the Paradox of Life:

Compared to Putin, the President of Ukraine, Volodymyr Zelenskyy, was considered by everyone to be an insignificant president. No one took him seriously, and they considered this president to be a mere puppet.

In reality, the war between Russia and Ukraine demonstrated that the "insignificant" president, disparaged by everyone, really became the most important person on the planet, who fights with the greatest courage for his country, his people, and the entire democracy of the planet. From a president belittled by everyone, Zelenskyy became appreciated by the whole planet, including by his rival, Putin.

A last aspect of the Law of the Paradox of Life between these two characters is that Putin hired hitmen to kill the president of Ukraine. To everyone's surprise, Zelenskyy sits fearlessly in his office in the center of Kyiv, and Putin is dying of fear, hiding in his most secret bunkers, terrified to meet even his subordinates, while everyone wants Zelenskyy to survive, and absolutely all the people on the planet want Putin to succumb as soon as possible.

Spiritual Psychoanalysis of the Manifestation of the President of Russia, Vladimir Putin

When I did the Spiritual Psychoanalysis of the COVID-19 pandemic, we saw that the Universe put our civilization before this coronavirus so that we could see in the mirror what we are. We became aware that the human beings and our civilization are as aggressive as the COVID-19 coronavirus, which destroys the habitat in which we live, as we destroy nature, the planet, and our Mother Earth.

In the case of the Russian War in Ukraine, the Universe once again put us face to face with the aggressor of our planet, Vladimir Putin. Why do you think the Universe did this? Is it not because each of us can see ourselves again in the mirror and realize again who we really are? I think yes, we are all facing the biggest aggressor of our civilization so that we can see another aggressive side of our nature as human beings, to see where the materialistic way of thinking of each of us is leading us.

Through this "mirror," we must realize that the genes of President Vladimir Putin are in the subconscious of each of us. All of us, like Vladimir Putin, think and build our principles of life according to the principles of the materialistic thinking, according to the principle of the satisfaction of bodily pleasures. Even if our bodily pleasures mean much less than Putin's bodily pleasures, they have the same structure, the same dynamics, the same evolution, and will lead to the same result that Putin has reached today.

The borderline between the so-called "normality" and "pathology" of materialistic thinking and desires is very thin. All of us with materialistic thinking can consider ourselves "normal" as long as we don't do too much harm to the world around us, but under favorable conditions, when we're allowed to do something, when we're allowed to satisfy any bodily desire without being punished or judged, we all reveal all our darkest thoughts and desires.

To better understand what I want to say, let's take a look at my father and the President of Russia, V. Putin, and the Russian soldiers who invaded Ukraine on February 24, 2022. If we look at all these people individually, we see that deep in their souls, they are all good people with good intentions:

- My father is a very tender, fragile nature, who wanted to build a family appreciated in society.

- The President of Russia is a good patriot and a man of his word, who wanted to bring his people to the forefront of the world.

- The Russian soldiers fighting in Ukraine are hard-working, good-natured, and obedient children of the country, who want to do their duty to their motherland.

But what happened with my father, who became aggressive towards my mother? What happened to Vladimir Putin as he became the aggressor and the marauder of all the countries around Russia? And what happened to the Russian soldiers, who assaulted and raped Ukrainian women, plundered people's properties, broke into the Ukrainian shops and banks, and shot civilians on the roadside for no reason? What happened to them all?

They all felt the freedom from the society in which they live to do everything their heart desires and everything they want to do. My father received the consent of his parents and the society in which he lived, where men had to punish their women for any mistake. Putin sensed a consensus from his people that he can do anything as a leader with one of the biggest armies in the world. And the Russian soldiers were told that all Ukrainians are Nazis and that they had permission from their leaders to do whatever their heart desires in the country they have conquered. They have the right to steal, kill people who rebel against the conquerors, etc.

The paradox is that even if all those named above committed and continue to commit a lot of crimes and injustice against the surrounding world, they are not aware that they are doing evil. Both my father and Putin consider that everything they do is ideally normal, because their principles of thinking are based on their convictions that they are very calculated, very meticulous, and everything they undertake is perfect. They both know what they want from life, and they know how to calculate and proceed in life in such a way that all the events around them unfold exactly as they have planned in their minds.

Unfortunately, we can't build life only according the desires of our minds, because the life we live is not built only on ideas generated by the mind of a single person. Life in the Universe in which we live is a harmony between all the surrounding worlds in the Universe. If we had a spiritual way of thinking and knew how to live in harmony and peace with the Universe we would listen to the situations and the world around us as my mother did, and then no one would end up straying from the "normality" of thoughts and from materialistic desires to "pathological" ones.

The difference between materialistic and spiritual thinking is that those with materialistic thinking are focused *only* on their own interests, on personal bodily pleasures, and on their personal principles of life. Those with spiritual thinking are focused on harmony with the surrounding world, the pleasure of the surrounding world, and the pleasures of the people around them. Those with spiritual thinking are very aware that the principle of our existence in this Universe is based on the Boomerang Law, that everything we create for the world around us, we create for ourselves. If we create positive energies, we will receive positive energies, and if we create negative energies, these energies, sooner or later, will return to us.

What each of us must be aware of is that for all of us with materialistic thinking, the border between the so-called "normality" of bodily pleasures and "pathology" is not so large. In other words, we all have to realize as soon as possible that our material thinking will lead us to self-destruction. The Material thinking that the human being has had since its naissance on earth must be changed, especially in the new generation that is focused 100 percent on the satisfaction of their bodily pleasures. They must realize that our civilization has reached the peak of the materialistic thinking and of their bodily satisfactions, and the time has come for our entire civilization to move on to a new way of thinking—the spiritual thinking—because as long as we think materialistically, our civilization will face characters like Hitler, Putin, my father, and aggressive and rapist Russian soldiers.

The decision will be up to you: follow the lead of my father and Putin, who know exactly what they want from life and how to satisfy their bodily pleasures, or choose the path of my mother, who lived in perfect harmony with the Universe and the surrounding world.

As you can see from Vladimir Putin's life history, he created a HUGE number of negative energies in this Universe. He started many wars and world conflicts. Tens of thousands of civilians, children, and soldiers were killed because of him. Even though he has made such a mess in this Universe, he can't realize what he's doing.

Not only is Putin unable to realize the mistakes he makes, but we all with materialistic thinking can't understand the materialistic mistakes we commit, because this form of thinking makes us very stubborn beings. To be aware of our own deeds, we need some extreme, out of the ordinary situations, some catastrophes in our lives so big as to wake us up from our sleep and idleness and shake our stubborn brains.

In the case of my father, for example, it was necessary for him to lose his wife and remain alone to appreciate the effort she had made for him and to become aware that he had to value and respect her.

In Putin's case, the Universe had to put him before all the negative energies that he created in this Universe; all his aggression and hatred towards democratic countries had to turn against him. While so far he has carried out hate propaganda against the democratic countries, now the time has come for all the people on the planet to hate him back and despise him and wish him dead. Now that he is faced with the hostility of the entire planet, Putin has all the conditions to understand the impact of his aggression against the whole world.

Even if here in the material world Putin never understands his mistakes, the Universe will not let him go off until he gets it to the depths of his soul. After the death of his body, Putin's soul will go to the Kingdom of Heaven like Hitler's soul did, but the consciousness of his body will remain in Hell, in the World of Darkness, where he accumulated all the negative energies that he created on earth during his lifetime.

Now imagine the amount of negative energy created by this person in the World of Darkness, and imagine the amount of negative energy of hatred and aggression that each of us has created for him. What's in stock for Vladimir Putin in the World of Darkness are not only the energies created by him against our civilization but also the negative energies of our civilization against him. How will Vladimir Putin manage to cope with all these invasive and aggressive energies?

In my books, I have written several times about the fate of the politicians and religious leaders who create conflicts and wars. I wrote that in their next lives, they will end up losing their mind. Just look at Putin's example. It demonstrates exactly what happens to such people. All these people being invaded by the negative energies they created themselves end up in their next lives becoming mentally ill, because the aggressive negative energies are so numerous and invasive that these people will completely lose their sense of reality. The world they will live in will be a world walled off by their own negative, aggressive, and invasive energies, which will have no end, and they won't be able to see anything that goes on around them.

THE ONGOING WAR BETWEEN RUSSIA AND UKRAINE

From a spiritual point of view, the war between Russia and Ukraine is a negative energy created by our civilization and accumulated in the World of Darkness for centuries. And now, reaching the peak of its accumulation, this cloud of negative energy returned it in the form of war to those who produced it. To figure out who created this energy and how, we have to look at the countries involved in this conflict.

The entire planet was involved in the COVID-19 pandemic, as our entire civilization is guilty of what is happening to the nature of our planet and to the human habitat. In the war started by the Russians, only Russia, Ukraine, the European Union, and the United States are involved, so the creators of the negative energy that descended to the earth in the form of war are precisely these countries.

In my opinion, Vladimir Putin, together with his Russian people, created approximately 80 percent of the entire number of negative energies of the war; Ukraine created about 5 percent of all negative energies brought down to earth in the form of war; and the European Union together with the USA created approximately 15 percent of these energies.

A) NEGATIVE ENERGIES CREATED BY RUSSIA

Since 1917, this country has not known the meaning of democracy and has been manipulated by its leaders to their heart's content.

To explain political dictatorship means, I'll cite Hitler's political dictatorship. In order to manipulate his nation, Hitler started with the propaganda that the German people were the purest nation, of the purest blood, and with the highest intelligence compared to all the nations of the world. In other words, Hitler took all measures to instill in the people's minds that his nation was superior to other nations. Under this pretext, the Germans had every right to conquer other countries and dominate them. Following Hitler's propaganda, a nation was created with the courage and will to dominate all other countries.

Communism, built by the Russians beginning in 1917, has always been a policy similar to Hitler's policy, but with much larger and wider proportions than Hitler's concepts. In the former communist countries and in the Soviet Union, there was propaganda that the Communist Party was the most perfect party in the whole world, that the Soviet Union (Russia) was the richest country, and that its Russian people were the best, the most patriotic, the most intelligent, the most soulful, etc. The other countries, the European countries and the United States, were countries where human rights and justice didn't exist.

I was educated by the Communist system, so I felt what Communist "patriotic" education means. This made me a blind patriot for my country; it made me a murderer against the Western countries. I felt hatred inside me for the capitalist (democratic) countries, and I wanted to go to Afghanistan to fight capitalism.

During the disintegration of the Soviet Union in the early 1990s, I became aware of what was behind the Communist Policy of Patriotism. I realized the Hitlerism of the Communists in manipulating the masses, which was a policy much more invasive and aggressive than the Hitlerist one. Most of all, I realized this when my country of origin, Moldova, broke away from Russia and ended up among the countries outside the former USSR, which Russia's policy considered as enemies.

While before the collapse of the Soviet Union Moldovans were flattered and treated as a part of the USSR, after the collapse, Moldova, like Ukraine,

Georgia, Chechnya, etc., landed on the list of countries detested by Russia, which continues to pursue a Communist-Hitlerite policy.

The Russians began to accuse all ex-USSR countries of Russophobia, stating that these countries violate the rights of the Russians in their territory, that the leadership of these countries was stupid, incompetent, incapable, backward etc. All this Russian policy was aimed at recovering the territories of the ex-USSR countries. Under the pretext of Russophobia in Moldova, Georgia, Azerbaijan, and Ukraine, the Russians initiated conflicts and wars in all these countries.

With Vladimir Putin's rise to power, Russia's policy has become much more aggressive. This president and his secret services discovered a new way of manipulating the masses. They discovered the mass media sources and the Internet, which became a subtle lever to fool the Russian people and make them pro-patriots and pro-Putinist zombified Russian citizens.

Initially, the secret services eliminated all the journalists who were outspokenly telling the truth, and then they ousted all the political opponents of Vladimir Putin and started a massive propaganda campaign both in Russia, the ex-USSR countries, and all the democratic countries of the world. Putin's leadership invested billions upon billions of dollars in pro-Russian, pro-Putinist propaganda in all these countries.

Under the pretext of "debunking" the information, the Russians managed to infiltrate the market of democratic countries and win in the minds of tens of thousands of Westerners. The pro-Russian and pro-Putinist propaganda were so strong that not only the natives from Russia or the ex-USSR, but even leaders of democratic countries started to have confidence in it, and people from European and American countries began to believe it themselves.

In essence, the Russian propaganda stated that all the democratic countries are dictatorial countries pursuing a policy of Russophobia, that these countries want to conquer Russia and seize its riches and destroy Russia as a nation. It's enough to turn on any Russian television channel (Pervii kanal or Rossia-1, for example), watch the TV shows like *Solovievlive* or *60 Minutes*, or visit any Russian social network (Odnoklassniki) to see that they speak only negatively about civilized countries. The Russians say that:

- the ex-USSR countries are backward countries with Nazi leadership that oppress the Russian minorities in their country;

- the European Union is a world of homosexuals;

- the USA is a nation of morons;

- all the democratic countries tell lies and only Russia speaks the truth and brings justice and peace to the earth;

- the Russians are the liberators of the democratic world;

- the Russians are the smartest, most intelligent, and most correct of all people.

Under such pretext, the Russian people became an aggressive people against all the democratic countries on the planet, and they became aggressive against all ex-USSR countries.

The pro-Russian and pro-Putinist propaganda have extensively zombified the Russian people. It has embedded so deeply in the Russians' brains that the democratic countries are Nazi countries that they don't even realize that they themselves have become a Nazi people as a result of the racist-Putinist propaganda. In other words, Putin's Nazi policy has turned a large part of the Russian people into a nation of Nazis and aggressive killers against the entire civilized world on the planet, a nation of zombified people, without a will, without rational thinking.

I apologize for the accusations I want to make against the Russian people. But for you to understand what I want to tell you, I want to give you an example. To understand the true feelings of a person who lost his mother, we can read a lot of books and say we understand, but true awareness of feelings reaches us only when we lose our mother, when we experience the feelings of this loss. In order to understand the Russian people and the consequences of their racist and aggressive thinking, we have to live and feel for ourselves the influence of Russian propaganda on the thinking of the Russian people and on the subjugated peoples.

I come from Moldova, the country that was subjugated by the Russians for seventy years until 1992, where I myself was under the influence of the communist propaganda of the Russians. Since then, Moldova, even if it got rid of the Russian leaders, did not get rid of their racist propaganda, their political and economic influence. I lived for several years in Russia, and I know exactly how Russians think. Of course, the Russian people don't differ at all from other peoples. They all think according to the same principles of life as any other peoples. Even the Germans were no different from other peoples, but don't forget what Hitler's propaganda did to the minds of this people in the last century. Now, imagine that the German people were influenced by Hitler's propaganda for only one generation, and the Russian people are influenced by racist propaganda for several generations, starting in 1917. Imagine how deeply racist propaganda is embedded in the brains of this people.

All this pro-Russian, pro-Putinist, anti-European, anti-American, anti-Ukrainian, anti-Georgian, anti-Moldova, anti-Chechen propaganda made a large portion of the Russian people hate all democratic countries in the world and all the former Soviet countries. The behaviour of President Vladimir Putin, together with the hatred and aggressiveness of a large part of the Russian people, in my opinion, generated approximately 80 percent of the negative energies from the World of Darkness that have descended upon the earth under the guise of war.

If we are to focus on the Law of the Paradox of Life in the case of the Russian people and Russia in general, we see that this people and their motherland truly considered themselves the greatest people and the greatest country on the planet. The Russian people were convinced to their innermost core that they are the most soulful people on the planet, that they are the greatest people on the globe, that their country is the fairest and most secure country on the planet. In the end, it turned out that this country, the majority of this people, is the most cowardly, the most aggressive people, with the most Nazi-like principles of life.

The majority of the Russian people who regarded themselves as the most revolutionary on the planet eventually proved to be a cowardly and fearful people. This war made us realize that the Russian people had many revolutions, but as a nation it had not contributed to these revolutions. The revolutions in Russia happened without the involvement of the Russian people. They were created only at a high level; only the top co-leaders killed each other, and the revolution was over. The Russians never came out to defend their personal interests as the Ukrainians, Moldovans, Georgians, and all other democratic nations on the planet did.

Even now, when they see that they are led by a Nazi-Putinist person and that their Putinism is leading them to economic disaster and demise, the Russian people have no courage to take to the streets to bring down their dictator.

The economic stability of this country, which was thought to be unconquerable, is now seen in its reality. The Russians don't have any personal economy developed by them. They don't produce cars, tractors, household appliances or computers—absolutely nothing. All they have is natural wealth such as gas, oil, and forests. So far, the majority of the Russian people and Russia have only taken advantage of their natural wealth and spent it to enrich themselves and create wars.

The Russian people were so fooled by the pro-Russian and pro-Putinist propaganda that they didn't realize the reality in which they live. They consider themselves the greatest people in the world, above the people of all the nations on the planet. They believe that the whole planet must bow before them and align according to their principles of life.

The thinking of a large part of the the people of this nation is so distorted that they can't see that they are a people who only take advantage of the riches of Mother Earth, that they use up all the riches of Mother Earth to enrich themselves and build weapons. They don't see that in reality, they failed to invent or build any industry specific to the Russian people.

Now, when all the democratic countries have withdrawn all their industry that they created in Russia, when the Russians are left only with their personal industry that doesn't exist, they'll see the real world in which they live, and a great part of the Russian people will realize what they have achieved so far as a nation. Then the Russian people who have been manipulated by pro-Russian propaganda will come down to earth and realize that they are no better than other nations, that any person of Russian nationality is a person identically equal to any other person of any other nationality on earth.

To understand the message of the Universe, we must wonder why the Universe put us face to face with the Russian people, who are a people manipulated by pro-Russian and pro-Putinist propaganda. I believe that the Universe did this so that we realize the negative impact that propaganda brings to our society with materialistic thinking.

In my books so far, I have talked about the materialist thinking and the ways of manipulating the masses: about the political ways to create patriots of countries and about the ways of religions to create religious patriots. Remember that the Russian people are an ideal example for our civilization to become aware of the techniques of manipulating the masses and creating patriots of the countries.

In order to create zombified patriots of the Putinist-Nazi policy, Putin has praised his people to the skies; he convinced them that the Russians and Russia are the supreme nation and country on earth, that only they can teach the countries of the world about justice and fairness.

To spread this patriotic propaganda, Putin killed all the journalists and all his political rivals who were against his principles. He appointed to the radio and television stations anchors who broadcast only pro-Putinist information. Putinist-Nazi propaganda has been carried through mass media sources, starting from cartoons and ending with information about weather and sports.

The Russians have spread their propaganda for years not only in Russia, but they have also distributed the pro-Russian and pro-Putinist propaganda in all ex-USSR countries, and they have established radio and television channels in all democratic countries in Europe and North America.

Pro-Russian and pro-Putinist propaganda has not only clouded the minds of Russians in Russia, but it has also befuddled the minds of more than 50 percent of the population in the ex-USSR countries (in Ukraine, Moldova, Georgia etc.) and blackened the minds of much of the population of democratic countries in Europe and America. Even now, during the war between Russia and Ukraine, when everyone knows that Putin and Russia are war criminals, the pro-Putinist policy makes a large percentage of people on the planet support him and not realize the crimes of Putin and Russia against democracy.

I want to remind you that I come from Moldova, and I know exactly how Russian propaganda works in these countries. In each of these countries with the propaganda, more than 50 percent of the pro-Russian parties came to power. These people who vote for these parties are so zombified that no explanation in the world can make them change their opinion or see reality. Even if you show them concrete examples of the European Union investing in Moldova, even if you show them the factories, the plants, and the roads that were built by the Europeans, still the pro-Russian people will say that Russia helped Moldova. Even if you show them concrete examples of Russia blackmailing Moldova with gas and selling to them at the highest price on the market, the pro-Russian peopl will ignore all this

Considering the mechanism for the creation of political patriots, I believe that our civilization and leaders should become aware of the impact of this mechanism of manipulating the masses, and they should make laws to take measures to prevent such techniques from reoccurring in our civilization.

I understand that our civilization has reached a high level of democracy, where everyone is allowed to do whatever they think. But you see that it's not really like that. Russians and pro-Russian politics reached the markets of democratic countries through media sources that conquered the minds of people. However, I am convinced that our society must take drastic measures to disallow propaganda in which a country or a people or a religion is privileged. In other words, our society must start up anti-propaganda against the propaganda of any origin, whether political, religious, racial, etc. Each time someone alludes to any nation, people, or religion as being superior to another nation or religion it should be taken as a NAZI policy advocating hatred and aggression against other nations or religions.

Important: What all the democratic countries must take into consideration is that the politics of the extremist religions follows the same principles as the Putinist politics. Putin glorifies his people and his country as being the greatest, and this is the same policy of extremist religions these days, which propagates the belief that men are superior to women and that their religion is the supreme religion. I am convinced that extremist religions, like Putinist politics, will at some point break out and create a warlike conflict within the whole world, much more serious than Russia's conflict against Ukraine.

Please don't think it's a joke, because the religious politics is much more convincing and much more invasive than Putinist politics. People educated in a religion will become much more aggressive towards our civilization than the Russians are against the Ukrainians.

In order to stop the religious propaganda in the world and succeed in making all believers aware of the negative effects of religious propaganda, our civilization must proceed with radical changes. It must move away from the materialistic to spiritual thinking.

You will say that this is impossible and that most people on the planet won't easily accept a radical change so quickly. Of course, no one will want to change their way of thinking or to give up on satisfying their personal bodily pleasures in order to focus on the pleasures of their neighbors (the surrounding world). The materialistic thinking has been embedded in our brains since the appearance of Homo sapiens on earth, and it's impossible to change. Let's see what the solution is.

In order to succeed in convincing the entire civilization on the planet about the importance of spiritual thinking scientists must accept spirituality as a form of science. Rather, scientists should accept the research of the Supreme Consciousness of the Universe as a new form of scientific research.

Currently there is already a lot of scientific research to convince scientists to accept spirituality in their research. Even Albert Einstein said that he believed in life after death, because energies can't disappear. Currently, quantum physics has demonstrated that there is a Supreme Consciousness of the Universe. I am no longer talking about the near-death experiences, which are specific research activities, and I am no longer talking about the Spiritual Psychoanalysis conceived by me, in which we clearly and obviously see the influence of the Supreme Consciousness of the Universe on the course of everyone's life between us and our entire civilization.

If scientists seriously started researching the Supreme Consciousness of the Universe and bringing irrefutable evidence about the spiritual world in which we live, and accepted the Essential Law of the Universe, Family Bond, and followed this law with sanctity and accepted the Spiritual Psychoanalysis as an essential way of collaborating with the Universe, the problem of the materialist propaganda of any origin would be solved by itself. Then our civilization would manage, without shedding a single drop of blood, to win all the wars against all the religions of the world and all the radical politicians on the planet.

When becoming aware of the true Laws of the Universe (the Laws of the Universe described by me in my first book, *The Destiny and Signs of God*), every citizen of this planet will willingly give up all the religious and political policies in which they believe.

Why the Universe Brought Us Face to Face with Putinist Propaganda from Russia

Precisely when I was writing this chapter, the Universe created a rather incomprehensible situation for me, one that I considered as an undeserved negative energy but which still lingers and affects me.

Last year I had to travel a lot to Quebec City, which is more than four hundred kilometers away from our house. Driving more than a thousand kilometres a month, I had to change the oil of my car's engine more often than I usually did. In March 2022, when we reached the limit of the car's mileage regarding the oil in the engine, my wife and I had to travel to Quebec City twice, which required a car journey of another two thousand kilometers. I didn't have many days left, and I had to have the oil changed as soon as possible.

It was too late to call my mechanic, because he had a lot of customers waiting in line, and the appointment had to be made in advance. The solution was to call the car dealers in the city, because the oil could be changed at their shop at any time. I usually avoid taking my car to the dealer, because every time I go to them for a problem, they suggest that more service should be provided. But in this case, I had no choice.

I called customer service at the dealership and an advisor answered. I introduced myself and said, "I want to make an appointment for my car to change the oil."

The man said, "We will do an inspection of the brakes and check the condition of the car."

Before the man finished speaking, I interrupted him. "I don't need you to check the brakes, because I changed the brakes a few months ago. What

I need is for you to change the oil in my car as soon as possible." I said this more forcefully.

The man didn't comment on anything I said, and we continued to agree on the time when I would bring the car to the garage. He confirmed my appointment for the next day.

The next morning, arriving by car, I went to the service advisor where I had to register. I introduced myself and said, "I have a reservation for 10:00 for an oil change."

The advisor looked on the computer and told me, "We're going to check the brakes."

I didn't pay too much attention to what she said, because I was convinced that everything was in order, and I thought that when the lady talked about brakes, that meant a routine inspection.

Among other things, the garage I usually use to check the brakes doesn't charge me. They do the general inspection of the car just to spare me from any further problems that should be solved. In the case of this advisor, I was convinced that it was only a routine inspection and that everything was going according to the agreement. I handed them the car key and stepped out.

After a few hours, I returned to the garage to pick up my car. I went to the service advisor, and she gave me the keys and said, "We checked the brakes, the engine oil, the windshield wipers, and the pressure in the car's wheels. Everything is in order. The price is $70."

I didn't quite understand everything the advisor told me, and I was surprised that the oil change cost me so little. I paid the bill. The lady gave me the keys to the car and the receipt with all the work the garage had done on my car, and I went to the car with a feeling that something wasn't right.

I got in the car and saw that the garage hadn't changed the decal on the left corner of the windshield, where the mileage is usually written for the next oil change. I couldn't believe it, and I started to read the statement from the advisor listing the work done by the garage on my car. It said that the garage had checked the oil in the car's engine, the brakes, the tire pressure, the wipers, and for all that they had charged me seventy dollars. I couldn't believe what was happening; I thought such a thing was not real.

I went back to the advisor to see what was going on, because in my brain there was no way the garage wouldn't change the oil.

The advisor asked me, "Is there a problem?"

I answered, "I don't know. I just wanted to know if you changed the oil of the car."

The scared advisor said to me, "No. We did inspection number one."

I couldn't believe what I was hearing. I had no idea what "inspection number one" meant, and I told her, "Ma'am, I had an appointment with you for an oil change. I don't need all these checks. When I came by, I told you that I had a reservation for an oil change."

The lady was embarrassed and went to talk to the dealership manager, the one who deals with the most important jobs.

The head mechanic came to me and said, "In the morning, I was there when you ordered the brakes to be checked."

I didn't blame the garage guy for lying about the fact that he was there when I talked to the secretary, but I told him, "Sir, I came here for the oil change."

"Your car doesn't need an oil change," argued the garage man.

Without letting him finish, I told him, "Yesterday, when I made the appointment for the oil change and the man talked to me about the brakes, I told him twice that I don't need to have the brakes checked because I changed the brakes a few months ago; I just need the oil changed."

Seeing that I'd caught him red-handed, the main garage man told to me, "Well, we can change the oil right now. It will be ready in ten minutes."

It was already the second time that they made me pay for some unjustified and unnecessary services. The employees are so focused on imposing additional checks on vehicles and fooling customers that neither the customer service man nor the secretary even heard the essential reason for which I took the reservation. They both wanted to forcefully impose the "Number One Program" on me, which I neither needed nor had any idea about, so they were caught red-handed.

I no longer wanted to deal with this company so I left, refusing the manager's offer. I went directly to a private garage, where I would usually go, and solved the problem very easily.

After the situation at the garage, I was angry and didn't understand why it had happened to *me*? I didn't create any negative energy to deserve all this.

I came home and told my wife what had happened. Then I talked to a friend of mine, and only in the evening when I went to bed and everything was quiet could I understand the reason why the Universe had created that situation for me. I realized that I had just finished writing what you read so far, and an adjustment was needed to make each of the readers aware of why the Universe made us face up to pro-Russian propaganda from Russia.

Here is the message of the Universe for our civilization that confirms the consequences of our materialistic thinking. To begin, I'll describe the structure of Russia.

Russia, like any other country in the world, is similar to the structure of a corporation, with an executive director or a country leader. The director imposes laws, and employees must execute these laws. In the case of Russia, Putin felt the freedom to impose his own laws.

Putin's concept was to create an anti-democratic, anti-European, and anti-American country. He wanted all the countries of the world to be afraid of Russia, to accept it as the second power in the world to which it would cede the territories that once belonged to the Soviet Union. He needed these countries under his command to carry out his diabolical plan to have all these countries worship him as an almighty god.

To achieve such a feat, Putin needed loyal people who would fulfill all his orders with sanctity, and he needed the entire Russian people to support him. In order to make his people think like him, a radical reform in journalism and in the leadership of the country was needed. It was necessary for all the Russian media to talk only about what Putin wanted. In order to make journalists report only Putinist propaganda, Putin killed absolutely all the journalists who tried to speak the truth, so that there would be no opponents of his policy at the helm of the country. He also killed all the smartest politicians.

By killing all the people who opposed his regime, Putin managed to zombify the majority of the Russian people with the help of the Internet and mass media in such a way that everyone thinks like him. Now a large part of the people in Russia want to take revenge against the United States and Europe, and the majority of the Russians want to destroy Ukraine as a state; they want to destroy this nation and wipe it off the face of the earth.

Surprisingly, the people with a higher education, who are aware of the Nazi-Putinist policy, still continue to support this policy at all levels of leadership. I'm talking about the foreign minister, the Russian diplomats, and Russian ambassadors from the embassies of all the countries of the world. I'm talking about Russia's representatives at the UN. It's surprising that all these people, aware of the Nazism-Putinist agenda, continue to support this policy.

At one point, I asked myself: Why do these people continue to support the Nazi-Putinist policy of their country? They surely are aware that what they're doing is not good. Later, I realized what was happening. These people continue to lie to the world because they aren't afraid that they will have to answer for their acts in front of the justice system, or that a moment will come when they are responsible for the Nazi-Putinist policy—the policy that kills innocent people, that destroys an entire nation, that destroys the economy of their country and of the entire planet.

Let's see what happens at the management level of a corporation. Let's take the car dealership I told you about. The director of this company, like the directors of all corporations, wants to make as much profit as possible. In order to squeeze out as much money as possible from their patrons, they have a well-defined policy of making reliable cars but not really that reliable. The cars must last as long as the company's warranty exists. For this reason, they employ engineers to upgrade their vehicles and they invent mechanisms to reduce the reliability of the parts over time. They also extort money from customers at the dealership level by inventing all kinds of mandatory vehicle check-ups. Based on these rules, company employees have no fear of taking advantage of the clientele to extort money from them.

If we compare Russia and its Hitlerist Putinist policy with the car company and its policy, we see that the essential construction principle between them is identical. Just as Putin imposed his anti-human policy, the car company has an anti-customer policy. Even if the difference between Russia, which kills people, and the car company, which extorts money from their clientele, is quite large, their organizing principle is the same: Putin killed all the journalists and the politicians in opposition, and the car company simply does not hire staff that contradict the company's policy of robbing the clientele.

Just as the employees of Russia aren't afraid of justice but spread Hitlerist-Putinist propaganda all over the world, the car company's engineers do the same by inventing defective parts, and the dealerships impose mandatory and unnecessary checks of consumers' vehicles.

What happens? Why are the representatives of a village or a company not afraid of justice? Why do they hurt people and not even realize that they're doing it? Countries and corporations are like "cars on wheels," in which everything works according to laws dictated by the leaders and their politics. Each wheel/personnel must fulfill its functions to perfection. Otherwise, the whole policy is ruined. Journalists and official representatives of Russia must lie to the world in order to impose their Hitlerist-Putinist policy, and dealership employees must take advantage of the naivety of their customers to milk them of their money.

Unfortunately, if we look at the essential mechanism of the construction of countries and corporations, we see that all of them are built according to the principle of the materialistic thinking, where the policy of domination or enrichment is more important than the human being.

If the representatives of Russia and the employees of the dealership had a spiritual thinking, they would be aware that all of them will end up before justice as a result of their actions, because in the spiritual world in which we live, in this Universe, *nothing* goes unnoticed. We all, sooner or later, end up before justice. All the negative energies created by us, regardless of whether they were created at our workplaces or in our daily lives, have to happen to us.

What happens to the people suffering the influence of extreme political and religious propaganda? Caught in the crosshairs of persuasive political and religious propaganda, people's mindset becomes aggressive and turns against the surrounding world, claiming that everyone is disrespectful of their own country, their own religion, their own culture and traditions.

The Russians for example, point accusatory fingers at the civilized world and prosecute everybody of Russophobia and hostility. But they have no idea that who accuses the others are actually accusing themselves, because they themselves are like that. I don't mean that extremist Russians or extremist Islamists are unsensible to empathy, love, or respect. No. They are highly respectful of the surrounding world, and very generous and ready to commit self-sacrifice for the sake of others, simply because both the political and religious propaganda speaks a lot about love, understanding, patriotism, sacrifice, etc. But they direct their faithful love and patriotism only where the propaganda urges and guides them to do.

The Russians are very respectful of their own people, and extremist Islamists are reverent and thoughtful of their own fellow nationals and traditions, but when it comes to dealing with the world from outside the propaganda "bubble," they become belligerent and accuse everyone of disrespectfulness. And this happens when the extremists in any group get together and a "collective energy" of aggressiveness builds up towards those living outside their "bubble" of influence.

Both the Russians and the Islamists believe that they know best how to build their lives; they believe that they have the most lucid mind and are free from all the bodily temptations possessed by all other categories of people. What I would like for all of them to realize is that any form of propaganda, be it political or religious, makes all believers to be subjugated to that propaganda policy. The beliefs of believers that they are free is just an illusion; in reality, they are all slaves to propaganda. These people don't have a shred of democracy. They don't know what it means to be free or to stand out in life as an independent personality. They are slaves of faith and propagandistic beliefs.

In reality, political and religious propaganda uprooted the independence and personality of each person. In Russia, for example, patriotic people following Russian propaganda idolize their president and look at their lives through the lens of Putin. They don't know how to think about their personal desires and life principles, but they listen to the propaganda and are ready to go and die for their idol. The same thing happens in religions: believers orientate their lives through the prism of prophets and religious propaganda that was written several thousand years ago.

But God didn't leave us a "prism"/prophet every two thousand years so that we all focus only on them. From my personal experience following the Spiritual Psychoanalysis of God's signs, I know perfectly well that each of us is a prophet, both for us and for the people we are in contact with throughout our lives; I know that each of us is a future universe. We all have to learn to communicate with the Universe/God exactly as those prophets of old communicated with Him.

In my first book, I wrote about ways to communicate with the Universe/ God. We can all do this. God taught me that each of us has a unique communication link with Him. No one can better understand the language of our communication with the Universe. Only we alone know exactly what God's message is for us. God speaks to each of us exactly as parents speak to their children. Just as parents take into consideration the age, character, and abilities of their child and speak to them depending on their level of understanding, God does exactly the same with each of us. He appreciates us according to our true value and gives us recommendations based on who we are, and we are unique in the Universe. No one else is like us. So God behaves with each of us as a unique personality in the Universe.

Each of us is a unique creation and has unique importance in the Universe that no one else can replace. When each of us becomes aware of what I want to say, learns to communicate with the Universe, finds his personal identity with the unique path of his life in the Universe, and sees the miracles that God creates for each of us at every crossroads of our lives, then I am sure that no one will want to continue the ways of other prophets/religions or political leaders.

The universe does not owe anything to anyone. It returns absolutely everything that we create. If we create positive energies for the surrounding world, we receive positive energies from the Universe, and if we carry out the policy of mass destruction, or the policy of robbing customers, all these energies will surely return to haunt us until we realize that we must stop producing such negative energies.

As you can see, the Universe has brought us face to face with the Hitlerist-Putinist policy so that we all understand that our entire civilization is governed by the same principle as the Hitlerist-Nazi Policy of Russia—that we all and all the Russians think materialistically, and that absolutely everything that is built in our civilization is built according to the same principle of Hitler-Nazi politics and materialist thinking.

I understand that it's very difficult to accept and become aware of the mechanism of the materialistic thinking described by me. "We are not murderers like the majority of the Russians are," you may say. But even the Russians don't find it easy to believe that they are Nazis. It's equally difficult for them to accept that they are a nation of Hitlerist-Putinist people. But try not to think like the Russians. Try not to look at the aggressiveness of the Russians and compare it with the gullibility of the corporation employees. Try to focus on the essential structure of the materialist thinking and the ensuing disasters in our society if we follow it.

Imagine that the Russians were ruled by the Nazi policy for only one hundred years. They were fooled by the Nazi policy from 1917 until now, and just look how hard it is for them to give up their way of thinking. Now imagine each of us, our civilization, directed by the materialistic thinking since the appearance of the first human being on earth. Imagine again how hard it must be for us to give up something that is embedded in our brains from time immemorial.

I understand that this is difficult for all of us, but we have to do it, otherwise extreme outbreaks, such as the Russian war, will await us at every step. We will never get rid of extremism as long as we think materialistically, as long as we focus only on our own person and do nothing for the world around us.

The corporations are not the only ones designed according to the materialistic structure described above; our entire society is built according to the materialistic principles, and this is what makes us not fear the consequences of our actions and not realize that we are acting incorrectly.

The Nazi-Putinist policy made Russians hardened killers, and the materialist thinking of our civilization made us today, in the twenty-first century, face a global pandemic organized by the Universe against us. We came face to face with the Russian politics and Nazism, and we came face to face with the global warming of the planet, which is leading us to brinkmanship of self-destruction.

I hope that these situations will convince our civilization that it must give up on our materialistic thinking and move to a new form of thinking and evolution.

B) THE NEGATIVE ENERGIES CREATED BY UKRAINE

Ukraine in this war is the one that suffers the most because of the negative energies from the World of Darkness. Even if they created approximately 5 percent of all the negative energies of this conflict, it is Ukraine who had to sacrifice herself for the entire democracy of the planet.

The negative energy created by this country and its people is the fact that they took the democratic course of evolution and didn't want to join the Putinist dictatorship of Russia. I want to remind you that from a spiritual point of view, we must treat aggression with love. Even when the aggression comes from the biggest aggressor on the planet, namely Russia, we still have to treat it with love.

In the case of Ukraine in relation to Russia, I believe that had Ukraine yielded to Russia and ceded Crimea and Donbas, as requested, then I 50 percent of the Putinist aggression would have diminished, and had Ukraine declared itself a demilitarized country, then Russia would certainly not have started this war.

A year before the start of the war in Ukraine, I wrote several letters to the President of Moldova, Maia Sandu, stating that neither Moldova nor Ukraine stand any chance against the biggest aggressor on the planet, and the only way to defend them is to cede to Russia the territories requested and to declare themselves demilitarized countries.

In my books, I have written several times about sacrifice, about the fact that in order to succeed in evolving spiritually, we have to sacrifice something we care a lot about to the negative energies of the Dark World. The reward for any sacrifice made to the World of Darkness is a reward with enormous benefit.

In the case of Ukraine, the country did not deserve to be attacked by the most aggressive bully in the world with the most fearful weapons, but most certainly the country and its people will have the most to gain in spiritual evolution.

The Law of Life Paradox: While so far no one has drawn attention to Ukraine, which has suffered permanently from Russia's Putinist policy, no one has taken this people seriously. Look at how now the whole planet has admiration for this country and this people, who fight fearlessly against the biggest aggressor of the world. No one ever dared to fight against Russia, but the insignificant people of Ukraine not only had the courage to face off against the most aggressive army on the planet, but also to demonstrate the greatest courage ever on this earth. The insignificant army of Ukraine has become the most important army on the planet—the army that defends the highest values of democracy on earth

C) THE NEGATIVE ENERGIES CREATED BY THE UNITED STATES AND THE EUROPEAN UNION

The essential reason why Putin became so aggressive against these countries was that they were involved in wars with different countries of the world, and that they considered themselves the essential power of the planet. Putin was very jealous of these countries and was quite dissatisfied with the democratic countries, not only because they created wars in different countries, but also because they spread democracy to the ex-Communist countries of Europe. Putin became most dissatisfied when he saw that even the countries of the ex-USSR took the democratic path of evolution and wanted to join the European Union.

Putin accepted that he had lost his influence over Poland and Romania, but when he saw that in Moldova, Georgia, and Ukraine democrats willing to join the European Union came to power, he lost his mind and went for an extreme version of his actions, and he invaded Ukraine.

What Putin wanted was to be accepted by the democratic countries and be given at least the ex-USSR countries, so he can disregard them to his heart's content. Unfortunately, neither the European Union nor the United States accepted that anti-democracy penetrated the countries with a democratic tendency, even if they were once part of a territory occupied by Russia under the USSR.

Based on the above, I want to say that the North Atlantic Treaty Organization (the United States and the European Union) is guilty of interfering with the domestic affairs of other countries and intervening militarily in Vietnam, Afghanistan, Iraq, etc. The invasion carried out by the USA and NATO in several countries that Putin considers as "a playground" for these countries made him jealous and wish that he had the same favor as the USA and NATO: he wanted the former Soviet states back, where he could feel that he is the boss.

Had the USA and NATO had spiritual thinking, they would have known that according to the Laws of the Universe, no one has the right to interfere with someone's domestic affairs. We don't have the right to interfere in someone's life or family, and even more, we don't have the right to meddle with the domestic affairs of other countries.

But because the USA and NATO have materialistic thinking and deploy their armies to the soil of other countries to make order, they are also to be blamed for approximately 15 percent of the war in Ukraine. In other words, the USA and NATO created negative energies for the World of Darkness because they intervened militarily in other countries. Even if their invasion was 100 percent justified and they wanted to defend the interests of democracy, the military invasion of a foreign country is a negative energy.

The universe created a situation for the USA and NATO with Afghanistan when the Taliban conquered that country. Through that situation, the Universe showed the democratic countries that they have nothing to do with their armies on the soil of another country. They can support it militarily, as they do with the Ukrainians, but every country owes it to itself to have the courage to fight for its rights.

Just as we can't change a person, or the relationships of the members of a family, we can't change the political course of a country. That country alone must be aware and want to choose the course of its life, and absolutely no one can do it for her. Look at Ukraine, look at this determined people who are fighting with the greatest resolution to break free from Russia's imperialist and dictatorial influence. Look at their desire to become a free and democratic country. No one can stop this people, not even the most aggressive and powerful army in the world can conquer this people and their country.

Let's ask ourselves questions from Spiritual Psychoanalysis: Why do you think that the Universe brought the USA and NATO on Ukraine's side? Why do you think Russia forced NATO not to get involved militarily? The universe has done it so that all the democratic countries of the world can see the way in which they can interfere in other countries; even if NATO and the USA have the most powerful army in the world, they do not have the right to interfere with the domestic affairs of another country.

Even if Ukraine is desperately asking for help, the situations created by the Universe tell us that NATO and the USA have the right to give the Ukrainians defensive weaponry, offensive weaponry, but they do not have any right to deploy their army to the *soil of another country!*

Just as we don't have the right to interfere with the intimate affairs of a family, the USA and NATO must not interfere with the affairs of other countries. The only solution that democratic countries can take against countries with extreme dictatorship is to cut off all economic relations, just like they did with Russia.

Spiritual Psychoanalysis of the War in Ukraine

A) THE PERIOD OF OUR CIVILIZATION'S ADOLESCENCE:

In the context of the war in Ukraine, significant international conflicts emerged between the democratic and non-democratic countries. Conspicuous among them is the conflict between the United States of America and Russia and China. The conflicts between these countries reminded me of my classmates in my teen years who perfectly embodied the above states.

On the one hand, there was my seatmate (he embodied the United States), who at that time had the most impressive muscular body of all the boys and was also one of the top students in the classroom. On the other hand, there were two twin brothers (who embodied Russia and China), who were marginally as well built as the other boy, but not as good at learning as him.

One of the twins (the Russian) was aggressive and jealous of my seatmate (the USA) and wanted to humiliate him. He would bully him almost every day. He knew he had no chance of defeating my classmate, so he relied on his twin brother (the Chinese) jumping in to help, and together they managed to beat down my mate.

Several times in my books, I wrote that our civilization finds itself in the adolescent period of spiritual evolution, the crucial period of our evolution when we must make the most important evolutionary choice for our future—to continue the materialistic path of evolution, which is a path of self-destruction, or to start on a new path of evolution, spiritual evolution.

Through their belligerent actions, the United States, Russia, and China demonstrate that our civilization behaves like a teenager who has the impression that he will succeed in the future through his materialistic behavior of domination, power, and enrichment.

B) WHAT PRECIPITATED THE WAR IN UKRAINE?:

The war in Ukraine demonstrated and highlighted the fact that our civilization is really divided into two sides: the side of the democratic countries, and the side of the anti-democratic ones. The anti-democratic countries include imperialist countries such as Russia and China, and countries with religious dictatorships, such as Iran, Syria, etc.

All countries with a political or religious dictatorship accuse the United States and the European Union of (1) interfering with the domestic affairs of other countries, and of (2) being the infidel, the unfaithful to God.

From the point of view of Spiritual Psychoanalysis, all these accusations against the democratic countries are gaps in the democracy and should be thoroughly analyzed through a Spiritual Psychoanalysis, taken seriously, and solved.

Democracy in our civilization was not easy to build, and it's not at all easy to keep it. History has shown that on this planet there have been several forms of democracy so far, but they all failed precisely because they didn't know how to listen to the signs of God and didn't take seriously the recommendations/signs that the Universe/God gave them. They didn't know and didn't want to think spiritually in order to do a deep Spiritual Psychoanalysis of all the events that took place around them. Basically, they destroyed themselves because they didn't know how to live in harmony with the Universe.

Had the democracy in today's democratic countries accepted the spiritual thinking and behavior of our evolution, we could have avoided both the war in Ukraine and the major international conflicts between the democratic countries and countries with political or religious dictatorships.

In the early 1990s, during the time when the USSR fell apart, the basis of all the countries with a political dictatorship was dismantled. At that time, the democratic countries were the strongest ones on Earth with the most developed economies and the greatest influence on this planet. Had they accepted the spiritual thinking, our civilization would have enjoyed all the conditions for a prosperous and continuous evolution.

The USSR comprised fifteen countries that Russia had once conquered. After disintegration, all these countries became independent, extremely poor, and with an enormous desire to start a new form of evolution—the democratic one. All the countries had an intense feeling for democracy except Russia. All ex-USSR countries were fed up with the Communist dictatorship of the Russians; they'd had enough of the aggression, lies, and injustice that the Russians had propagated during the USSR era for seventy years.

Russia was the only country out of the fifteen that disfavored democracy. The country had acquired the imperialist taste for manipulation of the masses, submission, theft, domination, exploitation, etc. Not only did Russia manipulate the countries inside the USSR, but it was the sponsor of terrorist and anti-democratic states in the world; it manipulated almost half of the countries on the planet and could not easily abandon its materialistic pleasures for the sake of some "democracy."

At that time, I was a student at the Faculty of Medicine and was on the front line of the revolutionary events in the USSR. We all saw exactly what was happening in the world. We saw the imperialist tendency of the Russians, who after the collapse of the USSR did not change their old habit of sowing terror in the world. In addition to sponsoring terrorism around the globe, the Russians added a new dirty occupation to their foreign policy: they initiated a new pro-Russian propaganda in the former USSR countries, which easily precipitated dirty and illegitimate wars in Moldova, then in Chechnya, then in Georgia, Armenia, Azerbaijan, Ukraine etc.

We knew exactly how the "mechanism" of their propaganda and the political terror and the Russian army work, because day after day, all of us from the fourteen countries of the former USSR lived the terror organized by the Russians against us. We were eagerly waiting for the democratic countries together with the United Nations to open their eyes and see the Russian aggression and terror against us; we were impatiently waiting for the world's democracies to come to our aid to defend our democratic interests according to democratic laws, to save us from the Russian terror and aggressiveness that befell us every day.

Unfortunately, not even the United Nations Organization reacted to our demands, and none of the democratic countries came to our aid. We felt alone, abandoned by the civilized world. We were surprised by the fact that all of us, the ordinary people, saw the Russian aggression and terror, and the democratic countries of the world, together with the UN, did not see any of what was going on. We were mistreated by the Russians and ignored by the democratic countries of the world until 2022, when Russia invaded Ukraine, and the democratic countries themselves felt threatened by Russian belligerence and militancy. Throughout this period, we faced not only the communist aggression of the Russians, but also the discrimination by the democratic countries of the small and "insignificant" states.

The early 1990s were the time when the democratic countries showed the true colors of their "democracy." Instead of choosing the democratic pathway and supporting countries eager to pursue democracy, the United States, together with the countries of the European Union, chose to invest in dictatorship and imperialism, in Russia and China; they let the Russian billionaires with their dirty money tap in the financial markets of the democratic countries. They guided themselves according to the principle of the materialist thinking of superiority, enrichment, and domination. The greed for money made the European countries dependent on Russian gas and oil, so the democratic countries as a whole became dependent on cheap labor from imperialist China.

Had the democratic countries had a spiritual thinking, they would surely have known that when you see a negative energy, you must avoid feeding it with your energies that are based on materialistic thinking, because the negative energy will transform all your materialistic energies into negative energies that will turn ten times against you.

In the given case, everyone knew that Russia was and continued to be the sponsor of terrorism in the world, that the country is the major negative energy of our civilization. The country didn't build its terrorist principles in a single day, or change it under Putin's leadership—no! The country has always been a terrorist country. From the birth of communism, it was known that the country is much more aggressive, destructive, murderous, and manipulative than Hitlerism. With the disintegration of the USSR, Russia didn't change its habits; on the contrary, under the pretext of "democracy," it began to put into practice its diabolical plans that it propagated all the time during Communism.

Had the European Union and the United States not invested in Russia, then Russia would not have had the resources to continue sponsoring the terrorist and anti-democratic countries in the world. It would not have had the resources to become aggressive against the countries around it. In other words, if the United States and the European Union had not fed Russia with materialistic energies of enrichment, then Russia would not have ended up being the major negative energy of our civilization, with a global level of destruction.

In early 1990s, Russia, like all the former USSR countries, was one of the poorest countries in the world. There, absolutely nothing worked. The entire economy built during Communism was completely destroyed, and there was nothing to compensate for it. If the democratic countries had not invested in the economy of this country, they wouldn't have bought all the gas and oil from it, then practically, Russia wouldn't have had any development resources. Having no resources for development, it would surely have given up its imperialist principles of conquest, domination, aggression, and manipulation, and at some point, it would have realized that their solution to salvation was to pursue a democratic evolution.

Had the democratic countries had a spiritual thinking, they would have focused on the democratic states of the world. They would have defended and invested not only in the ex-USSR countries eager for democracy, but they would have also invested in all democratic countries around the world. Investing in the democratic countries would have boosted the flourishing of democracy and prosperity; then all democratic countries would have been on the same level as both the USA and all developed democracies. On the other hand, by cutting the investment in the Russian and the Chinese economies, the democratic countries would have managed to convince these countries to give up their imperialist principles and would have managed to convert them into democratic countries without any effort. The poverty of these countries would have made them relinquish their imperialistic and terrorist ambitions.

CONCLUSION

The war in Ukraine and the conflicts between anti-democratic and demo-cratic countries are not random situations; they are all the signs of God, organized by the Consciousness of the Universe/God, which always brings us to face the truth and our own energies that we ourselves have created so that we can become aware of what we have to change in ourselves.

Emerging from the conflict between anti-democratic and democratic countries, we see that democracy is superior to anti-democracy, and we see that democracy is the biggest power on Earth; in other words, in order to have a continuous future and an eternal evolution, we do not need religious or political conservatism. We need a political and spiritual democracy.

To spare democracy of being accused by the anti-democratic countries of "Satanism," or "lack of belief in God," scientists should accept spiritual-ity as a new form of scientific research, especially since a solid basis already exists in this area. Also, scientists should accept the research of the Supreme Consciousness of the Universe as a new form of scientific research.

In order for the anti-democratic countries not to accuse the USA or the European countries of meddling in the domestic affairs of other countries, a certain kind of Third Energy should be created, as I have mentioned in my books. The United Nations Organization should be completely rebuilt in such a way as to have the right to protect all the countries of the world that are in danger and to create their laws of justice in such a way that no country or president in the world would even think to attack another country or engage in political or religious manipulations.

Imagine that our civilization has always invested and continues to invest only in materialist thinking, exactly as democratic countries have invested in anti-democratic countries since the 1990s. Here is the result

And now imagine that our civilization begins to invest in spiritual thinking, just as democratic countries would begin to invest in countries with a democratic tendency. Imagine the result.

FOR THE FUTURE:

Right now, our civilization has reached the peak of extreme events on earth. It was attacked by a global pandemic, it is involved in Russia's "Nazi war," it is faced with pollution and global warming, and all this speaks about the fact that our civilization is facing the negative energies created by it due to our materialistic thinking. I hope that my books and the events in which our civilization is involved will make the reader aware that the time has come for us to realize that we have to give up our materialistic thinking, exactly as the Russians have to give up their Nazi-Putinist ideology.

Albert Einstein once said that the world is a dangerous place to live, not because of those who do evil, but because of those who look on and do nothing (Princeton N.J., March 30, 1953).

If only you knew how easy life is when you're able to live in harmony with the Supreme Consciousness of the Universe.

Bibliographie

Ötzi, le mystère révélé (2020): https://www.youtube.com/watch?v=M34BSF0V0Mk

Who made the virus? : https://www.gandul.ro/diverse/China to be called before international court for mass creating weapons of destruction and should pay enormous damages 19413297?fbclid=IwAR10YqdKP0jlouXef4aWEfmonpqXGPfgZH9rjKd2YoGYJu1CslhWJVXLIqU#live_close

Meditation guide avec les Archanges (15 octobre 2018) : https://www.youtube.com/watch?v=sTqj9HP0Yv4

The documentary TV series "The Story of God with Morgan Freeman" episode 2019 "Search for the devil": https://www.telequebec.tv/documentaire/l-histoire-de-dieu/en-quete-du-diable/

The Shack" (2017 Movie): https://www.youtube.com/watch?v=VZwpQ3CZ7Ck

Wikipedia „Abiogeneza": https://ro.wikipedia.org/wiki/Abiogenez%C4%83

health-InfoBase. Canada COVID-19 epidemiology update: Summary : updated: 2023-09-06: https://health-infobase.canada.ca/src/data/covidLive/Epidemiological-summary-of-COVID-19-cases-in-Canada-Canada.ca.pdf https://health-infobase.canada.ca/covid-19/#a4

José Rodrigues dos Santos (juillet 2019) „LA FORMULE DE DIEU": https://fr.wikipedia.org/wiki/La_Formule_de_Dieu

Ernst Mach in 1893 „Mach's principle": https://fr.wikipedia.org/wiki/Principe_de_Mach

Astrologie: https://fr.wikipedia.org/wiki/Astrologie

„L'histoire de Dieu" „Vision de Dieu" (2019) : https://www.telequebec.tv/documentaire/l-histoire-de-dieu/vision-de-dieu/

Esprit Spiritualité Métaphysiques: https://www.espritsciencemetaphysiques.com/lignes-de-ley-chakras-de-la-terre.html

Chakras des animaux: https://charline74420.wixsite.com/theanimal/single-post/2017/06/04/Chakras-des-animaux

Business Insider 29/04/2019; „L'univers est plus jeune et grandit plus vite que ce que l'on pensait" : https://www.businessinsider.fr/lunivers-est-plus-jeune-et-grandit-plus-vite-que-ce-que-lon-pensait/

HOLA SPANIOLA, 28 august 2016, „LAS ETAPAS DE LA VIDA": http://holas-paniola.blogspot.com/2016/08/las-etapas-de-la-vida-etapele-vietii.html?m=1

Le Temps, 3 august 2019 „Horizons lointains. Variations sur le thème des dimensions de l'Univers" : https://blogs.letemps.ch/pierre-brisson/2019/08/03/horizons-lointains/

How The Universe Works season 8 „Secrets of Time Travel" 31 january 2020 : https://www.youtube.com/watch?v=zL4aX87Kpj8

" *Mon enfant, son fantome*" Canal D august 13, 2015: https://www.canald.com/emissions/mon-enfant-son-fantome-1.1440775?tab=a-propos

Ephesians 5:22-33 New International Version (NIV) : https://www.biblegateway.com/passage/?search=Ephesians+5%3A22-33&version=NIV

„Les grands reportages", epizod „Antibiotiques: la fin du miracle?" (2020) http://video.lefigaro.fr/tvmag/video/antibiotiques-la-fin-du-miracle-vf-diffuse-le-21-03-19-a-09h25-sur-arte/6015931908001/

The 12 Chakras: December 4, 2019 : https://www.chakras.info/12-chakras/

Il est où le bonheur (07 avr. 2016) : https://www.youtube.com/watch?v=m5qXr9lLdwA

„L'histoire de Dieu" "Dieu existe" (2019): https://www.telequebec.tv/documentaire/l-histoire-de-dieu/dieu-existe/

„Histoires d'ancêtres" „La grande aventure de la Préhistoire" Dominique Grimaud-Hervé, Frederic Serre, Jean-Jacques Bahain, Roland Nespoulet, Romain Pigeaud 2015 „Arbre généalogique des hominidés" : https://www.hominides.com/html/references/histoires-d-ancetres-0986.php Last updated decembre 02, 2015.

Gandul, February 30, 2020 Who made the virus? : https://www.gandul.ro/diverse/China to be called before international court for mass creating weapons of destruction and should pay enormous damages 19413297? fbclid=IwAR10YqdKP0jlouXef4aWEfmonpqXGPfgZH9rjKd2YoGYJu1Cslh WJVXLIqU#live_close

Global, Christopher Nehring, 07 mai 2020 : https://www.dw.com/ro/coronavirus-creat-de-oameni-%C3%AEn-laborator/a-53357409

Wikipedia 1, 18, June 2020: https://en.wikipedia.org/wiki/World_population

"LUCY IN THE SKY", 2019, Natalie Portman plays Lucy Cola; Directed by: Noah Hawley Screenplay by: Brian C Brown & Elliott DiGuiseppi and Noah Hawley Story by: Brian C Brown & Elliott DiGuiseppi Produced by: Reese Witherspoon, Bruna Papandrea, p.g.a., Noah Hawley, p.g.a., John Cameron, p.g.a.

INSPQ Centre d'expertise et de référence en santé publique (10 juillet 2020) https://www.inspq.qc.ca/covid-19/donnees

Robyn Dixon, June 21, 2020: https://www.washingtonpost.com/world/europe/russia-uses-prizes-and-patriotism-to-urge-vote-on-changing-constitution-but-scant-mention-of-keeping-putin-in-power/2020/06/20/e79ea850-afcb-11ea-98b5-279a6479a1e4_story.html

Holy Bible, New International Version. 2011. Biblica.

Albert Einstein (March 30, 1953) https://2.bp.blogspot.com/-hHK2LkY4enE/WstyFzpWYSI/AAAAAAAAO54/DNGRsYsZtbQNGvv7IEeEUwryHGlFSx80gCLcBGAs/s640/Einstein.tif https://falschzitate.blogspot.com/2018/04/die-welt-wird-nicht-bedroht-von-den.html

Albert Einstein https://www.express.co.uk/news/weird/1415278/afterlife-albert-einstein-relativity-life-after-death-google-mo-gawdat-big-bang-spt

Guardians of the Galaxy Vol. 2 (2017) https://www.imdb.com/title/tt3896198/

Jean Jacques Rousseau (1712 – 1778) https://cafephilo93.fr/philosophelumiere/30-thomas-hobbes-1588-1679

Ionel Rotaru, (2024) *The Destiny and Signs of God—Spiritual Psychoanalysis,* second edition.

Printed in the USA
CPSIA information can be obtained
at www.ICGtesting.com
LVHW091121021124
795328LV00001B/95